NCERT
SOLUTIONS
Science

CLASS
VII

by

Rashmi Jain *(Physics)*
Nirusheel *(Chemistry)*
Meenakshi, Barkha *(Biology)*

✳ arihant
Arihant Prakashan (School Division Series)

✻arihant

Arihant Prakashan (School Division Series)

All Rights Reserved

ꙮ **Administrative & Production Offices**

Regd. Office

'Ramchhaya' 4577/15, Agarwal Road, Darya Ganj, New Delhi -110002
Tele: 011- 47630600, 43518550

ꙮ **Head Office**

Kalindi, TP Nagar, Meerut (UP) - 250002
Tel: 0121-7156203, 7156204

ꙮ **Sales & Support Offices**

Agra, Ahmedabad, Bengaluru, Bareilly, Chennai, Delhi, Guwahati, Hyderabad, Jaipur, Jhansi, Kolkata, Lucknow, Nagpur & Pune.

ꙮ **ISBN**   978-93-27197-09-9

PO No : TXT-XX-XXXXXXX-X-XX

Published by Arihant Publications (India) Ltd.

For further information about the books published by Arihant, log on to
www.arihantbooks.com or e-mail at info@arihantbooks.com

Follow us on

Preface

Feeling the immense importance and value of NCERT books, we are presenting this book, having the **NCERT Exercises' Solutions.** This book presents not only solutions but also detailed explanations. Through these detailed explanations, students can learn the concepts which will enhance their thinking and learning abilities. Along with the solutions, we have covered the text material of NCERT books in Notes form covering all Definitions, Key Words, Important Points, etc.

We have introduced some Additional Features with the solutions which are given below:

- All questions covered including questions given in-between the chapter, **Paheli & Boojho Questions and Chapter End Exercises.**
- This book also covers solutions to selected problems of **NCERT Exemplar Problems.**
- **Explanatory Solutions** Along with the solutions to questions we have given all the points that tell how to approach to solve a problem. Here we have tried to cover all those loopholes which may lead to confusion. All formulae and hints are discussed in full detail.

For such a wonderful work, a special note of thanks goes to our Authors (Rashmi Jain, Nirusheel, Meenakshi, Barkha) and our production team.

We are confident that this book will be highly useful for the students. Suggestions for the improvement of the book shall be received with great appreciation and gratitude.

Publisher

Contents

Chapter 1

Nutrition *in* Plants

Important Points

- **Nutrients** Carbohydrates, proteins, fats, vitamins and minerals are the components of food. These components of food are necessary for our body and are called nutrients.
- **Nutrition** It is the process of taking food by an organism and its utilisation by the body.
- **Autotrophic nutrition** (*auto*–self; *trophos*–nourishment) The mode of nutrition in which organisms make their own food from simple substances (e.g. CO_2 and H_2O) by the process of photosynthesis is called autotrophic nutrition. Therefore, green plants are called **autotrophs**. Animals and most other organisms take in ready made food prepared by the plants.
- **Heterotrophs** Those organisms which cannot prepare their own food and take food from green plants or animals, are called heterotrophs and the mode of nutrition is called **heterotrophic nutrition**.
- **Photosynthesis** The process by which green plants synthesise food themselves by using carbon dioxide and water in the presence of sunlight (energy) and chlorophyll is called photosynthesis.

  The process can be represented as an equation :

$$\text{Carbon dioxide} + \text{Water} \xrightarrow[\text{Chlorophyll}]{\text{Sunlight}} \text{Carbohydrate} + \text{Oxygen}$$

- **Cell** The bodies of living organisms are made of tiny functional units called cells. The cell is enclosed by a thin outer boundary, called **cell membrane**. There is a large spherical structure floating in the centre of a cell which is called as **nucleus**. The nucleus is surrounded by a jelly-like substance called **cytoplasm**.

- **Stomata** The plants take carbon dioxide gas from air through tiny pores present on the surface of the leaves. These pores are surrounded by **guard cells**. Such pores are called stomata.

  Note Water and minerals are transported to the leaves by the vessels which run like pipes throughout the root, the stem, the branches and the leaves.

- **Chlorophyll** It is green pigments which is present in the leaves of plants. This pigment captures the energy of the sunlight.

- **Solar energy** Sun is the ultimate source of energy for all living organisms. The solar energy is captured by the leaves and stored in the plant in the form of food.

- **Algae** It is a large group of simple plant like organisms. They contain chlorophyll which gives them the green colour. Algae can also prepare their own food by the process of photosynthesis.

- **Host** It is the organism or plant in which parasite lives.

- **Parasite** The organism which lives on or inside another organism (host) and derives the food from it, is called a parasite. An example of parasite plant is *Cuscuta*. It is also called amarbel. *Cuscuta* plant does not have chlorophyll.

- **Insectivorous plants** Those green plants which obtain their food (partly) from insects are called **insectivorous plants** or **carnivorous plants**, e.g. pitcher plant.

- **Fungi** It is non-green plant that derive their nutrition from dead and decaying organic matter, i.e. saprotrophs.

- **Saprotrophic nutrition** The mode of nutrition in which organisms take in nutrients in solution form from dead and decaying matter is called saprotrophic nutrition.

- **Saprotrophs** Plants which use saprotrophic mode of nutrition are called saprotrophs.

- **Symbiotic relationship** The condition where two different organisms live together and share shelter and nutrients, called symbiotic relationship, e.g. lichen, *Rhizobium*.

- **Lichen** In organisms called lichens, a chlorophyll-containing partner, which is an algae and a fungus live together.

  The fungus provides shelter, water and minerals to the algae and in return, the algae provide food which it prepares by photosynthesis.

▪ **Replenishment of nutrients in soil** Usually crops require a lot of nitrogen to make proteins. After the harvest, the soil becomes defficient in nitrogen. Plants cannot use the nitrogen gas available in atmosphere. *Rhizobium* bacteria live in the root nodules of leguminous plants. This bacteria takes nitrogen gas from the atmosphere and converts it into water soluble nitrogen compounds and give them to the leguminous plants for their growth.

In returns, leguminous plants provide food and shelter to the bacteria. They thus have a symbiotic relationship. This association is very important for the farmers, as they do not need to add nitrogen fertilisers to the soil in which leguminous plants are grown.

Intext Questions

Que 1. How plants prepare their own food? *(Pg 1)*

Ans. Green plants can make their own food from simple substances like carbon dioxide and water present in their surroundings by the process of photosynthesis.

In plants, water and minerals present in the soil are absorbed by roots and CO_2 from air is taken through the stomata. The leaves have green pigment called chlorophyll, which help it to capture the energy of the sunlight. So, leaves of green plants containing chlorophyll synthesise carbohydrates in the presence of sunlight, water and carbon dioxide.

$$CO_2 + H_2O \xrightarrow[\text{Chlorophyll}]{\text{Sunlight}} \text{Carbohydrate (glucose)} + O_2 \text{ (oxygen)}$$

Que 2. Why our body cannot make food from the carbon dioxide, water and minerals like plants do? *(Pg 1)*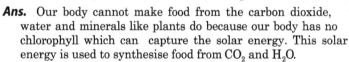

Ans. Our body cannot make food from the carbon dioxide, water and minerals like plants do because our body has no chlorophyll which can capture the solar energy. This solar energy is used to synthesise food from CO_2 and H_2O.

Que 3. Answer the following questions *(Pg 1)*

   (a) Where the food factories of plants are located?

   (b) How do plants obtain the raw materials from the surroundings?

Ans. (a) Leaves are the food factories of plants.

(b) The synthesis of food in plants occurs in leaves. Therefore, all the raw materials must reach there. Water and minerals obtained from soil, CO_2 taken from air through pore on leaves called stomata and solar energy is captured by leaves.

Que 4. How water and minerals absorbed by roots reach the leaves? *(Pg 2)*

Ans. Water and minerals are transported to the leaves by the vessels which run like pipes throughout the root, stem, branches and the leaves. They form a continuous path or passage for the nutrients to reach the leaf.

Que 5. What is so special about the leaves that they can synthesise food but other parts of the plant cannot? *(Pg 2)*

Ans. The leaves have a green pigment called chlorophyll which helps leaves to capture the energy of the sunlight and to synthesise food. Other parts of the plants do not have chlorophyll therefore they are unable to synthesise food.

Que 6. "In the absence of photosynthesis, life is impossible on the earth". Explain. *(Pg 2)*

Ans. In the absence of green plants, there would not be the process of photosynthesis. Without photosynthesis it will affect the plant as it could not make food. The survival of almost all living organism directly or indirectly depends upon the food made by the plants. Besides oxygen which is essential for the survival of all living organisms is produced during photosynthesis. Thus, we can say that life would be impossible on the earth in the absence of photosynthesis.

Que 7. Some plants have deep red, violet or brown leaves. Can these coloured leaves also carry out the process of photosynthesis? *(Pg 3)*

Ans. Yes, these leaves can also carry out the process of photosynthesis because they contain chlorophyll. The large amount of red, brown and violet pigment mask the green colour of chlorophyll in these leaves.

Que 8. Why algae are green in colour? *(Pg 4)*

Ans. Algae contain chlorophyll which gives them the green colour.

Que 9. From where do the plants obtain nitrogen? *(Pg 4)*

Ans. Soil has certain bacteria that convert gaseous nitrogen into a usable form and release it into the soil. These soluble forms are absorbed by the plants along with water.

Que 10. Are mosquitoes, bed bugs, lice and leeches that suck our blood also parasites? *(Pg 5)*

Ans. Yes, the animals such as mosquitoes, bed bugs, lice and leeches that suck our blood are also parasites because these organisms derive their nutrition from host (human).

Que 11. If the pitcher plant is green and carries out photosynthesis, then why does it feed on insects? *(Pg 5)*

Ans. The insectivorous plants grow in soil which do not contain sufficient nitrogen mineral. These plants (e.g. pitcher plant) are green and carry out photosynthesis to obtain a part of the food required by them. But they do not get the nitrogen from the soil in which they grow. So, insectivorous or carnivorous plants feed on insects to obtain the nitrogen needed for their growth.

Que 12. Some organisms do not have mouths like animals. They are not like green plants as they lack chlorophyll and cannot make food by photosynthesis. How do these organisms acquire nutrients? *(Pg 6)*

Ans. These organisms have a different mode of nutrition. They secrete digestive juices on the dead and decaying matter and convert it into a solution, then they absorb the nutrients from it. These organisms are called saprotrophs.

Que 13. Paheli is keen to know whether her beautiful shoes which she wore on special occasions, were spoiled by fungi during the rainy season. She wants to know how fungi appear suddenly during the rainy season. *(Pg 6)*

Ans. The fungal spores are generally present in the air and grow on article (e.g. pickles, leather shoes, clothes, etc.) that are left in hot and humid weather for a long time. During rainy season, they land on wet and warm things and begin to germinate and grow.

Que 14. Boojho says once his grandfather told him that his wheat fields were spoiled by a fungus. He wants to know, does fungi cause diseases also? *(Pg 7)*

Ans. Yes, fungi cause diseases in plants, animals and humans.

Que 15. Farmers spread manure or fertilisers in the fields, or gardeners use them in lawns or in pots, why these are added to the soil? *(Pg 7)*

Ans. As plants absorb mineral nutrients from the soil, their amounts in the soil keep on declining. Fertilisers and manures contain plant nutrients such as nitrogen, potassium, phosphorus, etc which need to be added from time to time to enrich the soil.

Exercises

Que 1. Why do organisms need to take food?

Ans. The organisms need to take food to build their bodies, to grow, to repair damaged part of their bodies and to obtain the energy to carry out life processes. Food provide resistance to fight against diseases and protection from different infections.

Que 2. Distinguish between a parasites and a saprotroph.

Ans. Differences between parasites and saprophytes

	Parasite	Saprotroph
1.	The organism that lives inside the body of another organism (host) and derives the food from it.	The organism that feeds on dead and decaying organic matter. They do not require any host.
2.	They harm the body of host.	They are cleaning agents.
3.	*Cuscuta* plant is a parasite.	Fungi is a saprotroph.

Que 3. How would you test the presence of starch in leaves?

Ans. Presence of starch in leaves can be tested by iodine test. Iodine turns starch solution into blue-black colour. Pour few drops of dilute iodine solution on the boiled leaf. The leaf becomes blue-black which proves the presence of starch in it. The starch is a carbohydrate.

Que 4. Give a brief description of the process of synthesis of food in green plants.

Ans. Plants prepare their own food by the process of photosynthesis. Leaves of the plants have green pigment called chlorophyll, which helps them to capture the energy of the sunlight and they synthesise food from carbon dioxide and water. Thus, chlorophyll, sunlight, carbon dioxide and water help to carry out the process of photosynthesis. The solar energy is captured by the leaves and stored in the plant in the form of food.

The reaction for the process of photosynthesis can be shown as follows:

$$\text{Carbon dioxide} + \text{Water} \xrightarrow[\text{Chlorophyll}]{\text{Sunlight}} \underset{\text{(food)}}{\text{Carbohydrate}} + \text{Oxygen}$$

During photosynthesis, food is synthesised and oxygen is released in the process.

Que 5. Show with the help of a sketch that the plants are the ultimate source of food.

Ans. The following sketch shows that the plants are the ultimate source of food.

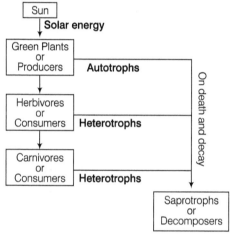

Que 6. Fill in the blanks.

   (a) Green plants are called .... since they synthesise their own food.

   (b) The food synthesised by the plants is stored as ....

   (c) In photosynthesis solar energy is captured by the pigment called ....

   (d) During photosynthesis, plants take in .... and release ....

Ans. (a) Green plants are called **autotrophs** since they synthesise their own food.

   (b) The food synthesised by the plants is stored as **starch**.

   (c) In photosynthesis solar energy is captured by the pigment called **chlorophyll**.

   (d) During photosynthesis, plants take in **carbon dioxide** and release **oxygen**.

Que 7. Name the following.

(a) A parasitic plant with yellow, slender and tubular stem.

(b) A plant that has both autotrophic and heterotrophic mode of nutrition.

(c) The pores through which leaves exchange gases.

Ans. (a) *Cuscuta* (amarbel)

(b) Pitcher plant (insectivorous plant)

(c) Stomata

Que 8. Tick (✔) the correct option.

(a) Amarbel is an example of

    (i) autotroph   (ii) parasite

    (iii) saprotroph   (iv) host

(b) The plant which traps and feeds on insects is

    (i) *Cuscuta*   (ii) China rose

    (iii) pitcher plant   (iv) rose

Ans. (a) Amerbel is an example of parasite.

(b) The plant which traps and feeds on insects is pitcher plant.

Que 9. Match the items given in Column I with those in Column II.

	Column I		Column II
(a)	Chlorophyll	(i)	Bacteria
(b)	Nitrogen	(ii)	Heterotrophs
(c)	Amarbel	(iii)	Pitcher plant
(d)	Animals	(iv)	Leaf
(e)	Insects	(v)	Parasite

Ans. The correct match of the both columns :

	Column I		Column II
(a)	Chlorophyll	(iv)	Leaf
(b)	Nitrogen	(i)	Bacteria
(c)	Amarbel	(v)	Parasite
(d)	Animals	(ii)	Heterotrophs
(e)	Insects	(iii)	Pitcher plant

Que 10. Mark 'T' if the statements is True and 'F' if it is False.
(a) Carbon dioxide is released during photosynthesis.
(b) Plants which synthesise their food themselves are called saprotrophs.
(c) The product of photosynthesis is not a protein.
(d) Solar energy is converted into chemical energy during photosynthesis.

Ans. (a) F, oxygen is released during photosynthesis.
(b) F, plants which synthesise their own food are called autotrophs.
(c) T, the product of photosynthesis is starch (carbohydrates).
(d) T

Que 11. Choose the correct option from the following :
(a) Which part of the plant takes in carbon dioxide from the air for photosynthesis?

     (i) Root hair   (ii) Stomata
     (iii) Leaf veins   (iv) Sepals

(b) Plants take carbon dioxide from the atmosphere mainly through their

     (i) roots   (ii) stem
     (iii) flowers   (iv) leaves

Ans. (a) (ii) Stomata, carbon dioxide from the air is taken in through the tiny pores present on the surface of leaves. Such pores are called stomata.
(b) (iv) Leaves, plants take carbon dioxide from the atmosphere mainly through their leaves.

Selected NCERT Exemplar Problems

> Multiple Choice Questions

Que 1. Organisms which prepare food for themselves using simple naturally available raw materials are referred to as
(a) heterotrophs   (b) autotrophs
(c) parasites   (d) saprophytes

Ans. (b) Organisms which prepare food for themselves using simple naturally available raw materials are referred to as **autotrophs**.

Que 2. Which of the following statements is/are correct?
   (i) All green plants can prepare their own food.
   (ii) Most animals are autotrophs.
   (iii) Carbon dioxide is not required for photosynthesis.
   (iv) Oxygen is liberated during photosynthesis.
   Choose the correct answer from the options below :
   (a) (i) and (iv)   (b) (ii) only
   (c) (ii) and (iii)   (d) (i) and (ii)

Ans. (a) (i) and (iv) are correct statements, and (ii) and (iii) are incorrect. Because (ii) animals are heterotrophs and (iii) CO_2 is necessary for photosynthesis. Green plants prepare their own food from CO_2 and H_2O.

Que 3. Pitcher plant traps insects because it
   (a) is a heterotroph.
   (b) grows in soils which lack in nitrogen.
   (c) does not have chlorophyll.
   (d) has a digestive system like human beings.

Ans. (b) Pitcher plant traps insects because it grows in soils which lack in nitrogen.

Que 4. The term that is used for the mode of nutrition in yeast, mushroom and bread-mould is
   (a) autotrophic   (b) insectivorous
   (c) saprophytic   (d) parasitic

Ans. (c) The term that is used for the mode of nutrition in yeast, mushroom and bread-mould is saprophytic. The mode of nutrition in which organisms take nutrition in solution form from dead and decaying matter is called saprophytic or saprotrophic nutrition.

Que 5. When we observe the lower surface of a leaf through a magnifying lens, we see numerous small openings. Which of the following is the term given to such openings?
   (a) Stomata   (b) Lamina
   (c) Midrib   (d) Veins

Ans. (a) When we observe the lower surface of a leaf through a magnifying lens, we see numerous small openings. Such openings are called stomata. These openings are surrounded by guard cells.

Que 6. Two organisms are good friends and live together. One provides shelter, water, and nutrients while the other prepares and provides food. Such an association of organisms is termed as
(a) saprophyte (b) parasite
(c) autotroph (d) symbiosis
Ans. (d) Two organisms are good friends and live together. One provides shelter, water and nutrients while the other prepares and provides food. Such an association of organisms is termed as symbiosis, e.g. lichen.

Que 7. Which of the following raw material is available in the air for photosynthesis?
(a) Oxygen (b) Carbon dioxide
(c) Nitrogen (d) Hydrogen
Ans. (b) Carbon dioxide (raw material) is available in the air for photosynthesis.

❯ Very Short Answer Type Questions

Que 8. Potato and ginger are both underground parts that store food. Where is the food prepared in these plants?
Ans. In both the plants, shoot system and leaves are above ground. They prepare food through photosynthesis and transport it to the underground part for storage.

Que 9. Photosynthesis requires chlorophyll and a few other raw materials. Add the missing raw materials to the list given below:
Water, minerals, ... (a) .... , ... (b) ....
Ans. (a) sunlight (b) carbon dioxide.

❯ Short Answer Type Questions

Que 10. A goat eats away all the leaves of a small plant (balsam). However, in a few days, new leaves could be seen sprouting in the plant again. How did the plant survive without leaves?
Ans. The plant of balsam survived on the food stored in the stem and roots.

Que 11. Unscramble the following to form terms related to modes of nutrition.
(i) RASPAEIT (ii) ROPEHYTSAP
(iii) TOROPHAUT (iv) SIBIOMSYS
Ans. (i) PARASITE (ii) SAPROPHYTE
(iii) AUTOTROPH (iv) SYMBIOSIS

Que 12. Nitrogen is an essential nutrient for plant growth. But farmers who cultivate pulse crops like green gram, bengal gram, black gram, etc do not apply nitrogenous fertilisers during cultivation. Why?

Ans. Roots of pulses (leguminous plants) have a symbiotic association with a bacterium called *Rhizobium*. This bacteria convert gaseous nitrogen of air into water soluble nitrogen compounds and give them to the leguminous plants for their growth. Hence, farmers need not use nitrogenous fertilisers.

Que 13. Wheat dough if left in the open, after a few days, starts to emit a foul smell and becomes unfit for use. Give reason.

Ans. Carbohydrates in wheat dough encourage the growth of yeast and other saprophytic fungi which breakdown carbohydrates into simpler compounds like CO_2 and alcohol and emit a foul smell.

Que 14. Sunlight, chlorophyll, carbon dioxide, water and minerals are raw materials essential for photosynthesis. Do you know where they are available? Fill in the blanks with the appropriate raw materials.
   (a) Available in the plant : ....
   (b) Available in the soil : ....
   (c) Available in the air : ....
   (d) Available during day : ....

Ans. (a) Available in the plant : Chlorophyll
     (b) Available in the soil : Water, minerals
     (c) Available in the air : Carbon dioxide
     (d) Available during day : Sunlight

Que 15. Observe the given figure and label the following terms given in the box.

Stomatal opening, Guard cell

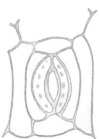

Ans. Labelled figure is given below:

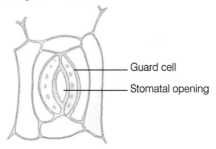

— Guard cell
— Stomatal opening

> Long Answer Type Questions

Que 16. Match the organisms given in Column I with their mode of nutrition given in Column II.

	Column I		Column II
(a)	Mango tree	(i)	Insectivorous plant
(b)	Mushroom	(ii)	Heterotroph
(c)	Pitcher plant	(iii)	Autotroph
(d)	*Cuscuta*	(iv)	Saprophyte
(e)	Elephant	(v)	Parasitic

Ans. The correct match of the both columns :

	Column I		Column II
(a)	Mango tree	(iii)	Autotroph
(b)	Mushroom	(iv)	Saprophyte
(c)	Pitcher plant	(i)	Insectivorous plant
(d)	*Cuscuta*	(v)	Parasitic
(e)	Elephant	(ii)	Heterotroph

Que 17. Wild animals like tiger, wolf, lion and leopard do not eat plants. Does this mean that they can survive without plants? Can you provide a suitable explanation?

Ans. Animals like tiger, wolf, lion and leopard are carnivores and do not eat plants. They hunt and eat herbivorous animals like deer, gaur, bison, zebra, giraffe, etc which are dependent on plants for food. If there are no plants, herbivorous animals will not survive and ultimately animals like tiger, wolf, lion and leopard will have nothing to eat.

Que 18. Spot as many organisms as possible in the puzzle given below figure by encircling them as shown. Write the names on a sheet of paper and categorise them into autotrophs and heterotrophs. Classify the heterotrophs into herbivores, carnivores, omnivores and saprophytes.

B	R	O	S	E	A	T	C	R	O	W
A	A	G	N	B	H	I	N	D	I	B
N	B	N	G	I	N	G	E	R	C	L
Y	B	A	N	H	B	E	C	O	W	F
A	I	M	U	S	H	R	O	O	M	F
N	T	G	B	E	R	M	W	F	I	O
E	L	E	P	H	A	N	T	S	C	X
T	S	A	E	Y	N	P	H	B	E	E
C	A	R	R	O	T	U	L	S	I	X

Ans. Number of organisms : 21

(Some examples are given. You may find the rest of the organisms.)

B	R	O	S	E	A	T	C	R	O	W
A	A	G	N	B	H	I	N	D	I	B
N	B	N	G	I	N	G	E	R	C	L
Y	B	A	N	H	B	E	C	O	W	F
A	I	M	U	S	H	R	O	O	M	F
N	T	G	B	E	R	M	W	F	I	O
E	L	E	P	H	A	N	T	S	C	X
T	S	A	E	Y	N	P	H	B	E	E
C	A	R	R	O	T	U	L	S	I	X

Autotrophs — Rose, Mango, Bhindi, Carrot, Banyan, Tulsi, Ginger,

Heterotrophs — Elephant, Ant, Yeast, Tiger, Mushroom, Fox, Mice, Owl, Cow, Crow, Rabbit, Bee, Fish, ox

Herbivores — Elephant, Cow, Rabbit, Bee, ox

Carnivores — Fox, Tiger

Omnivores — Ant, Mice, Owl, Crow, Fish

Saprophytes — Mushroom, Yeast

Chapter **2**

Nutrition *in* Animals

Important Points

- Plants can prepare their own food by the process of photosynthesis but animals get their food from plants, either directly by eating plants or indirectly by eating animals that eat plants. Some animals eat both plants and animals.

- **Animal nutrition** All animals require food for obtaining energy, growth, repair of damaged parts and functioning of the body. The process of taking food by an animal and its utilisation in the body is called animal nutrition.

- **Complex substances and simpler substances** The components of food such as carbohydrates are complex substances which cannot be utilised by the body. So, they are broken down into simpler substances.

- **Digestion** The process of breakdown of complex components of food into simpler substances is called digestion.

- **Different ways of taking food** Different organisms have different mode of taking food into the body. Animals take in food by different mode of feeding, e.g. scraping (snail), sucking (mosquito), siphoning (butterfly) and sponging (housefly), chewing (ant), capturing and swallowing (eagle).

- **Starfish** It feeds on animals covered by hard shells of calcium carbonate. After opening the shell, the starfish pops out its stomach through its mouth to eat the soft animal inside the shell and then stomach goes back into the body and the food is easily digested.

▪ **Digestion in humans** We take in food through the mouth, digest and utilise it. The unused parts of the food are defecated. The human digestive system consists of **alimentary canal** (digestive tract) and its **associated glands.** The canal can be divided into various compartments : (i) the **buccal cavity,** (ii) foodpipe or **oesophagus,** (iii) **stomach,** (iv) **small intestine,** (v) **large intestine** ending in the **rectum** and (vi) the **anus.**

The main digestive glands which secrete digestive juices are

(i) salivary gland (ii) liver and   (iii) pancreas.

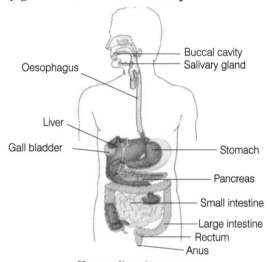

Human digestive system

▪ Digestion in animals takes place in five steps :

(i) The process of taking food into the body is called **ingestion.**

(ii) The process by which the food containing large insoluble substances is broken down into small water soluble substances is called **digestion.**

(iii) The process by which the digested food passes through the intestinal wall into blood stream is called **absorption.**

(iv) The process by which the absorbed food is taken in body cells and used for energy, growth and repair is called **assimilation.**

(v) The process by which the undigested food is removed from the body is called **egestion.**

- **The mouth and buccal cavity** Food is taken into the body through the mouth. The buccal cavity consists of **teeth, tongue** and **salivary** glands.

- **Salivary glands** These are a pair of small and branched structures situated in the mouth cavity. Secretion of salivary glands is known as **saliva** which contains starch splitting enzyme namely amylase and mucin for easy swallowing of food.

- **Teeth** We chew the food with the teeth and break it down mechanically into small pieces. Each tooth is rooted in a separate socket in the gums and perform different functions. There are four types of teeth :

  (i) **Incisors** There are four chisel shaped incisors at centre of each jaw for biting and cutting the food.

  (ii) **Canines** These are two large pointed teeth just behind incisors in each jaw, for piercing and tearing the food.

  (iii) **Premolars** There are four (two on each side) large premolars with flat surface behind the canines in each jaw.

  (iv) **Molars** In an adults, there are six (three on each side) large molars with flat surface behind the premolars in each jaw.

  Note Molars and premolars are used for chewing and grinding food.

- **Milk teeth and permanent teeth** The **first set** of teeth grows during infancy and they fall off at the age between six to eight years. These are termed milk teeth.

  The **second set** that replaces them are the permanent teeth. The permanent teeth may last throughout life or fall off during old age or due to some dental disease.

- **Tooth decay** Bacteria are present in our mouth but they are not harmful to us. However, if we do not clean our teeth and mouth after eating, many harmful bacteria also begin to live and grow in it. These bacteria breakdown the sugars present from the leftover food and release acids. The acids gradually damage the teeth. This is called tooth decay.

  Note Chocolates, sweets, soft drinks and other sugar products are the major culprits of tooth decay.

- **Causes of hiccups** The windpipe carries air from the nostrils to the lungs. It runs adjacent to the foodpipe. During the act of swallowing, a flap-like valve closes the passage of the windpipe and guides the food into the foodpipe. If, by chance, food particles enter the windpipe, we feel choked, get **hiccups** or **cough**.

- **Tongue** It is a muscular organ attached at the back to the floor of buccal cavity. It is free from front and can help to mix saliva with the food, swallowing food, talking or speaking and tasting with the help of taste buds for sweet, salty, sour and bitter food. **Salivary glands** secrete **saliva** which breaks down starch into sugars.

- **Foodpipe or oesphagus** The swallowed food passes into oesophagus or foodpipe. The foodpipe runs along the neck and the chest. Food is pushed down by movement of the wall of the foodpipe. Actually this movement takes place throughout the alimentary canal and pushes the food downwards.

- **Stomach** It is a thick-walled bag. It receives food from the foodpipe at one end and opens into the small intestine at the other.

  The inner lining of the stomach secretes mucous, hydrochloric acid and digestive juices. The mucous protects the lining of the stomach.

  The acid kills many bacteria that enter along with the food and makes the medium in the stomach acidic and helps the digestive juices to act. The digestive juices breakdown the **proteins** into simpler substances.

- **Working of the stomach** It was discovered by a strange accident. **William Beaumont** found that the stomach was churning food. Its wall secreted a fluid which could digest the food. He also observed that the end of the stomach opens into the intestine only after the digestion of the food inside the stomach is completed.

- **The small intestine** It is highly coiled and is about 7.5 m long. In small intestine, the carbohydrates get broken into simple sugars, fats into fatty acids and glycerides and proteins into amino acids. It receives secretions from the liver and the pancreas.

- **Fatty acids** An organic compound consisting of a long hydrocarbon chain and a terminal carboxylic acid. They are one of the main constituent of fats. Glycerol combines with fatty acid to form fats.

- **Glycerol** It is a colourless sweet-tasting viscous liquid, miscible with water. It is widely distributed in all living organism as a constituent of the **glycerides**.

- **Amino acid** It is a carboxylic acid that contains the amino group. These acids are the smallest unit that link together to form complex molecules like proteins.

- **Liver** It is a reddish brown gland situated in the upper part of the abdomen on the right side. It is the **largest gland** in the body. Liver secretes **bile juice** which is commonly known as bile. **Bile** juice is stored in a sac called the **gall bladder**. The bile plays an important role in the digestion of fats.

- **Pancrease** It is a large cream coloured gland which secretes pancreatic juice. These juices act on carbohydrates, fats and proteins and change them into simpler forms.

- **Villi** The inner walls of the small intestine have thousands of finger-like outgrowths. These are called villi (singular villus). The surface of the villi absorbs the digested food materials.

- **Diarrhoea** It may be caused by an infection, food poisoning or indigestion. Under severe conditions, it can be fatal. This is because of the excessive loss of water and salts from the body.

- **Oral Rehydration Solution (ORS)** Before a doctor is consulted, the patient should be given plenty of boiled and cooled water with a pinch of salt and sugar dissolved in it. This is called Oral Rehydration solution (ORS).

- **Large intestine** It is wider and shorter than small intestine. Its function is to absorb water and some salts from the undigested food material. The remaining waste passes into the rectum and remains there as semi-solid faeces. The faecal matter is removed through the anus from time-to-time. This is called **egestion.**

- **Digestion in grass-eating animals** These animals like as cows and buffaloes quickly swallow their food and store it in a part of their stomach called **rumen** (it is absent in humans).

- Here, food gets partially digested and is called **cud.** But later, the cud returns to the mouth in small lumps and the animal chews it, this is the reason why these animals chewing continuously. This process of digestion is called **rumination** and animals are called **ruminants.** Ruminants have a large sac-like structure called **caecum** between the small intestine and large intestine.
- **Cellulose** It is a type of carbohydrate. The grass is rich in cellulose. Many animals including humans, cannot digest cellulose. The cellulose of the food is digested here by the action of certain bacteria which are not present in humans.
- *Amoeba* It is a microscopic single-celled organism found in pond water. *Amoeba* has a cell membrane, a rounded, dense nucleus and many small bubble-like vacuoles in its cytoplasm.
- **Pseudopodia** *Amoeba* constantly changes its shape and position. It pushes out one or more finger-like projections, called pseudopodia or false feet for movement and capture of food.
- **Food vacuole** It is fluid filled membrane bound structure present inside the cytoplasm of the cell. The food is trapped in a food vacuole in *Amoeba* and by the action of digestive juices the food is broken down into simpler substances.

Intext Questions

Que 1. Complete the following table, from the options given below :

(Scraping, chewing, siphoning, capturing and swallowing, sponging, sucking, etc.)   *(Pg 11)*

Name of animal	Kind of food	Mode of feeding
Snail		
Ant		
Eagle		
Humming-bird		
Lice		
Mosquito		
Butterfly		
Housefly		

Ans. The complete table is

Name of animal	Kind of food	Mode of feeding
Snail	Leaves and insects	Scraping
Ant	Food particles	Chewing
Eagle	Small animals	Capturing and swallowing
Humming-bird	Nectar of flower	Sucking
Lice	Blood	Sucking
Mosquito	Blood	Sucking
Butterfly	Nectar of flower	Siphoning
Housefly	All most everything	Sponging

Que 2. How food moves in the opposite direction during vomiting? *(Pg 15)*

Ans. The intense pressure formed in the stomach when the food is not accepted by the stomach. The content in the stomach is then pushed back. This returned content is expelled out from the mouth in the form of vomiting.

Que 3. What are the reasons of vomiting? *(Pg 16)*

Ans. Some reasons of vomiting are
(i) Allergy in stomach
(ii) Food poisoning
(iii) Excessive eating
(iv) Bloating of stomach (gas in between food content).

Que 4. Why animals like cow cannot chew their food properly at the time they take it in? *(Pg 18)*

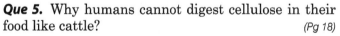

Ans. Animals like cow cannot chew their food properly due to presence of cellulose in their diet. At the time they take in food, the food only moistens and is sent for cellulose digestion and softening in rumen.

Que 5. Why humans cannot digest cellulose in their food like cattle? *(Pg 18)*

Ans. Humans cannot digest cellulose in their food like cattle due to the absence of rumen. The cellulose of the food is digested by the action of bacteria present in rumen.

Exercises

Que 1. Fill in the blanks.

(a) The main steps of nutrition in humans are ………,
………, ………, ……… and ……… .

(b) The largest gland in the human body is ……… .

(c) The stomach releases hydrochloric acid and ………
juices which act on food.

(d) The inner wall of the small intestine has many
finger-like outgrowths called ……… .

(e) *Amoeba* digests its food in the ……… .

Ans. (a) The main steps of nutrition in humans are **ingestion,
digestion, absorption, assimilation** and **egestion.**

(b) The largest gland in the human body is **liver.**

(c) The stomach releases hydrochloric acid and **digestive** juices
which act on food.

(d) The inner wall of the small intestine has many finger-like
outgrowths called **villi.**

(e) *Amoeba* digests its food in the **food vacuole.**

Que 2. Mark 'T' if the statement is True and 'F' if it is False.

(a) Digestion of starch starts in the stomach.

(b) The tongue helps in mixing food with saliva.

(c) The gall bladder temporarily stores bile.

(d) The ruminants bring back swallowed grass into their
mouth and chew it for some time.

Ans. (a) F, digestion of starch starts in the mouth.

(b) T

(c) T

(d) T

Que 3. Tick (✓) mark the correct answer in each of the
following.

(a) Fat is completely digested in the

(i) stomach

(ii) mouth

(iii) small intestine

(iv) large intestine

(b) Water from the undigested food is absorbed mainly in the
   (i) stomach
   (ii) foodpipe
   (iii) small intestine
   (iv) large intestine

Ans. (a) (iii) **Small intestine** is the site for complete digestion of fats by the action of bile juice.

(b) (iv) **Large intestine** absorbs the water from undigested food.

Que 4. Match the items of Column I with those given in Column II.

Column I (Food components)		Column II (Product(s) of digestion)	
(a)	Carbohydrates	(i)	Fatty acid and glycerol
(b)	Proteins	(ii)	Sugar
(c)	Fats	(iii)	Amino acids

Ans. The correct match of the both columns :

Column I (Food components)		Column II (Product(s) of digestion)	
(a)	Carbohydrates	(ii)	Sugar
(b)	Proteins	(iii)	Amino acids
(c)	Fats	(i)	Fatty acids and glycerol

Que 5. What are villi? What is their location and function?

Ans. Villi are the finger-like projections in the inner walls of the small intestine.

Function Villi increase the surface area for absorption of digested food.

Que 6. Where is the bile produced? Which component of the food does it help to digest?

Ans. Bile juice is produced by the liver and stored in gall bladder. It helps in digestion **fats** present in food.

Que 7. Name the type of carbohydrate that can be digested by ruminants but not by humans. Give the reason also.

Ans. Cellulose is the carbohydrate that can be digested by ruminants but not by humans because ruminants have a large sac-like structure called **rumen** which is located between the small intestine and large intestine. Certain bacteria are present in rumen which helps in digesting cellulose.

Que 8. Why do we get instant energy from glucose?

Ans. Glucose is a simple sugar or carbohydrates which is broken down in
the presence of oxygen into CO_2 and H_2O and releases instant energy.
Glucose is easily absorbed by the blood, hence provides instant energy
to the body.

Que 9. Which part of the digestive canal is involved in:
  (i) absorption of food ....
  (ii) chewing of food ....
  (iii) killing of bacteria ....
  (iv) complete digestion of food ....
  (v) formation of faeces ....

Ans. Parts of digestive canal that are involved in following process are
  (i) Absorption of food **small intestine**
  (ii) Chewing of food **buccal cavity**
  (iii) Killing of bacteria **stomach**
  (iv) Complete digestion of food **small intestine**
  (v) Formation of faeces **large intestine**

Que 10. Write one similarity and one difference between
nutrition in *Amoeba* and human beings.

Ans. Both *Amoeba* and humans require energy for the growth and
maintenance of their bodies. This energy is derived from the food they
eat. The food is in a complex form and is therefore broken down into
simple forms by the process of digestion. Both these organisms are
heterotrophs as they derive their food from other plants or animals.

Difference between nutrition in *Amoeba* and human beings is given
below :

	Digestion in humans	Digestion in *Amoeba*
1.	Humans have mouth and complex digestive system.	Mouth and digestive system are absent in *Amoeba*.
2.	Digestive juices are secreted in the buccal cavity, stomach and small intestine.	Digestive juices are secreted in the food vacuole.
3.	Digestion of carbohydrates proteins and fats starts in separate regions.	All the food components are digested in the food vacuole.

Que 11. Match the items of Column I with suitable items in Column II.

	Column I		Column II
(a)	Salivary gland	(i)	Bile juice secretion
(b)	Stomach	(ii)	Storage of undigested food
(c)	Liver	(iii)	Saliva secretion
(d)	Rectum	(iv)	Acid release
(e)	Small intestine	(v)	Digestion is completed
(f)	Large intestine	(vi)	Absorption of water
		(vii)	Release of faeces

Ans. The correct matching of the both columns :

	Column I		Column II
(a)	Salivary gland	(iii)	Saliva secretion
(b)	Stomach	(iv)	Acid release
(c)	Liver	(i)	Bile juice secretion
(d)	Rectum	(vii)	Release of faeces
(e)	Small intestine	(v)	Digestion is completed
(f)	Large intestine	(vi)	Absorption of water

Que 12. Label the given figure of the digestive system.

Ans. The digestive system is composed of following parts:

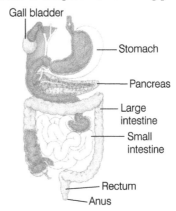

Gall bladder

Stomach

Pancreas

Large intestine

Small intestine

Rectum

Anus

Que 13. Can we survive only on raw, leafy vegetables/grass? Discuss.

Ans. Plants synthesise their own food by trapping solar energy in the form of glucose. Human beings and other animals do not have the ability to make their own food. They depend upon autotrophs for their food directly or indirectly. Therefore, we can say that raw, leafy vegetables and grasses provide sufficient energy to human and animals to survive.

Selected **NCERT Exemplar Problems**

❯ **Multiple Choice Questions**

Que 1. Given below from (i) to (iv) are some food items.

   (i) Boiled and mashed potato

   (ii) Glucose solution

   (iii) A slice of bread

   (iv) Mustard oil

Which of the above will give blue-black colour when tested with iodine?

(a) (i) and (ii)   (b) (i) and (iii)

(c) (ii) and (iii)   (d) (iii) and (iv)

Ans. (b) Among the given options, boiled and mashed potato and a slice of bread will show the presence of starch by giving blue-black colour when tested with iodine.

Que 2. Which of the following pair of teeth differ in structure but are similar in function?

    (a) Canines and incisors   (b) Molars and premolars

    (c) Incisors and molars   (d) Premolars and canines

Ans. (b) Molars and premolars differ in structure but perform the same function, i.e. chewing and grinding food.

Que 3. Read carefully the terms given below. Which of the following set is the correct combination of organs that do not carry out any digestive functions?

    (a) Oesophagus, large intestine, rectum

    (b) Buccal cavity, oesophagus, rectum

    (c) Buccal cavity, oesophagus, large intestine

    (d) Small intestine, large intestine, rectum

Ans. (a) Among the given options, the correct set with combination of organ that do not perform any digestive function is oesophagus, large intestine and rectum. The function of these organs is

  (i) **Oesophagus** It serves as a pipe for conduction of food.

 (ii) **Large intestine** Its function is to absorb water and some salts from undigested food.

(iii) **Rectum** It stores the undigested food.

Que 4. The swallowed food moves downwards in the alimentary canal because of

    (a) force provided by the muscular tongue

    (b) the flow of water taken with the food

    (c) gravitational pull

    (d) the contraction of muscles in the wall of foodpipe

Ans. (d) The swallowed food moves downwards in the alimentary canal because of the contraction of muscles in the wall of foodpipe.

Que 5. The acid present in the stomach

    (a) kills the harmful bacteria that may enter along with the food

    (b) protects the stomach lining from harmful substances

    (c) digests starch into simpler sugars

    (d) makes the medium alkaline

Ans. (a) The acid present in the stomach kills the harmful bacteria that may enter along with the food.

Que 6. The finger-like outgrowths of *Amoeba* helps to ingest food. However, the finger-like outgrowths of human intestine helps to

    (a) digest the fatty food substances

    (b) make the food soluble

    (c) absorb the digested food

    (d) absorb the undigested food

Ans. (c) The finger-like outgrowths of the human intestine is called the **villi**. It increases the surface area of the intestine and helps in absorption of digested food.

Que 7. Read the following statements with reference to the villi of small intestine.

    (i) They have very thin walls.

    (ii) They have a network of thin and small blood vessels close to the surface.

    (iii) They have small pores through which food can easily pass.

    (iv) They are finger-like projections.

Identify those statements which enable the villi to absorb digested food.

    (a) (i), (ii) and (iv)   (b) (ii), (iii) and (iv)

    (c) (iii) and (iv)   (d) (i) and (iv)

Ans. (a) The villi present in the small intestine help to absorb the digested food as

    (i) they have very thin walls.

    (ii) they have a network of thin and small blood vessels close to the surface.

    (iii) they are finger-like projections.

Que 8. The false feet of *Amoeba* are used for

    (a) movement only

    (b) capture of food only

    (c) capture of food and movement

    (d) exchange of gases only

Ans. (c) The false feet of *Amoeba* are used for movement and capturing the food.

Que 9. The enzymes present in the saliva convert
  (a) fats into fatty acids and glycerol
  (b) starch into simple sugars
  (c) proteins into amino acids
  (d) complex sugars into simple sugars
Ans. (b) The enzymes present in the saliva convert starch into simple sugars.

Que 10. Cud is the name given to the food of ruminants which is
  (a) swallowed and undigested
  (b) swallowed and partially digested
  (c) properly chewed and partially digested
  (d) properly chewed and completely digested
Ans. (b) The swallowed and partially digested food of ruminants is called cud.

Que 11. Choose the correct order of terms that describes the process of nutrition in ruminants.
  (a) Swallowing → partial digestion → chewing of cud → complete digestion
  (b) Chewing of cud → swallowing → partial digestion → complete digestion
  (c) Chewing of cud → swallowing → mixing with digestive juices → digestion
  (d) Swallowing → chewing and mixing → partial digestion → complete digestion
Ans. (a) The correct order of terms that describes the process of nutrition in ruminants is
  swallowing → partial digestion → chewing of cud → complete digestion

Que 12. Cellulose-rich food substances are good source of roughage in human beings because
  (a) human beings do not have cellulose-digesting enzymes
  (b) cellulose gets absorbed in the human blood and converts into fibres
  (c) the cellulose digesting bacteria convert cellulose into fibres
  (d) cellulose breaks down into smaller components which are egested as roughage
Ans. (a) The cellulose-rich food substances are good source of roughage in human beings because human beings do not have cellulose digesting-enzymes.

❯ Very Short Answer Type Questions

Que 13. Name the parts of the alimentary canal where
   (i) water gets absorbed from undigested food
   (ii) digested food gets absorbed
   (iii) taste of the food is perceived
   (iv) bile juice is produced

Ans. The part of alimentary canal where
   (i) water gets absorbed from undigested food is **large intestine.**
   (ii) digested food gets absorbed is **small intestine.**
   (iii) taste of the food is perceived by **tongue.**
   (iv) bile juice is produced in **liver.**

Que 14. Choose the odd one out from each group and give reasons.
   (i) liver, salivary gland, starch, gall bladder
   (ii) stomach, liver, pancreas, salivary gland
   (iii) tongue, absorption, taste, swallow
   (iv) oesophagus, small intestine, large intestine, rectum

Ans. (i) **Starch** because rest all are glands and starch is a type of carbohydrate.
   (ii) **Stomach** because rest all are digestive glands and stomach it is a digestive organ.
   (iii) **Tongue** because rest all are digestive processes and tongue is a part of digestive system.
   (iv) **Small intestine** because it carriers the process of digestion and rest are not involved in digestion.

Que 15. You were blindfolded and asked to identify the drinks provided in two different glasses. You could identify drink *A* as lime juice and *B* as bitter gourd juice. How could you do it inspite of being blindfolded?

Ans. Inspite of being blindfolded, one could identify two different drinks with the help of taste buds present in the tongue.

Que 16. Following statements describe the five steps in animal nutrition. Read each statement and give one word for each statement. Write the terms that describe each process.
   (a) Transportation of absorbed food to different parts of body and their utilisation.

(b) Breaking of complex food substances into simpler and soluble substances.

(c) Removal of undigested and unabsorbed solid residues of food from the body.

(d) Taking food into the body.

(e) Transport of digested and soluble food from the intestine to blood vessels.

Ans.   (a) Assimilation   (b) Digestion

         (c) Egestion   (d) Ingestion

         (e) Absorption

❯ Short Answer Type Questions

Que 17. Match the animals in Column I with their mode of feeding in Column II.

Column I (Animals)		Column II (Mode of feeding)	
(a)	Housefly	(i)	Biting and chewing
(b)	Cockroach	(ii)	Suckling
(c)	Mosquito	(iii)	Sponging
(d)	Infants	(iv)	Sucking

Ans. The correct match of both the columns :

Column I (Animals)		Column II (Mode of feeding)	
(a)	Housefly	(iii)	Sponging
(b)	Cockroach	(i)	Biting and chewing
(c)	Mosquito	(iv)	Sucking
(d)	Infants	(ii)	Suckling

Que 18. 'A' got her gall bladder removed surgically as she was diagnosed with stones in her gall bladder. After the surgery, she faced problems in digestion of certain food items when consumed in bulk. Can you tell which kind of food items would they be and why?

Ans. After surgical removal of gall bladder, 'A' would face problems in digestion of fat and fatty substances when consumed in bulk. This is because the bile juice from the gall bladder helps in digestion of fats.

Que 19. Ruminants such as cows and buffaloes swallow their food hurriedly and then sit restfully and chew their food. Give reason.

Ans. Ruminants such as cows and buffaloes swallow their food hurriedly and store it in a part of the stomach called rumen. The cellulose of the food is digested here by the action of certain bacteria which are not present in humans. Later, this partially digested food is returned to the buccal cavity of the animals in small lumps and animal chews it to complete the process of digestion. This process is called rumination.

Que 20. Boojho and Paheli were eating their food hurriedly so that they could go out and play during the recess. Suddenly, Boojho started coughing violently. Think of the reasons, why he was coughing and discuss with your friends.

Ans. Sometimes when we eat hurriedly, talks or laughs while eating, the flap like valve (called epiglottis) which closes the passage of windpipe remains open. Therefore, the food may enter into the windpipe. Coughing helps to clear the passage and returns the food particle back to the food pipe.

> Long Answer Type Questions

Que 21. Label the below given figure as directed below in (a) to (d) and give the name of each type of teeth.

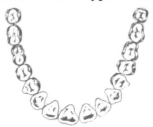

(a) The cutting and biting teeth as 'A'
(b) The piercing and tearing teeth as 'B'
(c) The grinding and chewing teeth as 'C'
(d) The grinding teeth present only in adult as '*D*'

Ans.

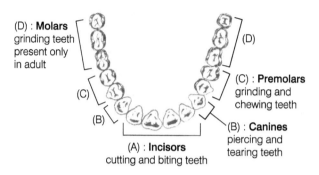

(D) : **Molars**
grinding teeth
present only
in adult

(D)

(C) : **Premolars**
grinding and
chewing teeth

(C)

(B)

(B) : **Canines**
piercing and
tearing teeth

(A) : **Incisors**
cutting and biting teeth

Que 22.

Label the following parts of above figure and name them.

(a) The largest gland in our body.

(b) The organ where protein digestion starts.

(c) The organ that releases digestive juice into the small intestine.

(d) The organ where bile juice gets stored.

Ans.

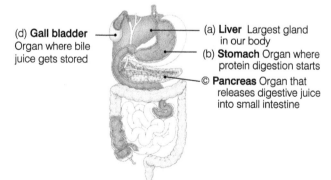

(d) **Gall bladder**
Organ where bile
juice gets stored

(a) **Liver** Largest gland
in our body

(b) **Stomach** Organ where
protein digestion starts

© **Pancreas** Organ that
releases digestive juice
into small intestine

Que 23. Solve the crossword given as figure.

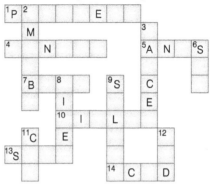

	Across		Down
1.	Cream coloured digestive gland	2.	Feeds with the help of pseudopodia
4.	Organ that mixes saliva with the food	3.	Undigested excretory solid residues
5.	Point of defecation	6.	Total number of molars in one jaw of an adult
7.	Stored in gall bladder	8.	Largest gland
10.	Finger-like outgrowth in the small intestine	9.	Watery secretion in the mouth
13.	Kind of taste buds	11.	A ruminant
14.	Kills bacteria in the stomach	12.	Form of food chewed by ruminants

Ans.

Chapter **3**

Fibre *to* Fabric

Important Points

- **Fibre** A thread or filament from which a vegetable tissue, mineral substances or textile is formed.

  Textile fibre can be spun into a yarn or made into fabric by various methods including weaving, knitting, braiding and twisting.

  Two types of fibres are
    - (i) Natural fibre (silk, wool)
    - (ii) Man-made fibre (nylon, rayon)

- **Animal fibres : wool and silk** We know that some fibres like jute and cotton are obtained from plants. We also obtain fibres like wool and silk from some animals.

- **Wool** It is the textile fibre obtained from **fleece** (hair) of sheep, goat or yak, etc.

  Skin of the sheep has two types of fibres :
    - (i) The coarse beard hair.
    - (ii) The fine soft under-hair close to skin.

  Note The fine hair provide the fibres for making wool.

- **Selective breeding** Some breeds of sheep possess only fine under-hair. Their parents are specially chosen to give birth to sheep which have only soft under-hair. This process of selecting parents is termed as selective breeding.

- **Animals that yield wool** The fleece of sheep is not the only source of wool. Other sources of wool are
    - (i) **Yak** wool in Tibet and Ladakh.
    - (ii) **Angora** wool obtained from angora goats in Jammu and Kashmir or in hilly regions.

(iii) **Kashmiri goat** The under fur of Kashmiri goat is soft and it is woven into fine shawls called **pashmina shawls**.

(iv) **Camels** The fur (hair) on the body of camels is used as wool.

(v) **Llama** and **Alpaca** These are found in South America and also yield wool.

■ **Rearing** It is a process of taking care livestock (e.g. cows, buffaloes, goats, etc.) for commercial purposes. These animals are fed, provided shelter and are breed for better yield like meat, wool, etc. e.g. Sheep are reared mainly for the wool. They are mainly reared in areas with low rainfall. In winters, they are kept indoors and fed on dry fodder, leaves and grains.

■ **Processing fibres into wool** It involves the following steps :

Step I The process of removing fleece (hair) from the body of sheep, is called **shearing**. Machines similar to those used by barbers are used shave off hair.

Step II The process of washing sheared skin in tanks to remove grease, dust and dirt, is called **scouring**. Now-a-days, scouring is done by machines.

Step III Separation of hair of different textures known as **sorting**.

Step IV The small fluffy fibres, called burrs are picked out from the hair.

Step V Fibres are dyed in various colours.

Step VI Fibres are straightened, combed and rolled into yarn. The longer fibres are made into wool for sweaters and the shorter fibres are spun and woven into woollen clothes.

Note Sorter's job is risky as sometimes, they get infected by a bacterium, **anthrax**, which causes a fatal blood disease called sorter's disease. Such risks faced by workers in any industry are called occupational hazards.

■ **Silk** It is a natural protein fibre, some forms of which can be woven into textiles. The protein fibre of silk is composed mainly of fibroin and is produced by certain insect larvae to form cocoons.

■ **Sericulture** The breeding and management of silkworms for the production of silk is known as sericulture. Different types of silk (e.g. mulberry silk, tasaar silk, etc) with different textures are obtained from different varieties of silk moths.

- **Life cycle of silk moth** There are the four stages in the development of silk moth :

  Eggs → caterpillars → pupa → silk moth
         Silkworms   (Adult)
         (larvae)

- **Silkworms or caterpillars** The female silk moth lays eggs from which hatch larvae that are called silkworms or caterpillars. The moth is important because it makes the silk and no longer live.

- **Pupa** Silkworm grow in size and when the caterpillar is ready to enter the next stage of its life called pupa or an insects in its inactive immature form between larvae and adult.

- **Cocoon** Silkworm swing its head from side to side and secretes fibre made up of protein, which hardens on exposure to air and becomes silk fibre. Soon the silkworm completely covers itself by silk fibres. This covering is known as cocoon.

- Tassar silk, mooga silk, kosa silk, etc are obtained from cocoons spun by different types of moths. The most common silk moth is the **mulberry silk moth**.

- **From cocoon to silk** For obtaining silk, moths are reared and their cocoons are collected to get silk threads.

  (i) **Rearing silkworms** The caterpillar larvae are reared by feeding them on mulberry leaves. They spin a cocoon around themselves.

  (ii) **Processing of silk** Cocoons are collected and kept under the sun or boiled, or exposed to steam. This helps in separating the silk fibres. The process by which silk thread is separated from the cocoon is called **reeling the silk**. Then the spinning of silk fibres into threads is done. The silk threads obtained are woven into the desired clothes.

- **Discovery of silk** Silk is supposed to be discovered in China. Accidently, a cocoon dropped into the cup of tea of empress si-lung-chi, and a tangle of delicate threads separated from the cocoon. Silk industry began in China and was left a closely guarded secret for hundreds of years. Later on, traders and travellers introduced silk to other countries. The route they travelled is still called the 'silk route'.

Intext Questions

Que 1. Why yak, goat, sheep have a thick coat of hair? *(Pg 25)*

Ans. As we know, air is a poor conductor of heat and the hair of these animals trap a lot of air due to which animals feel warm.

Que 2. Does shearing hurt the sheep? *(Pg 26)*

Ans. Shearing does not hurt the sheep because the uppermost layer of the skin is dead. Also, the hair of sheep grow again.

Que 3. What type of disease may be caused by wool industry? *(Pg 28)*

Ans. A fatal blood disease known as 'sorter's disease' caused by a bacterium, **anthrax** produced in wool industry.

Que 4. Why a cotton garment cannot keep us as warm in winter as woollen sweater does? *(Pg 28)*

Ans. Cotton clothes are thin and do not have space in which air can be trapped. Thus, cotton clothes do not prevent heat coming out of our body.

Woollen clothes keep us warm during winter because wool is a poor conductor of heat and it has air trapped in between the fibres.

Que 5. What happens when synthetic silk and woollen silk burn? *(Pg 29)*

Ans. Since, synthetic silk is made up of plant, so it smells like burning paper or plastic but woolen silk is made up of protein molecule and hence it gives burning hair smell on burning.

Exercises

Que 1. You must be familiar with the following nursery rhymes.

(i) 'Baa Baa! Baa Baa! Black sheep, have you any wool.'

(ii) 'Mary had a little lamb, whose fleece was white as snow.'

Answer the following :

(a) Which parts of the black sheep have wool?

(b) What is meant by the white fleece of the lamb?

Ans. (a) The black sheep in the poem seems to have wool on almost all the parts as it in the poem, it offers wool enough to fill three bags full.

(b) Here, the white fleece of the lamb refers to pure white coloured hairy skin of the lamb.

Que 2. The silkworm is (i) a caterpillar, (ii) a larva. Choose the correct option.

    (a) (i)   (b) (ii)

    (c) Both (i) and (ii)   (d) Neither (i) nor (ii)

Ans. (c) Both (i) and (ii), larva and caterpillar are silkworms.

Que 3. Which of the following does not yield wool?

    (a) Yak   (b) Camel

    (c) Goat   (d) Woolly dog

Ans. (d) Woolly dog does not yield wool.

Que 4. What is meant by the following terms?

    (a) Rearing   (b) Shearing

    (c) Sericulture

Ans. (a) **Rearing** It is taking care of livestock (e.g. goats, cows, sheep, etc) for commercial purpose by taking them out in herds for grazing, feeding them on a mixture of pulses. Corn, jawar, oil cakes (material left after taking out oil from seeds) and minerals for better growth and yield of produce like meat, milk, wool. Beside this in extreme climate conditions like winter, these are also provided shelter and fed on leaves, grain and dry fodder.

    (b) **Shearing** It is the process in which fleece (hair) of the sheep along a thin layer of skin is removed from its body. Machines similar to those used by barbers are used to shave off hair. Generally, the hair are removed during the hot weather which enables the sheep to survive without their protective coat of hair. Shearing does not hurt the sheep as the uppermost layer of the skin is dead.

    (c) **Sericulture** Sericulture or silk farming is the rearing of silkworms for the production of raw silk. For obtaining silk, silkworm moths are reared and their cocoons are collected to get silk threads. Silk yarns come from the cocoon of the silkworm. The caterpillar hatches from a very small egg and is an eating machine. When the silkworms start its spinning process in the cocoon, the worm's head is coated with a gummy protein called sericin.

    The silkworm rotates its body thousands of times producing one continuous strand of silk of length of 12 football fields. The silk adheres to itself forming the cocoon.

Que 5. Given below is a sequence of steps in the processing of wool. Which are the missing step? Add them.

Shearing, ... sorting .... , ..., ...

Ans. (i) Shearing   (ii) Scouring,   (iii) Sorting,

(iv) Fibre spinning,   (v) Dyeing,   (vi) Rolling into the yarn.

Que 6. Make sketches of the two stages in the life history of the silk moth. Which are directly related to the production of silk.

Ans.

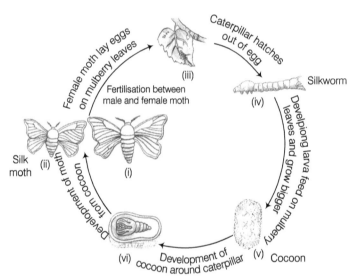

Life history of silk moth

(i) Male adult silk moth   (ii) Female adult silk moth

(iii) Eggs on mulberry leaves   (iv) Silkworm

(v) Cocoon

(vi) Cocoon with developing moth

Que 7. Out of the following which are the two terms related to silk production?

Sericulture, floriculture, moriculture, apiculture, and silviculture

Hints

(i) Silk production involves cultivation of mulberry leaves and rearing silkworms.

(ii) Scientific name of mulberry is *Morus alba*.

Ans. Sericulture, moriculture terms related to silk production.

Que 8. Match the words of Column I with those given in Column II.

	Column I		Column II
(a)	Scouring	(i)	Yields silk fibres
(b)	Mulberry leaves	(ii)	Wool yielding animal
(c)	Yak	(iii)	Food of silkworm
(d)	Cocoon	(iv)	Reeling
		(v)	Cleaning sheared skin

Ans.

	Column I		Column II
(a)	Scouring	(v)	Cleaning sheared skin
(b)	Mulberry leaves	(iii)	Food of silkworm
(c)	Yak	(ii)	Wool yielding animals
(d)	Cocoon	(i)	Yields silk fibres

* Reeling It is a rotator device used for reeling of silk .

Que 9. Given below is a crossword puzzle based on this lesson. Use hints to fill in the blank spaces with letters that complete the words.

Down	Across
(D) 1. Through washing	(A) 1. Keeps warm
2. Animal fibre	2. Its leaves are eaten by silkworms
3. Long thread like structure	3. Hatches from egg of moth

Ans.

		1D S		2D S			
		C		I			
3D F	1A W	O	O	L			
I	U	K					

1D → Scour
2D → Silk
3D → Fibre
1A → Wool
2A → Mulberry
3A → Caterpillar

Selected **NCERT Exemplar Problems**

≫ **Multiple Choice Questions**

Que 1. The rearing of silkworms for obtaining silk is called
    (a) cocoon   (b) silk
    (c) sericulture   (d) silviculture
Ans. (c) Rearing of silkworm for obtaining silk is called sericulture.

Que 2. Which of the following is not a type of silk?
    (a) Mulberry silk   (b) Tassar silk
    (c) Mooga silk   (d) Moth silk
Ans. (d) Moth silk is not a type of silk. It is an adult silkworm.

Que 3. Paheli wanted to buy a gift made of animal fibre obtained without killing the animal. Which of the following would be the right gift for her to buy?
    (a) Woollen shawl   (b) Silk scarf
    (c) Animal fur cap   (d) Leather jacket
Ans. (a) Woollen shawl is made up of only by fleece (hair) of sheep.

Que 4. Silk fibre is obtained from
    (a) fleece of sheep   (b) cotton ball
    (c) cocoon   (d) shiny jute stalk
Ans. (c) Silk fibre is obtained from cocoon.

Que 5. Wool fibre cannot be obtained from which of the following?

    (a) Goat   (b) Llama

    (c) Alpaca   (d) Moth

Ans. (d) Wool fibre cannot be obtained from moth.

Que 6. Selective breeding is a process of

    (a) selecting the offsprings with desired properties

    (b) selecting the parents with desired properties

    (c) selecting an area for breeding

    (d) selecting fine hair for good quality wool

Ans. (b) The process of selecting parents for obtaining desired characters in their offsprings such as soft under hair in sheep is termed as selective breeding.

Que 7. The general process that takes place at a sheep shearing shed is

    (a) removal of fleece

    (b) separating hair of different textures

    (c) washing of sheep fibre to remove grease

    (d) rolling of sheep fibre into yarn

Ans. (a) Removal of fleece takes place at a sheep shearing shed.

Que 8. The term sericulture is used for

    (a) culture of bacteria

    (b) rearing of silkworm

    (c) making silk fabric from silk yarn

    (d) production of sarees

Ans. (b) The term sericulture is used for rearing of silkworm.

Que 9. Reeling of silk is

    (a) a process of making silk reels

    (b) spinning of silk fibres

    (c) weaving of silk cloth

    (d) the process of taking silk threads from cocoon

Ans. (d) Reeling of silk is the process of taking silk threads from cocoon.

Que 10. Silkworms secrete fibre made of

    (a) fat   (b) cellulose

    (c) protein   (d) nylon

Ans. (c) Silk is a natural protein fibre.

≫ Very Short Answer Type Questions

Que 11. Fill in the blanks in the following statements.

(a) .... and .... fibres are obtained from animals.

(b) Silk fibres come from .... of silk ....

(c) Wool yielding animals bear .... on their body.

(d) Hair trap a lot of ...., which is a poor .... of heat.

Ans. (a) Silk, wool   (b) cocoons, moth

(c) hair   (d) air, conductor

Que 12. State whether the following statements are True or False. If False, correct them.

(a) Silkworms are caterpillars of silk moth.

(b) In India, camels and goats are generally reared for obtaining wool.

(c) The rearing of silkworms for obtaining silk is called silviculture.

(d) In the process of obtaining wool from fleece, sorting is done after scouring.

(e) Yak hair are not used to make woollen fabric.

Ans. (a) True

(b) False, generally sheep are reared.

(c) False, it is sericulture.

(d) True

(e) False, yak hair are used to make woollen fabric.

Que 13. How do the hair of certain animals help in keeping their bodies warm?

Ans. Hair traps a lot of air which is a poor conductor of heat resulting their body warm.

≫ Short Answer Type Questions

Que 14. Various steps involved to obtain wool from fleece are given here.

(i) Picking out the burrs   (ii) Dyeing in various colours

(iii) Shearing   (iv) Scouring

(v) Sorting

Write the above steps in the correct sequence in which they are carried out.

Ans. Correct sequence is

    (iii) Shearing

        ↓

    (iv) Scouring

        ↓

    (v) Sorting

        ↓

    (i) Picking out the burrs

        ↓

    (ii) Dyeing in various colours

Que 15. Some words related with silk are jumbled up. Write them in their correct form.

    (a) TURECULRISE   (b) WILSMORK

    (c) BELMURRY   (d) RINGLEE

Ans. (a) Sericulture   (b) Silkworm

    (c) Mulberry   (d) Reeling

Que 16. Figure shows three rings of circles with letters in them. Some of these letters in each ring can form the name of one wool yielding animal. Find the names of these animals.

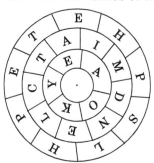

Ans. These animals are yak, camel and sheep.

Que 17. Write a caption for each of the figures given as figure (a-d)

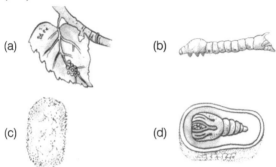

(a)

(b)

(c)

(d)

Ans. (a) Eggs of silk moth on mulberry leaves
(b) Silkworm
(c) Cocoon
(d) Cocoon with developing moth

Que 18. A wholesale woollen fibre dealer gets the woollen fibre of different textures sorted for various purposes. Match the items in Column I with the woollen fibre in Column II.

Column I	Column II
(a) Pashmina shawl	(i) Camel wool
(b) Woollen carpet	(ii) Angora wool
(c) Baby blanket	(iii) Kashmiri goat
(d) Woollen sweater	(iv) Sheep wool

Ans. (a)—(iii), (b)—(i), (c)—(ii), (d)—(iv)

❯ Long Answer Type Questions

Que 19. Complete the paragraph related to the life history of silk moth by filling in the blanks.

The ......(a)...... silk moth lays ......(b)...... , from which hatch ......(c)...... called ......(d)...... or ......(e)....... . They grow in size and when the caterpillar is ready to enter the next stage of its life history called ......(f)...... , it first weaves a covering to hold itself, which is known as ......(g)....... .

Ans. The missing words are
(a) female   (b) eggs   (c) larvae   (d) caterpillars
(e) silkworms   (f) pupa   (g) cocoon

Que 20. Paheli went to the market to buy sarees for her mother. She took out a thread from the edge of the two sarees shown by the shopkeeper and burnt them. One thread burnt with a smell of burning hair and the other burnt with the smell of burning paper. Which thread is from a pure cotton saree and which one from a pure silk saree? Give reason for your answer.

Ans. In first saree, one thread which burnt with a smell of burning hair is from pure silk, silk and hair are protein fibres. So, on burning these thread, a smell of burning hair comes out.

In second saree, second thread which burnt with the smell of burning cotton and paper because cotton and paper both are carbohydrates and on burning they give similar smell.

Que 21. Explain the phrase – 'Unity is Strength' on the basis of the making of fabric from fibre.

Ans. Fibres and fabric play a large role in everyday applications. A fibre is a hair-like strand of material. They are the smallest visible unit of a fabric and denoted by being extremely long in relation to their width. Fibres can be spun into yarn and made into fabric. A single fibre is too weak to break but when it once made a fabric it is difficult to tear. Fabric needs more energy to tear apart as compared to a single fibre.

Que 22. Write various steps for processing fibres into wool.

Ans. The various steps for processing fibres into wool are
   (a) Removal of fleece from the body of sheep, the process called shearing.
   (b) Washing of sheared skin in tanks, the process called scouring.
   (c) Separation of hair of different textures called sorting.
   (d) The small fluffy fibres, called burrs are picked out from the hair.
   (e) Fibres are dyed in various colours.
   (f) Fibres are straightened, combed and rolled into yarn. The longer fibres are made into wool for sweaters.

Chapter 4

Heat

Important Points

- **Heat** It is the form of energy which produces the sensation of warmth.

- **Temperature** In our daily life, there are many objects, some of them are hot and some are cold. Some objects are hotter than others while some are colder than others. We normally decide the hotness or coldness by touching an object, but our sense of touching an object is not reliable to determine the degree of hotness and coldness of a body. A reliablement measurement of the hotness and coldness of a body or object is called its temperature.

  Note We should not touch objects which are more hot and should be careful when handling the candle flame or stove in the home.

- **Thermometer** Temperature is measured by a device called thermometer.

- **Clinical thermometer** Thermometer that measures our body temperature is called a clinical thermometer. It consists of long, narrow, uniform glass tube and a bulb at one end which contains mercury. The clinical thermometer is designed to measure the temperature of human body. A clinical thermometer reads temperature from 35°C to 42°C.

  The normal average temperature of human body is about 37°C. The temperature of every person may not be 37°C. It could be slightly higher or slightly lower.

  Note Mercury is very toxic and is difficult to dispose off. So, thermometer must be handled carefully. Clinical thermometer should not be used to measure the temperature of objects other than the human body. It should not be kept in the sun or near a flame, otherwise it may break. Now-a-days, digital thermometers are used which do not use mercury.

- **Laboratory thermometer** To measure the temperature of any object other than the human body, we use laboratory thermometer. The temperature range of laboratory thermometer is –10°C to 110°C.

- **Maximum-minimum thermometer** The maximum and minimum temperature of a day is measured by maximum-minimum thermometer.

  Temperature is described in degree celsius (°C) in **celsius scale**. It is used earlier time. The other scale with the range 94-108 degree is the **fahrenheit scale** (°F).

- **Transfer of heat** Heat flows from a hotter object to a colder object. This flow of heat is called transfer of heat. Transfer of heat takes place from three methods, i.e. conduction, convection and radiation.

- **Conduction** The process of transfer of heat from hotter end to colder end of a body is called as conduction. Generally, solids transfer heat through conduction.

- **Insulators** The materials which do not allow heat to pass through them easily are poor conductors of heat such as plastic and wood. Poor conductors are known as insulators.

- **Conductors** The materials which allow heat to pass through them easily are called conductors, e.g. aluminium, iron and copper.

- **Convection** In this process of transfer of heat in a medium, in which the particles of the medium take heat from the source and move, and new particles (cold particles) take their place, this movement continues till whole of the medium heated. This mode of heat transfer is called as convection. Normally, transfer of heat in liquid and gases takes place through convection.

- **Sea breeze** The movement of cool air from sea towards the land during the day is called sea breeze.

- **Land breeze** The movement of cool air from land towards the sea at the night is called land breeze.

  Note The phenomena of land breeze and sea breeze occur due to convection and cold air moves to take place of hot air.

- **Radiation** When transfer of heat takes place without any medium, then it is called radiation, e.g. Heat comes from the sun to the earth.

  All hot bodies radiate heat, our body also, gives heat to the surroundings and receive heat from radiation. When heat through radiation falls on an object, then a part of it is reflected, a part is transmitted and a part is absorbed. The temperature of an object increases due to absorbed part.

- We should use light coloured clothes in summer because they reflect most of the heat that falls on them and dark coloured clothes in winter because dark surfaces absorb more heat.

- In winter, we use woollen clothes. They keep us warm in winter. Wool is poor conductor of heat, also the air trapped in between the woollen fibres. They prevent the flow of heat from our body to the surroundings, so we feel warm.

Intext Questions

Que 1. How do we find out how hot an object really is? *(Pg 36)*

Ans. By using thermometer, we can measure the degree of hotness of a body.

Que 2. Is the body temperature of every person 37°C? *(Pg 38)*

Ans. No, the body temperature of every person is not 37°C. It is an average temperature. It could be slightly higher or slightly lower.

Que 3. How do we measure the temperature of other object rather than human body? *(Pg 38)*

Ans. Temperature of other object rather than human body is measured with laboratory thermometer because clinical thermometer is not suitable for higher temperature.

Que 4. The clinical thermometer is not used to measure high temperature, why? *(Pg 39)*

Ans. Clinical thermometer has the range 35°C to 42°C. If we use it to measure high temperature, it may break and mercury present in the clinical thermometer is harmful. So, we cannot use clinical thermometer to measure high temperature.

Que 5. Why does the mercury not fall or rise in a clinical thermometer when taken out of the mouth?   *(Pg 40)*

Ans. Because of the kink present in the thermometer, the mercury does not fall or rise in a clinical thermometer when taken out of the mouth.

Que 6. When a pan is removed from the fire, why does it cool down?   *(Pg 40)*

Ans. When a pan is removed from the fire, it loses heat to the surroundings by radiation and it cools down.

Que 7. How does the heat travel in air? In which direction, does the smoke go?   *(Pg 42)*

Ans. Heat travels in air through convection. Smoke goes up in the air because hot air is lighter than cool air.

Que 8. Why are you advised to use an umbrella when you go out in the sun?   *(Pg 43)*

Ans. We use an umbrella to protect us from heat coming from the sun in the form of radiation.

Que 9. Why we wear dark coloured clothes in winter and light coloured clothes in summer?   *(Pg 44)*

Ans. We wear dark coloured clothes in winter to keep us warm as they absorb all the heat radiation coming from the sun whereas light coloured clothes reflect most of the heat radiation that falls on them and therefore we feel more comfortable wearing them in the summer.

Que 10. Why it is preferred to use two thin blankets rather than one thick blanket?   *(Pg 44)*

Ans. In case of two thin blankets, there is an air gap which does not allow heat pass out from the body and it is not as such in case of one thick blanket.

Exercises

Que 1. State similarities and differences between the laboratory thermometer and the clinical thermometer.

Ans. **Similarities** Both thermometers are used to measure temperature and both of them use mercury.

Differences Clinical thermometer is used to measure human body temperature whereas laboratory thermometer is used to measure temperature of other object which has higher temperature than human body temperature.

Que 2. Give two examples each of conductors and insulators of heat.

Ans. Examples of conductors are metal, steel and examples of insulators are wood and plastic.

Que 3. Fill in the blanks.

     (a) The hotness of a body is determined by ....

     (b) Temperature of boiling water cannot be measured by a .... thermometer.

     (c) Temperature is measured in degree ....

     (d) No medium is required for transfer of heat by the process of ....

     (e) A cold steel spoon is dipped in a cup of hot milk. It transfer heat to its other end by the process of ....

     (f) Clothes of .... colour absorb heat better than clothes of light colours.

Ans. (a) temperature (b) clinical (c) celsius (d) radiation (e) convection (f) black or dark.

Que 4. Match the following.

(a) Land breeze blows during	(i) Summer
(b) Sea breeze blows during	(ii) Winter
(c) Dark coloured clothes are preferred during	(iii) Day
(d) Light coloured clothes are preferred during	(iv) Night

Ans. (a) — (iv)   (b) — (iii)

       (c) — (ii)   (d) — (i)

Que 5. Discuss why wearing more layers of clothing during winter keeps us warmer than wearing just one thick piece of clothing.

Ans. Wearing more number of clothes makes air gap which do not allow heat to pass out but in case of one thick cloth it is not as such, so we should wear more layers of clothing during winter to keep us warmer.

Que 6. Look at the figure, mark where the heat is being transferred by conduction, convection and radiation.

Ans. (i) Heat is being transferred in the steel vessel by conduction.

(ii) Heat is being transferred from vessel to water by convection.

(iii) Heat is being transferred from vessel to surroundings by radiation.

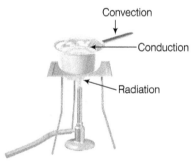

Que 7. In places of hot climate, it is advised that the outer walls of house be painted white. Explain.

Ans. In places of hot climate, it is advised that the outer walls of house be painted white because white colour does not absorb any heat radiation from the sun which keep inside cool even if there is hot climate outside the house.

Que 8. One litre water at 30°C is mixed with one litre of water at 50°C. The temperature of the mixture will be

(a) 80°C

(b) more than 50°C but less than 80°C

(c) 20°C

(d) between 30°C and 50°C

Ans. (d) Temperature of mixture is in between 30°C to 50°C because water at 50°C losses some heat and water at 30°C gains some heat.

Que 9. An iron ball at 40°C is dropped in a mug containing water at 40°C. The heat will
    (a) flow from iron ball to water
    (b) not flow from iron ball to water or from water to iron ball
    (c) flow from water to iron ball
    (d) increase the temperature of both

Ans. (b) As heat can only flow from higher temperature to lower temperature. Thus, the heat will not flow from iron ball to water or *vice-versa*.

Que 10. A wooden spoon is dipped in a cup of ice-cream, then its other end
    (a) becomes cold by the process of conduction
    (b) becomes cold by the process of convection
    (c) becomes cold by the process of radiation
    (d) does not become cold

Ans. (d) It does not become cold because it is an insulator.

Que 11. Stainless steel pans are usually provided with copper bottoms. The reason for this could be that
    (a) copper bottom makes the pan more durable
    (b) such pan appear colourful
    (c) copper is a better conductor of heat than the stainless steel
    (d) copper is easier to clean than the stainless steel

Ans. (c) As copper is a better conductor of heat than the stainless steel. So, stainless steel pans are usually provided with copper bottoms.

Selected **NCERT Exemplar Problems**

❯ **Multiple Choice Questions**

Que 1. A marble tile would feel cold as compared to a wooden tile on a winter morning because the marble tile
    (a) is a better conductor of heat than the wooden tile
    (b) is polished while wooden tile is not polished
    (c) reflects more heat than wooden tile
    (d) is a poor conductor of heat than the wooden tile

Ans. (a) Since, marble is a good conductor of heat as compared to the wood.

Que 2. A beggar wrapped himself with a few layers of newspaper on a cold winter night. This helped him to keep himself warm because

    (a) friction between the layers of newspaper produces heat

    (b) air trapped between the layers of newspaper is a bad conductor of heat

    (c) newspaper is a conductor of heat

    (d) newspaper is at a higher temperature than the temperature of the surroundings

Ans. (b) The air trapped between the newspaper does not allow to heat pass through, so it helps to keep beggar warm.

Que 3. Paheli & Boojho measured their body temperature. Paheli found her to be 98.6°F and Boojho recorded 37°C. Which of the following statements is true?

    (a) Paheli has a higher body temperature than Boojho.

    (b) Paheli has a lower body temperature than Boojho.

    (c) Both have normal body temperature.

    (d) Both are suffering from fever.

Ans. (c) These two temperatures are different scales but their actual value is equal.

Que 4. Boojho has three thermometers as shown in figure. He wants to measure the temperature of his body and that of boiling water. Which thermometer(s) should he choose?

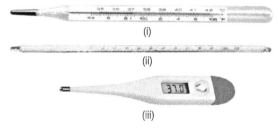

    (i)

    (ii)

    (iii)

    (a) Thermometers (i) and (iii) for measuring body temperature and (ii) for measuring the temperature of boiling water

    (b) Thermometer (i) for measuring temperature of both

    (c) Thermometer (ii) for measuring temperature of both

    (d) Thermometer (iii) for measuring temperature of both

Ans. (a) Thermometers (i) and (iii) are clinical thermometer and (ii) is laboratory thermometer.

Que 5. Four arrangements to measure temperature of ice in beaker with laboratory thermometer are shown in figure (a, b, c, d). Which one of them shows the correct arrangement for accurate measurement of temperture?

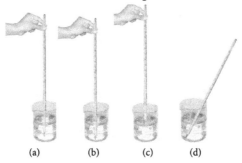

(a)   (b)   (c)   (d)

Ans. (a) Thermometer (a) has been put in correct way to measure the temperature.

Que 6. Figure (a, b, c, d) shows the reading on four different thermometers. Indicate which of the reading shows the normal human body temperature?

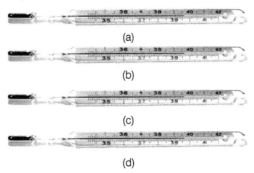

(a)

(b)

(c)

(d)

Ans. (c) As we know that normal body temperature is 37°C. So, correct option is (c).

Que 7. Figure (a, b, c, d) shows a student reading a doctor's thermometer. Which of the figure indicates the correct method of reading temperature?

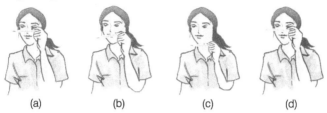

    (a)   (b)   (c)   (d)

Ans. (a) In first case, eyes of student are in level of the thermometer, so it is correct way to measure temperature using clinical thermometer.

> Very Short Answer Type Questions

Que 8. Shopkeepers selling ice blocks usually cover them with jute sacks. Explain why.

Ans. As we know that jute sacks is thermal insulators, it helps ice not to be melt immediately. So, shopkeepers used to cover ice blocks with jute sacks.

Que 9. A laboratory thermometer *A* is kept 7 cm away on the side of the flame while a similar thermometer *B* is kept 7 cm above the flame of a candle as shown in figure. Which of the thermometer *A* or *B* will show a greater rise in temperature? Give reason for your answer.

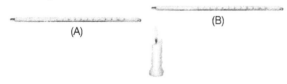

                                  (B)
               (A)

Ans. Thermometer *B* will show a greater rise in temperature because heated air above the candle rises immediatly and increase the temperature of bulb of thermometer *B* quite greater than *A*.

Que 10. To keep her soup warm Paheli wrapped the container in which it was kept with a woollen clothes. Can she apply the same method to keep a glass of cold drink cool? Give reason for your answer.

Ans. Yes, she can apply the same method to keep a glass of cold drink cool because wool is a thermal insulator, i.e. poor conductor of heat and it cannot allow to heat pass through.

Que 11. In a mercury thermometer, the level of mercury rises when its bulb comes in contact with a hot object. What is the reason for this rise in the level of mercury?

Ans. As the temperature increases, then expansion in mercury takes place which leads to the rise in the level of mercury in thermometer.

❯ **Short Answer Type Questions**

Que 12. A circular metal loop is heated at point O as shown in figure.

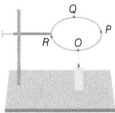

(i) In which direction, would heat flow in the loop?

(ii) In which order the pins at points P, Q and R fixed with the help of wax fall if points O, P, Q and R are equidistant from each other?

Ans. (i) Heat will flow in both the directions from O to P and from O to R.

(ii) First of all pin at P and R will fall simultaneously after that pin at Q will fall.

Que 13. In the arrangements A and B as shown in figure, pins P and Q are fixed to a metal loop and an iron rod with the help of wax. In which case are both the pins likely to fall at different times? Explain.

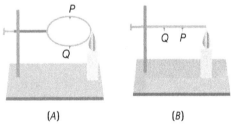

(A)   (B)

Ans. As in the given figures A and B, in case (A) P and Q got equal heat, so pin fix at P and Q in case of a fall simultaneously.

But in case of (B) pin at point P falls first than after pin at Q will fall as because heat received at P is greater than Q at the same time.

Que 14. For setting curd, a small amount of curd is added to warm milk. The microbes present in the curd help in setting if the temperature of the mixture remains approximately between 35°C to 40°C. At places, where room temperature remains much below the range, setting of curd becomes difficult. Suggest a way to set curd in such a situation.

Ans. For the setting of curd where temperature is below room temperature, the container in which curd is to be made must be kept in a thermally insulated cover or it can be wrapped with wool or jute sacks, so that temperature is maintained for the setting of curd.

Que 15. You may have noticed that a few sharp jerks are given to clinical thermometer before using it. Why is it done so?

Ans. Jerks are given to clinical thermometer before using it to settle down the mercury level below normal temperature, so that the measurement taken of a body be accurate.

Que 16. Why is it advised not to hold the thermometer by its bulb while reading it?

Ans. We are not advised to hold the thermometer bulb while reading it as the level of mercury increases from the actual reading by our body temperature.

Que 17. At a camp site there are tents of two shades. One made with black fabric and the other with white fabric. Which one will you prefer for resting on a hot summer afternoon? Give reason for your choice. Would you like to prefer the same tent during winter?

Ans. We will prefer white fabric tent in case of summer because it reflects all the radiations from the Sun and keeps us cool inside the tent.

But in case of winter, we should not use white fabric tent, we should use black fabric tent as it absorbs all colours of light from the sun and keeps us warm inside the tent.

Que 18. While constructing a house in a coastal area, in which direction should the windows preferably face and why?

Ans. While constructing a house in a coastal area, window should preferably towards the sea beach, so that the sea breeze coming from sea keeps the house cool during the day time.

Chapter 5

Acids, Bases *and* Salts

Important Points

- **Acids** The substances that are sour in taste (e.g. curd, lemon juice, orange juice and vinegar), turns blue litmus to red and corrosive in nature are called acids. Other examples are tamarind, amla, unripe grapes and mangoes.

- **Acidic substances** The substances that show the properties of acid are called acidic substances and the chemical nature of these substances is acidic.

- **Bases** The substances that are bitter in taste, soapy to touch and turns red litmus to blue, are called bases.

- **Basic substances** The substances that show the properties of base are called basic substances and the chemical nature of these substances is basic.

- **Indicators** Solution of substances that show different colours in acidic and basic solution are called indicators. They are used to test whether a substance is acidic or basic in nature.

  Turmeric, litmus, China rose petals (gudhal), etc are some of the naturally occurring indicators.

- **Litmus** It is the most commonly used natural indicator. It is extracted from **lichens**. It has a mauve (purple) colour in distilled water. In an acidic solution, it turns red and in basic solution, it turns blue.

- It is available in the form of a solution, or in the form of strips of paper, known as litmus paper. It is available as red and blue litmus paper.

- **Neutral solutions** The solutions which do not change the colour of either red or blue litmus are known as neutral solutions. These substances are neither acidic nor basic.
- **China rose indicator** China rose (gudhal) indicator turns acidic solutions to dark pink (magenta) and basic solutions to green.
- **Turmeric indicator** It turns from yellow to red in basic solution.
- **Acid rain** The rain containing excess of acids called an acid rain. The rain becomes acidic because carbon dioxide, sulphur dioxide and nitrogen dioxide dissolve in rain drops to form carbonic acid, sulphuric acid and nitric acid respectively. It can cause damage to buildings, historical monuments, plants and animals.
- **Phenolphthalein** It is an indicator used in neutralisation process. When the solution is basic, phenolphthalein gives a pink colour but if solution is acidic, it remains colourless.
- **Neutralisation** The reaction between an acid and a base is known as neutralisation. Salt and water are produced in this process with the evolution of heat.

$$\text{Acid} + \text{Base} \longrightarrow \text{Salt} + \text{Water (Heat is evolved)}$$

e.g. $\underset{\substack{\text{Hydrochloric} \\ \text{acid}}}{\text{HCl}} + \underset{\substack{\text{Sodium} \\ \text{hydroxide}}}{\text{NaOH}} \longrightarrow \underset{\substack{\text{Sodium} \\ \text{chloride}}}{\text{NaCl}} + \underset{\text{Water}}{\text{H}_2\text{O}}$

- **Salt** In neutralisation reaction, a new substance is formed that is called salt. Salt may be acidic, basic or neutral in nature.
- **Neutralisations in everyday life**
  (i) **Indigestion** Stomach contains HCl acid that sometimes leads to acidity or indigestion. To relieve indigestion, we take an **antacid** such as milk of magnesia which contains magnesium hydroxide which neutralises the effect of excessive acid.
  (ii) **Ant bite** When an ant bites, it injects the formic acid into the skin. To neutralise the effect, we rub moist baking soda or calamine solution containing zinc carbonate.
  (iii) **Soil treatment** Plants do not grow well, when the soil is either too acidic or too basic.
    (a) When the soil is too acidic, it is treated with bases like quicklime (calcium oxide) or slaked lime (calcium hydroxide).

(b) When the soil is too basic, organic matter is added to it. The organic matter releases acids which neutralise the basic nature of the soil.

(iv) **Factory wastes** It contains acids that are neutralised by adding basic substances otherwise as factory wastes allowed to flow into the water bodies can harm the aquatic life.

Intext Questions

Que 1. In the given table, identify among the given substances having the same taste.   *(Pg 49)*

Substance	Taste (sour/bitter/any other)
Lemon juice	
Orange juice	
Vinegar	
Curd	
Tamarind (imli)	
Sugar	
Common salt	
Amla	
Baking soda	
Grapes	
Unripe mango	

Ans. No, all substances do not have the same taste. Hence, the complete table is shown in the sense of taste.

Substance	Taste (sour/bitter/any other)
Lemon juice	Sour
Orange juice	Sour
Vinegar	Sour
Curd	Sour
Tamarind (imli)	Sour
Sugar	Sweet
Common salt	Salty
Amla	Sour
Baking soda	Bitter
Grapes	Sweet
Unripe mango	Sour

Que 2. Check the effect of given substances on turmeric solution and also remark. *(Pg 52)*

Test solution	Effect on turmeric solution	Remarks
Lemon juice		
Orange juice		
Vinegar		
Milk of magnesia		
Baking soda		
Lime water		
Sugar		
Common salt		

Ans. The complete table is shown below :

Test solution	Effect on turmeric solution	Remarks
Lemon juice	Blue	Acidic
Orange juice	Blue	Acidic
Vinegar	Blue	Acidic
Milk of magnesia	Red	Basic
Baking soda	Red	Basic
Lime water	Red	Basic
Sugar	No change	Neutral
Common salt	No change	Neutral

Que 3. What is acid rain? Where do these acids come from? What is the effect of acid rain? *(Pg 54)*

Ans. The rain containing excess of acids is called acid rain. It is very acidic because carbon dioxide, sulphur dioxide and nitrogen dioxide present in it which dissolve in rain drops to form carbonic acid, sulphuric acid and nitric acid respectively. It can cause damage to buildings, historical monuments, plants and animals.

Que 4. Why acids and bases should be handled in laboratory very carefully? *(Pg 54)*

Ans. We handle acids and bases in laboratory very carefully because these are corrosive in nature and irritating, and harmful to skin.

Exercises

Que 1. State differences between acids and bases.

Ans. Differences between acids and bases are as follows :

Acids	Bases
They are sour in taste.	They are bitter in taste.
They turn blue litmus to red.	They turn red litmus to blue.
They are not soapy to touch.	They are soapy to touch.
They are soluble in water.	They may or may not be soluble in water.
They are corrosive in nature.	They are not corrosive in nature.

Que 2. Ammonia is found in many household products such as window cleaners. It turns red litmus to blue. What is its nature?

Ans. The substances that turn red litmus to blue are basic in nature. Thus, ammonia is basic in nature.

Que 3. Name the source from which litmus solution is obtained. What is the use of this solution?

Ans. Litmus solution is obtained from lichens. It has mauve (purple) colour in distilled water. This solution is used as indicator.

Que 4. Is the distilled water acidic/basic/neutral? How would you verify it?

Ans. Distilled water is neither acidic nor basic. When we test its nature through litmus paper strips, we have found neither red nor blue changes in colour which verifies its neutral nature.

Que 5. Describe the process of neutralisation with the help of an example.

Ans. The reaction between an acid and a base is known as neutralisation reaction. In this reaction, both acid and base cancel each other's effect. Neutralisation reaction result in the formation of salt and water. During this reaction, energy in the form of heat is evolved.

$$\text{Acid} + \text{Base} \longrightarrow \text{Salt} + \text{Water} + \text{Heat} \uparrow$$

e.g. When sodium hydroxide (NaOH) is added to hydrochloric acid (HCl), sodium chloride (NaCl) and water (H_2O) are obtained.

$$\underset{\substack{\text{Sodium} \\ \text{hydroxide}}}{\text{NaOH}} + \underset{\substack{\text{Hydrochloric} \\ \text{acid}}}{\text{HCl}} \longrightarrow \underset{\substack{\text{Sodium} \\ \text{chloride}}}{\text{NaCl}} + \underset{\text{Water}}{H_2O} + \text{Heat}\uparrow$$

Que 6. State whether the following statements are true or false, and correct the false statements.

(a) Nitric acid turns red litmus to blue.

(b) Sodium hydroxide turns blue litmus to red.

(c) Sodium hydroxide and hydrochloric acid neutralises each other and form salt and water.

(d) Indicator is a substance which shows different colours in acidic and basic solutions.

(e) Tooth decay is caused by the presence of a base.

Ans. (a) False, nitric acid turns blue litmus to red because it is an acid.

(b) False, sodium hydroxide is a base, so it will turn red litmus to blue.

(c) True

(d) True

(e) False, tooth decay is caused by the presence of acid.

Que 7. Dorji has a few bottles of soft drink in his restaurant. But unfortunately, these are not labelled. He has to serve the drinks on the demand of customers. One customer wants acidic drink, another wants basic and third one wants neutral drink. How will Dorji decide which drink is to be served to whom?

Ans. Dorji will decide which drink is to be served to whom (customer) by doing the following litmus paper tests :

(i) If the drink turns blue litmus paper to red, then the drink is acidic and hence will be served to first customer who wants acidic drink.

(ii) If the drink turns red litmus paper to blue, then the drink is basic and hence will be served to another customer who wants basic drink.

(iii) If the drink shows no change in colour with litmus paper, then it will be neutral drink. Thus, it will be served to third customer.

Since, the soft drinks are edible. Dorji can take the decision by tasting the drinks. Acidic drinks will be sour to taste whereas basic drinks will be bitter to taste and neutral drinks will have no taste.

Que 8. Explain why

    (a) an antacid tablet is taken when you suffer from acidity.

    (b) calamine solution is applied on the skin, when an ant bites.

    (c) factory waste is neutralised before disposing it into the water bodies.

Ans. (a) We take an antacid tablet such as milk of magnesia to neutralises the excessive acid released in stomach.

    (b) When an ant bites, it injects the formic acid into the skin. The effect of acid can be neutralised by applying calamine solution that contains zinc carbonate.

    (c) The factory wastes contain acids if are allowed to flow into the water bodies and can kill fishes and other organisms. The factory wastes are thus neutralised by adding basic substances.

Que 9. Three liquids are given to you. One is hydrochloric acid, another is sodium hydroxide and third is a sugar solution. How will you identify them? You have only turmeric indicator.

Ans. We will put a drop each of hydrochloric acid, sodium hydroxide and sugar solution on the turmeric indicator. The liquid which changes the colour of turmeric indicator to red is basic in nature that is sodium hydroxide. Now, we will put a drop of sodium hydroxide on a drop of each of the other two liquids separately. After that we will put the drops of their mixtures on turmeric indicator. The drop which will change the colour of the turmeric indicator to red contains sugar solution.

This is because the mixture of base and neutral solution is basic in nature. On the other hand, the drop which will not change the colour of turmeric indicator contains hydrochloric acid because hydrochloric acid reacts with sodium hydroxide forms a neutral solution.

Sodium hydroxide + Hydrochloric acid/sugar solution $\longrightarrow$ Mixture

$$\downarrow$$

Hydrochloric acid $\xleftarrow{\text{No change in colour}}$ Drop on turmeric solution

$$\downarrow \text{Colour changes to red}$$

Sugar solution

Que 10. Blue litmus paper is dipped in a solution. It remains blue. What is the nature of the solution? Explain.

Ans. The nature of the solution could be basic or neutral, as if it is acidic it will change its colour to red but instead it remains same. Also, bases always turn to blue and if the solution is neutral even then its colour will not change.

Que 10. Consider the following statements :

(i) Both acids and bases change colour of all indicators.

(ii) If an indicator gives a colour change with an acid, it does not give a change with a base.

(iii) If an indicator changes colour with a base, it does not change colour with an acid.

(iv) Change of colour with an acid and a base depends on the type of the indicator.

Which of the above statements is/are correct?

(a) Only (iv) (b) (i) and (iv)
(c) (ii) and (iii) (d) All of these

Ans. (a) Only (iv)

All indicators do not change colour with acids as well as bases, e.g. turmeric changes its colour to pink with base but it remains yellow with acid. Therefore, statement (i) is incorrect. There are some indicators which changes colour with both acid and base, e.g. methyl orange, litmus, thus statement (ii) and (iii) are also incorrect. Statement (iv) is the correct conclusion about indicators.

Selected **NCERT Exemplar Problems**

> **Multiple Choice Questions**

Que 1. The correct way of making a solution of acid in water is to

(a) add water to acid

(b) add acid to water

(c) mix acid and water simultaneously

(d) add water to acid in a shallow container

Ans. (b) To make a solution of acid, we always add acid to water.

Que 2. Products of a neutralisation reaction are always

(a) an acid and a base (b) an acid and a salt
(c) a salt and water (d) a salt and a base

Ans. (c) The products of neutralisation reaction are salt and water.

Que 3. 'Litmus' a natural dye is an extract of which of the following?

(a) China rose (Gudhal) (b) Beetroot
(c) Lichen (d) Blueberries (Jamun)

Ans. (c) Litmus is extracted from lichen.

Que 4. Turmeric is a natural indicator. On adding its paste to acid and base separately, which colours would be observed?

 (a) Yellow in both acid and base
 (b) Yellow in acid and red in base
 (c) Pink in acid and yellow in base
 (d) Red in acid and blue in base

Ans. (b) Yellow in acid means no change in colour of turmeric indicator but red in base.

Que 5. Phenolphthalein is a synthetic indicator and its colours in acidic and basic solutions respectively are

 (a) red and blue   (b) blue and red
 (c) pink and colourless   (d) colourless and pink

Ans. (d) In acidic and basic solutions, phenolphthalein is colourless and pink respectively.

Que 6. When the soil is too basic, plants do not grow well in it. To improve its quality, what must be added to the soil?

 (a) Organic matter   (b) Quicklime
 (c) Slaked lime   (d) Calamine solution

Ans. (a) If the soil is basic, organic matter is added to it. Organic matter releases acids which neutralises the basic nature of the soil.

Que 7. Neutralisation reaction is a

 (a) physical and reversible change
 (b) physical change that cannot be reversed
 (c) chemical and reversible change
 (d) chemical change that cannot be reversed

Ans. (d) Neutralisation reaction is a chemical change that cannot be reversed.

Que 8. A solution changes the colour of turmeric indicator from yellow to red. The solution is

 (a) basic   (b) acidic
 (c) neutral   (d) either neutral or acidic

Ans. (a) A solution which changes the colour of turmeric indicator from yellow to red, is basic in nature.

Que 9. Which of the following sets of substances contains acids?

 (a) Grapes, lime water   (b) Vinegar, soap
 (c) Curd, milk of magnesia   (d) Curd, vinegar

Ans. (d) Curd and vinegar are acidic in nature because both have sour taste.

Que 10. Which of the following is an acid-base indicator?

(a) Vinegar   (b) Lime water

(c) Turmeric   (d) Baking soda

Ans. (c) We can use turmeric as an acid-base indicator.

⟫ Very Short Answer Type Questions

Que 11. Look at the given reaction.

Hydrochloric acid + Sodium hydroxide (base) ⟶

Sodium chloride (salt) + Water

Sodium chloride formed in this reaction remains in solution form. Can we get solid sodium chloride from this solution? Suggest a method (if any).

Ans. We can get solid sodium chloride by evaporation method. Evaporation is the process by which water changes from a liquid to a gas or vapour. Rate of evaporation increases with temperature.

Que 12. Paheli is suffering from indigestion due to acidity. Is it advisable to give her orange juice in this situation and why?

Ans. No, because orange juice is acidic in nature. Excess of acid in the stomach causes indigestion. We take an antacid such as milk of magnesia which contains magnesium hydroxide.

⟫ Short Answer Type Questions

Que 13. While playing in a park, a child was stung by a wasp. Some elders suggested applying paste of baking soda and others lemon juice as remedy. Which remedy do you think is appropriate and why?

Ans. Wasp sting inject a liquid in the skin which is acidic in nature. Hence, baking soda is the appropriate remedy, as it is basic in nature and neutralises the acid.

Que 14. Fill in the blanks in the following sentences :

(a) Lemon juice and vinegar taste .... because they contain ....

(b) Turmeric and litmus are .... acid-base indicators.

(c) Phenolphthalein gives .... colour with lime water.

(d) When an acidic solution is mixed with a basic solution, they .... each other forming .... and water.

Ans. (a) sour, acids   (b) natural   (c) pink   (d) neutralise, salt

Que 15. Look at the figure which shows solutions taken in test tubes *A, B, C* and *D*. What colour is expected, when a piece of red litmus paper is dropped in each test tube? Nature of the solutions is given in the table for your help.

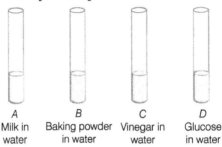

	A	B	C	D
	Milk in water	Baking powder in water	Vinegar in water	Glucose in water

Test tube	Nature of solution	Change in colour of red litmus
A	Neutral	
B	Basic	
C	Acidic	
D	Neutral	

Ans. Nature of solution is given below :

Test tube	Nature of solution	Change in colour of red litmus
A	Neutral	No change
B	Basic	Turn blue
C	Acidic	No change
D	Neutral	No change

Que 16. Match the substances in Column I with those in Column II.

	Column I		Column II
(a)	Tartaric acid	(i)	Soap
(b)	Calcium hydroxide	(ii)	Curd
(c)	Formic acid	(iii)	Unripe mangoes
(d)	Sodium hydroxide	(iv)	Ant's sting
(e)	Lactic acid	(v)	Lime water

Ans. (a)—(iii); (b)—(v); (c)—(iv); (d)—(i); (e)—(ii)

Que 17. Form a sentence using the following words :
baking soda, ant bite, moist, effect, neutralised, rubbing

Ans. The effect of an ant bite can be neutralised by rubbing moist baking soda.

> **Long Answer Type Questions**

Que 18. Fill in the crossword given as figure with the help of the clues provided.

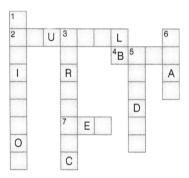

Across

(2) The solution which does not change the colour of either red or blue litmus.

(4) Phenolphthalein gives pink colour in this type of solution.

(7) Colour of blue litmus in lemon juice.

Down

(1) It is used to test whether a substance is acidic or basic.

(3) It is a natural indicator and gives pink colour in basic solution.

(5) Nature of ant's sting.

(6) It is responsible for increase in temperature during a neutralisation reaction.

Ans.

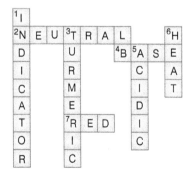

1. Indicator   2. Neutral   3. Turmeric   4. Base
5. Acidic   6. Heat   7. Red

Que 19. A farmer was unhappy because of his low crop yield. He discussed the problem with an agricultural scientist and realised that the soil of his field was either too acidic or too basic. What remedy would you suggest the farmer to neutralise the soil?

Ans. If the soil is too acidic, it should be treated with bases such as quicklime (calcium oxide) or slaked lime (calcium hydroxide). If the soil is too basic, organic matter should be added to it. Organic matter releases acids which neutralise the basic nature of the soil.

Que 20. Explain two neutralisation reactions related to daily life situation.

Ans. (i) **Ant bite** When an ant bites, injects the acidic liquid (formic acid) into the skin, the effect of the acid can be neutralised by rubbing moist baking soda (sodium hydrogen carbonate) or calamine solution, which contains zinc carbonate.

(ii) **Indigestion** Our stomach contains hydrochloric acid. It helps us to digest food, but too much of acid in the stomach causes indigestion. Sometimes, indigestion is painful. To relieve indigestion, we take an antacid such as milk of magnesia which contains magnesium hydroxide. It neutralises the effect of excessive acid.

Que 21. You are provided with four test tubes containing sugar solution, baking soda solution, tamarind solution, salt solution. Write down an activity to find the nature (acidic/basic/neutral) of each solution.

Ans. We can use both red and blue litmus solutions to find the nature (acidic/basic/neutral) of each solution.

In acidic media, blue litmus solution turns to red.

In basic media, red litmus solution turns to blue.

Solution	Effect on red litmus solution (change in colour)	Effect on blue litmus solution (change in colour)
Sugar solution	No change	No change
Baking soda solution	Red changes to blue colour	No change
Tamarind solution	No change	Blue changes to red colour
Salt solution (acidic)	No change	Blue changes to red colour
Salt solution (basic)	Red changes to blue colour	No change
Salt solution (neutral)	No change	No change

Que 22. You are provided with three test tubes *A*, *B* and *C* as shown in figure with different liquids. What will you observe when you put

    (a) a piece of blue litmus paper in each test tube?

    (b) a piece of red litmus paper in each test tube?

    (c) a few drops of phenolphthalein solution to each test tube?

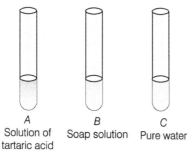

      A   *B*   *C*
Solution of   Soap solution Pure water
tartaric acid

Ans.

Test tube	Effect on blue litmus paper	Effect on red litmus paper	Effect on phenolphthalein solution
A	Turns red	Remains red	Colourless
B	Remains blue	Turns blue	Pink colour
C	Remains blue	Remains red	Colourless

Que 23. Paheli observed that most of the fish in the pond of her village were gradually dying. She also observed that the wastes of a factory in their village are flowing into the pond which probably caused the fish to die.

    (a) Explain, why the fish were dying?

    (b) If the factory waste is acidic in nature, how can it be neutralised.

Ans. (a) If the wastes of a factory flow into waterbodies, it can cause a threat to the lives of sea creatures and to anybody who drink the water. Since, factory wastes may contain acids or bases and it can kill the fish.

    (b) If the factory waste is acidic in nature, it can be neutralised by adding basic substances.

Chapter 6

Physical *and* Chemical Changes

Important Points

- Many changes occur in our surroundings on daily basis. All the changes occurred can be grouped into two types; physical changes and chemical changes.

- **Physical properties** A physical property can be measured and observed without changing the composition or identity of a substance, e.g. shape, size, colour, odour, volume, state (gas, liquid or solid), melting point and boiling point are physical properties of a substance.

- **Physical changes** Physical changes are the changes in the physical properties of substances. No new substances are formed in these changes. The changes may be reversible, e.g. melting of ice.

- **Chemical properties** Chemical properties of a substance is its ability to form new substances.

- **Chemical changes** The changes in which one or more new substances are formed are called chemical changes. In general, chemical changes are irreversible. The chemical properties of the substances formed are different from the original substances, e.g. rusting of iron, burning of magnesium ribbon and burning of coal, wood or leaves is also a chemical change. In fact, burning of any substance is a chemical change.

- **Chemical reaction** A chemical change is also called a chemical reaction, e.g.

  (i) When magnesium oxide is dissolved in water.

  Magnesium oxide (MgO) + water (H_2O) $\longrightarrow$
  $$\text{magnesium hydroxide } [Mg(OH)_2]$$

  (ii) Reaction between copper sulphate and iron.

  Copper sulphate solution $(CuSO_4)$ (blue) + Iron (Fe) $\longrightarrow$ Iron sulphate solution $(FeSO_4)$ (green)+ Copper (Cu) (brown deposit)

  (iii) Baking soda is treated with vinegar.

  Acetic acid (CH_3COOH) + Baking soda $(NaHCO_3)$
  $$\longrightarrow \text{Sodium acetate } (CH_3COONa) + \text{Carbon dioxide}$$
  $$(CO_2) + \text{Water } (H_2O)$$

  (iv) Carbon dioxide (CO_2) + Lime water $[Ca(OH)_2]$ $\longrightarrow$
  $$\text{Calcium carbonate } (CaCO_3) + \text{Water} (H_2O)$$

- **Characteristics of chemical change** New products are formed in a chemical reaction. The following may accompany a chemical change:

  (i) Heat, light or any other radiation (i.e. ultraviolet) may be given off or absorbed.

  (ii) Sound may be produced.

  (iii) A change in smell may take place or a new smell may be given off.

  (iv) A colour change may take place.

  (v) A gas may be formed.

- **Ozone layer** It protects us from the harmful ultraviolet radiation which come from the Sun. Ozone absorbs this radiation and breaks down to oxygen.

  Note If ultraviolet radiation were not absorbed by ozone, it would reach the earth's surface and cause harm to us and other life forms.

- **Rusting of iron** If you leave a piece of iron in the open for some time, it acquires a film of brownish substance. This substance is called **rust** and the process is called **rusting**, e.g. Iron gates of parks and iron benches kept in the open gets rusted.

The process of rusting can be represented by the following equation:

$$\text{Iron (Fe)} + \text{Oxygen (O}_2 \text{ from air)} + \text{Water (H}_2\text{O)} \longrightarrow$$

$$\text{Rust (iron oxide, Fe}_2\text{O}_3)$$

For rusting, the presence of both oxygen and water (or water vapour) is essential. If the content of moisture in air is high, i.e. it is more humid, rusting becomes faster.

- **Galvanisation** It is the process of applying a protective zinc coating to steel or iron, to prevent rusting. The iron pipes, we use in our homes to carry water are galvanised to prevent rusting.
- **Stainless steel** It is made by mixing iron with carbon and metals like chromium, nickel and manganese, it does not rust.
- **Crystallisation** Large crystals of pure substances can be formed from their solutions. The process of formation of crystals is called crystallisation. It is an example of physical change.

Intext Questions

Que 1. Cut a piece of paper in four squares and each square into further square pieces. Lay the pieces so that the pieces acquire the shape of original paper. Is there a change in the property of the paper?   *(Pg 58)*

Ans. No, the property of the paper does not change. Although, we cannot join the piece back to make the original piece of paper.

Que 2. Can we recover chalk by drying a paste of chalk dust and water?   *(Pg 58)*

Ans. Yes, if we make a paste of chalk dust and water, and allow it to dry, chalk will be recover. Chalk and chalk dust have same properties as chalk is broken into pieces, form chalk dust.

Que 3. What is photosynthesis? Is it a chemical reaction?
                                                          (Pg 63)

Ans. The process by which plants make their own food using carbon dioxide and water in the presence of chlorophyll and sunlight, is known as photosynthesis.

Chlorophyll is a green pigment present in the leaves of plants. The pigment capture the sun's energy which is used to prepare food from carbon dioxide and water.

$$6CO_2 + 6H_2O \xrightarrow[\text{Sunlight}]{\text{Chlorophyll}} \underset{\text{Glucose}}{C_6H_{12}O_6} + 6O_2$$

It is a chemical process.

Exercises

Que 1. Classify the changes involved in the following processes as physical or chemical changes.

(a) Photosynthesis

(b) Dissolving sugar in water

(c) Burning of coal

(d) Melting of wax

(e) Beating aluminium to make aluminium foil

(f) Digestion of food

Ans. (a) Photosynthesis – Chemical change

(b) Dissolving sugar in water – Physical change

(c) Burning of coal – Chemical change

(d) Melting of wax – Physical change

(e) Beating aluminium to make aluminium foil – Physical change

(f) Digestion of food – Chemical change

Que 2. State whether the following statements are true or false. In case a statement is false, write the correct statement in your notebook.

(a) Cutting a log of wood into pieces is a chemical change. (True/False)

(b) Formation of manure from leaves is a physical change. (True/False)

(c) Iron pipes coated with zinc do not get rusted easily. (True/False)

(d) Iron and rust are the same substances. (True/False)

(e) Condensation of steam is not a chemical change (True/False).

Ans. (a) False, cutting a log of wood into pieces is a physical change.

(b) False, formation of manure from leaves is a chemical change.

(c) True

(d) False, iron and rust are two different chemical substances.

(e) True

Que 3. Fill in the blanks in the following statements.

(a) When carbon dioxide is passed through lime water, it turns milky due to the formation of ....

(b) The chemical name of baking soda is ....

(c) Two methods by which rusting of iron can be prevented are ...... and ....

(d) Changes in which only ...... properties of a substance change are called physical changes.

(e) Changes in which new substances are formed are called ....

Ans. (a) calcium carbonate

$$Ca(OH)_2 + CO_2 \longrightarrow CaCO_3 + H_2O$$
$$\text{Lime water} \quad \text{Carbon} \qquad \text{Calcium} \quad \text{Water}$$
$$\text{dioxide} \qquad \text{carbonate}$$

(b) sodium hydrogen carbonate

(c) galvanisation, painting

(d) physical

(e) chemical changes

Que 4. When baking soda is mixed with lemon juice, bubbles are formed with the evolution of a gas. What type of change is it? Explain.

Ans. When baking soda (sodium bicarbonate) is mixed with lemon juice (citric acid), a chemical change occurs. In this reaction, new substances like carbon dioxide is formed and heat is evolved. This change is irreversible. It is a chemical change.

Sodium bicarbonate ($NaHCO_3$) + citric acid

↓

Sodium citrate + carbon dioxide + water + heat ↑

Que 5. When a candle burns, both physical and chemical changes take place. Identify these changes. Give another example of familiar process in which both the chemical and physical changes take place.

Ans. **Physical changes in burning candle** On heating, candle's wax melts, it is a physical change. Since, it again turns into solid wax on cooling. The change is reversible.

Chemical changes in burning candle The wax near to flame burns and gives new substances like carbon dioxide, carbon soot, water vapours, heat and light.

Cooking of food, boiling of eggs are examples of both physical and chemical changes. In both cases, the physical appearance of the substances change and new substances are formed.

Que 6. How would you show that setting of curd is a chemical change?

Ans. Setting of curd is a chemical change because we cannot get the original substance (milk) back. The new substance, i.e. curd is different from the milk in taste, smell and chemical properties.

Que 7. Explain why burning of wood and cutting it into small pieces are considered as two different types of changes.

Ans. Burning of wood is a chemical change while cutting of wood is a physical change because during burning, new substances are formed. After burning, we cannot get original substance, (i.e. wood) back. Cutting of wood into small pieces is a physical change because no new substance is formed.

Que 8. Describe how crystals of copper sulphate are prepared.

Ans. Crystals of copper sulphate are prepared in the following manner :
    (i) Take a cup full of water in a beaker.
    (ii) Add a few drops of dilute sulphuric acid.
        [**Caution** never add water to the acid as the acid may splash on you].
    (iii) Heat the water.
    (iv) When it starts boiling, add copper sulphate powder slowly with constant stirring.
    (v) Continue adding copper sulphate powder till no more powder can be dissolved.
    (vi) Filter the solution.
    (vii) Allow it to cool.

(viii) Do not disturb the solution, when it is cooling.

(ix) Look at the solution after sometime and wait till it changes into crystals.

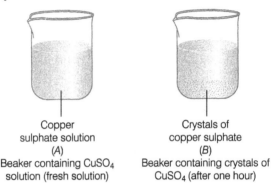

Copper
sulphate solution
(A)
Beaker containing CuSO₄
solution (fresh solution)

Crystals of
copper sulphate
(B)
Beaker containing crystals of
CuSO₄ (after one hour)

Que 9. Explain how painting of an iron gate prevents it from rusting.

Ans. Rusting of iron is due to the exposure of iron to the atmosphere for sometime. To prevent rusting of iron gate, we paint it. Painting prevents the iron gate to come in direct contact of atmosphere, water or both. Thus, a coat of paint cuts the contact between iron and atmosphere and it prevents rusting of iron.

Also we know that

Iron (Fe) + Oxygen (O_2) + Water (H_2O) $\longrightarrow$ Rust (iron oxide, Fe_2O_3)

Thus, it is necessary to cut the oxygen contact with iron to prevent rusting.

Que 10. Explain why rusting of iron objects is faster in coastal areas than in deserts.

Ans. We know that for rusting, the presence of both oxygen and water (water vapour) is essential.

Thus, in coastal areas, the air contains high moisture which means more humid environment and rusting becomes faster.

Whereas in deserts, moisture in air is less, hence rusting of iron is very slow there.

Que 11. The gas we use in the kitchen is called Liquefied Petroleum Gas (LPG). In the cylinder, it exists as liquid. When it comes out of the cylinder, it becomes a gas (change *A*). Then, it burns (change *B*). The following statements pertain to these changes. Choose the correct one.

    (a) Process *A* is a chemical change
    (b) Process *B* is a chemical change
    (c) Both processes *A* and *B* are chemical changes
    (d) None of the above processes is a chemical change

Ans. (b) Process *B* is a chemical change. Process *A* is a physical change. The LPG in cylinder is in liquid form because of high pressure. When it comes from cylinder, it turns into gas. It is a physical change.

Process *B* is a chemical change because burning of gas is a chemical change.

Que 12. Anaerobic bacteria digest animal waste and produce biogas (change *A*). The biogas is then burnt as fuel (change *B*). The following statements pertain to these changes. Choose the correct one.

    (a) Process *A* is a chemical change
    (b) Process *B* is a chemical change
    (c) Both processes *A* and *B* are chemical changes
    (d) None of the above processes is a chemical change

Ans. (c) Both processes *A* and *B* are chemical changes. Bacteria acts on waste and converts it to biogas (change *A*). Hence, it is a chemical change during biogas production (change *B*), it works as fuel and produces CO_2 and heat. Hence, *A* and *B* both are chemical changes.

Selected **NCERT Exemplar Problems**

> **Multiple Choice Questions**

Que 1. Which one of the following is a physical change?
    (a) Rusting of iron
    (b) Combustion of magnesium ribbon
    (c) Burning of candle
    (d) Melting of wax

Ans. (d) Melting of wax is a physical change.

Que 2. Which one of the following is a chemical change?

(a) Twinkling of stars   (b) Cooking of vegetables

(c) Cutting of fruits   (d) Boiling of water

Ans. (b) Cooking of vegetables is a chemical change.

Que 3. A chemical change may involve

(a) change in colour only

(b) change in temperature only

(c) evolution of gas only

(d) All of the above

Ans. (d) Change in colour, change in temperature and evolution of gas all are chemical changes.

Que 4. A man painted his main gate made up of iron, to

(i) prevent it from rusting

(ii) protect it from the sun

(iii) make it look beautiful

(iv) make it dust free

Which of the above statements is/are correct?

(a) (i) and (ii)   (b) (ii) and (iii)

(c) Only (ii)   (d) (i) and (iii)

Ans. (d) To prevent rusting of iron gate, we do paint on it. Painting makes it beautiful.

Que 5. Iron pillar near the Qutub Minar in Delhi is famous for the following facts. Which of these facts is responsible for its long stability?

(a) It is more than 7 m high

(b) It weighs about 6000 kg

(c) It was built more than 1600 years ago

(d) It has not rusted after such a long period

Ans. (d) The iron pillar located in Delhi in Qutub complex is famous for the rust-resistant composition of the metals used in its construction. It has not rusted after such a long period.

Que 6. Galvanisation is a process used to prevent the rusting of which of the following?

(a) Iron   (b) Zinc

(c) Aluminium   (d) Copper

Ans. (a) Galvanisation is the process of depositing a layer of zinc on iron.

Que 7. Paheli's mother made a concentrated sugar syrup by dissolving sugar in hot water. On cooling, crystals of sugar got separated.

This indicates a

(a) physical change that can be reversed

(b) chemical change that can be reversed

(c) physical change that cannot be reversed

(d) chemical change that cannot be reversed

Ans. (a) Dissolution of sugar in hot water is a physical change that can be reversed.

Que 8. Which of the following statements is incorrect for a chemical reaction?

(a) Heat may be given out but never absorbed

(b) Sound may be produced

(c) A colour change may take place

(d) A gas may be evolved

Ans. (a) Actually during the chemical reaction, heat may be given out or can be absorbed.

> Very Short Answer Type Questions

Que 9. State whether the following statements are true or false.

(i) When a candle burns, both physical and chemical changes take place.

(ii) Anaerobic bacteria digest animal wastes and produce biogas.

(iii) Ships suffer a lot of damage though they are painted.

(iv) Stretching of rubber band is not a physical change.

Ans. (i) True (ii) True (iii) True (iv) False

Que 10. Melting of wax is a change where a solid changes to liquid state. Give one more such change which you observe in your surroundings.

Ans. Melting of ice is also a change where solid changes into liquid state.

Que 11. What kind of change is shown by tearing of paper?

Ans. Tearing of paper is a physical change although it cannot be reversed.

❯ Short Answer Type Questions

Que 12. Match the items of Column I with the items of Column II.

	Column I		Column II
(a)	Large crystals	(i)	Turn lime water milky
(b)	Depositing a layer of zinc on iron	(ii)	Physical change
(c)	Souring of milk	(iii)	Rust
(d)	Carbon dioxide	(iv)	Sugar candy (mishri)
(e)	Iron oxide	(v)	Chemical change
(f)	Dissolving common salt in water	(vi)	Galvanisation

Ans. (a) — (iv), (b) — (vi), (c) — (v), (d) — (i), (e) — (iii), (f) — (ii)

Que 13. Fill in the blanks in the following statements using the words given in the box.

> rusted, colourful, substance, chemical, physical, reversible, iron oxide, object

(a) Making sugar solution is a .... change.

(b) A physical change is generally ....

(c) Grinding of wheat grain changes its size. It is a .... change.

(d) Iron benches kept in lawns and gardens get .... It is a .... change because a new .... is formed.

Ans. (a) physical   (b) reversible
(c) physical   (d) rusted, chemical, substance

Que 14. Classify the following processes into physical or chemical changes.

(a) Beating of aluminium metal to make aluminium foil

(b) Digestion of food

(c) Cutting of a log of wood into pieces

(d) Burning of crackers

Ans. Physical changes are

(a) Beating of aluminium metal to make aluminium foil.

(c) Cutting of a log of wood into pieces.

Chemical changes are

(b) Digestion of food.

(d) Burning of crackers.

Que 15. Write word equations for two chemical reactions with the help of materials given in the box.

> Air, copper sulphate, iron, vinegar, iron oxide, carbon dioxide, iron sulphate, copper, lime water, water

Ans. (i) Iron + air + water $\longrightarrow$ iron oxide

(ii) Copper sulphate + iron $\longrightarrow$ iron sulphate + copper

Que 16. Explain the following.

(a) Lime water turns milky on passing carbon dioxide gas into it.

(b) Bubbles are produced when acetic acid is added to a solution of sodium hydrogen carbonate.

Ans. (a) White coloured insoluble calcium carbonate is formed.

(b) Carbon dioxide is evolved due to the chemical reaction between acetic acid and sodium hydrogen carbonate.

> Long Answer Type Questions

Que 17. Give two examples for each of the following cases:

(a) Physical changes which are reversible.

(b) Physical changes which are not reversible.

(c) Chemical changes

Ans. (a) (1) Folding of paper   (2) Melting of ice

(b) (1) Tearing of paper   (2) Breaking of glass

(c) (1) Reaction between vinegar and baking soda.

    (2) Burning of a matchstick.

There are many other examples in each case which can be given.

Que 18. Give an example of a chemical reaction for each of the following situations:

(a) A change in colour is observed.

(b) A gas is evolved.

(c) Sound is produced.

Ans. (a) Reaction between copper sulphate solution and iron metal.

(b) Reaction between baking soda and vinegar (carbon dioxide is evolved).

(c) Burning of crackers.

Que 19. If you leave a piece of iron in the open for a few days, it acquires a film of brownish substance, called rust.

    (a) Do you think rust is different from iron?

    (b) Can you change rust back into iron by some simple method?

    (c) Do you think formation of rust from iron is a chemical change?

    (d) Give two other examples of a similar type of change.

Ans. (a) Yes, rust is quite different from iron.

    (b) No

    (c) Yes, it is a chemical change.

    (d) (i) Setting of curd from milk.

       (ii) Burning of magnesium ribbon to form magnesium oxide.

Que 20. A student took a solution of copper sulphate in a beaker and put a clean iron nail into it and left it for about an hour.

    (a) What changes do you expect?

    (b) Are these changes chemical in nature?

    (c) Write a word equation for the chemical change, if any.

Ans. (a) (i) Colour of the solution in the beaker changes from blue to green.

       (ii) A brown coloured deposit is found on the surface of the iron nail.

    (b) The changes are chemical in nature as new substances, iron sulphate (green) and copper (brown) are formed.

    (c) Copper sulphate + iron $\longrightarrow$ iron sulphate + copper
         (Blue)   (Green)   (Brown)

Chapter 7

Weather, Climate *and* **Adaptations** *of* **Animals** *to* **Climate**

Important Points

- **Weather** The day-to-day condition of the atmosphere at a place with respect to temperature, humidity rainfall wind-speed, etc is called the weather at that place. The temperature, humidity rainfall, wind speed and other factors are called the elements of the weather.

    Note The weather of a place changes day after day and week after week. That is why we often says, 'today's weather is too humid' or 'the weather was warm last week'.

- **Meteorological department** The **weather reports** are prepared by the meteorological department. This department collects data on temperature, wind, etc and make the weather prediction.

- **Rain gauge** Rainfall is measured by an instrument called rain gauge. It is basically a measuring cylinder with a funnel on top to collect rain water.

- **Humidity** The measurement of the moisture in the air is called humidity.

- **Maximum-minimum thermometer** It is a registering thermometer which can record the maximum and minimum temperatures reached at a period of time. It is also known as maxima-minima thermometer.

    Note The minimum temperature generally occurs in the early morning. While the maximum temperature of the day occurs in the afternoon.

■ **Sun** All changes in the weather are caused by the sun. Sun is a huge sphere of hot gases. The distance of the sun from us very large, even then energy sent out by the sun is so huge that it is the source of all heat and light on the earth. It is the primary source of energy that causes changes in the weather. Energy absorbed and reflected by the earth's surface oceans and the atmosphere plays important roles in determining the weather at any place.

■ **Climate** It is a measure of the average pattern of variation in temperature, humidity, atmospheric pressure, wind, precipitation, atmospheric particle count and other meteorological variables in a given region over long period of time.

■ **Hot and dry climate** The climate that have high temperature throughout the year and receives very little rainfall is called hot and dry climate, e.g. Rajasthan in India.

■ **Wet climate** The climate receiving rain for a major part of the year is called wet climate, e.g. North-Eastern region of India.

Note Kerala is very hot and wet in comparison to Jammu and Kashmir, which has a moderately hot and wet climate.

■ **Adaptation** An adaptation is a trait of an organism that has been favoured by natural selection.

Adaptations are of three types :

  (i) **Structural adaptations** Adaptation of special body parts of an organism that helps it to survive in its natural habitat, e.g. skin colour, shape, body covering.

  (ii) **Behavioural adaptations** Adaptation of special ways of a particular organism that helps it to survive in its natural habitat. It usually occurs in response to some external stimuli, e.g. Frogs and bear undergoes hibernation or winter sleep during hard winter season.

  (iii) **Physiological adaptations** Adaptation of systems present in an organism that allows it to perform certain biochemical reaction, e.g. Warm blooded animals are able to keep a constant body temperature.

■ **Polar region** These regions are covered with snow and it is very cold for most part of the year. For six months, the sun does not set at the poles while for the other six months, the sun does not rise.

In winters, the temperature may be as low as −37°C. Animals living there have adapted to these severe conditions. Polar bear and penguins are adapted for this region.

(i) **Polar bear** They have white fur so that they are not easily visible in the snowy white background. It protects them from their predators. It also helps them in catching their prey. They are so well-insulated that they have to move slowly and rest often to avoid getting over hated. It is a good swimmer. It has a strong sense of smell so that it can catch its prey for food.

(ii) **Penguin** It is also white and merges well with the white background. It also has a thick skin and lot of fat to protect it from cold.

- **Hibernation** Some animals go into deep sleep like state and their body temperature drops its heartbeat and respiration rate. It is called hibernation.

- **Migration** The regular seasonal journey undertaken by many species of animals and birds to escape the harsh and cold condition of weather is known as migration.

Many animals, birds and fishes migrate to warmer region in winter and come back when winter is over.

Some migration birds travel as much as 15000 km to escape the extreme climatic conditions at home. Generally they fly high where the wind flow is helpful and the cold conditions allow them to disperse the heat generated by their flight muscles.

It is not only birds that migrate; mammals, many types of fish and insects are also known to migrate seasonally in search of more hospitable climates.

- **Tropical region** It is present around the equator. It has generally very hot climate. Even in the coldest month, the temperature is generally higher than 15°C and in summer, the temperature may cross 40°C.

- **Tropical rainforest** Tropical rainforests are found in tropical region. Because of continuous warmth and rain, this region supports wide variety of plants and animals. The major types of animals living in the rainforests are monkeys, apes, gorillas, tigers, elephants, leopards, lizards, snakes, birds and insects.

- **Adaptation in animals living in tropical rainforests** Since, the numbers of animals living here is very large, there is intense competition for food and shelter. Many animals are adapted to live on the trees, e.g. Red-eyed frog has developed stickes pads on its fect to help it climb on trees, monkeys have long tails for grasping branches, etc. There is also competition for food, e.g. Bird taucan possesses a long and large beak, helping it to search the fruits on branches.

- **Camouflage** Some animals have sensitive hearing, sharp eyesight, thick skin and a skin colour which helps them to blend or match their skin colour with their surrounding. It is called camouflage.

- **Beard ape** The lion-tailed macaque (also called beard ape) live in the rainforests of Western Ghats. It is a good climber and spends a major part of its life on the tree.

- **Elephant** It is a well known animal of Indian tropical rainforest, has adapted to the conditions of rainforests in many remarkable ways. It uses its large trunk to smell, picking up food. Its trunks are modified teeth can tear the bark of trees. Large ears help it to wear even very soft sound and keep it cool in the hot and humid climate.

Intext Questions

Que 1. Who prepare weather report?   *(Pg 68)*

Ans. Meteorologists are the scientist in meteorological department of government prepare the weather report.

Que 2. Why weather changes so frequently?   *(Pg 70)*

Ans. The weather changes so frequently due to the revolution of the earth around the sun. It varies for a short period of time.

Que 3. Are the days shorter in winter than in summer?   *(Pg 71)*
Ans. Yes, the days are shorter and night larger in winter than in summer.

Que 4. Do fishes and butterflies also migrate like birds? *(Pg 74)*

Ans. Yes, fishes and butterflies also migrate like birds to protect themselves from the harsh climatic changes.

Exercises

Que 1. Name the elements that determine the weather of a place.

Ans. The elements that determine the weather of a place are temperature, humidity, rainfall, wind-speed, etc.

Que 2. When are the maximum and minimum temperatures likely to occur during the day?

Ans. The maximum temperature of the day occurs generally in the afternoon while the minimum temperature occurs generally in the early morning.

Que 3. Fill in the blanks :

   (a) The average weather taken over a long time is called ....

   (b) A place receives very little rainfall and the temperature is high throughout the year, the climate of that place will be........ and........ .

   (c) The two regions of the earth with extreme climate conditions are........ and........ .

Ans. (a) The average weather taken over a long time is called **climate**.

   (b) A place receives very little rainfall and the temperature is high throughout the year, the climate of that place will be **hot** and **dry**.

   (c) Two regions of the earth with extreme climate conditions are **tropical** and **polar region**.

Que 4. Indicate the type of climate of the following areas:

   (a) Jammu and Kashmir   (b) Kerala

   (c) Rajasthan   (d) North-East India

Ans. (a) Jammu and Kashmir : moderately hot and wet climate

   (b) Kerala : very hot and wet climate

   (c) Rajasthan : very hot and dry climate

   (d) North-East India : wet climate

Que 5. Which of the two changes frequently, weather or climate?

Ans. Weather changes frequently.

Que 6. Following are some of the characteristics of animals:
  (a) Diets heavy on fruits
  (b) White fur
  (c) Need to migrate
  (d) Loud voice
  (e) Sticky pads on feet
  (f) Layer of fat under skin
  (g) Wide and large paws
  (h) Bright colours
  (i) Strong tails
  (j) Long and large beak

For each characteristics indicate whether it is adaptation for tropical rainforests or polar regions. Do you think that some of these characteristics can be adopted for both regions?

Ans.

Characteristics of animals	Adaptation for
(a) Diets heavy on fruits	tropical rainforests
(b) White fur	polar regions
(c) Need to migrate	polar regions
(d) Loud voice	tropical rainforests
(e) Sticky pads on feet	tropical rainforests
(f) Layer of fat under skin	polar regions
(g) Wide and large paws	polar regions
(h) Bright colours	tropical rainforests
(i) Strong tails	tropical rainforests
(j) Long and large beak	tropical rainforests

Que 7. The tropical rainforest has a large population of animals. Explain why it is so?

Ans. The tropical rainforest has a large population of animals because continuous warmth and rain in this region support wide variety of plants and animals.

Que 8. Explain with examples, why we find animals of certain kind living in particular climatic conditions.

Ans. Climate has a profound effect on all living organisms. Animals are adapted to survive in the conditions in which they live. Animals living in very cold and hot climate must possess special features to protect themselves against the extreme cold or heat, e.g. Animals living in polar regions have adaptations such as white fur, strong sense of smell, thick skin, lot of fats to protect it from cold, wide and large paws for swimming, etc.

Que 9. How do elephant living in the tropical rainforest adapt itself?

Ans. Elephant living in the tropical rainforest has adapted to the conditions of rainforests in many remarkable ways. It uses its trunk as a nose because of which it has a strong sense of smell. The trunk is also used by it for picking up food. Its tusks are modified teeth. These can tear the bark of trees that elephant loves to eat. Large ears of the elephant help it to hear even very soft sound. They also help the elephant to keep cool in the hot and humid climate of the tropical rainforest.

Que 10. A carnivore with stripes on its body moves very fast while catching its prey. It is likely to be found in

    (a) polar regions   (b) deserts

    (c) oceans   (d) tropical rainforests

Ans. (d) tropical rainforests

Que 11. Which features adapt polar bears to live in extremely cold climate?

    (a) A white fur, fat below skin, keen sense of smell.

    (b) Thin skin, large eyes, a white fur.

    (c) A long tail, strong claws, white large paws.

    (d) White body, paws for swimming, gills for respiration.

Ans. (a) A white fur, fat below skin, keen sense of smell.

Que 12. Which option best describes a tropical region?

    (a) Hot and humid

    (b) Moderate temperature, heavy rainfall

    (c) Cold and humid

    (d) Hot and dry

Ans. (a) Hot and humid

Selected **NCERT Exemplar Problems**

> **Multiple Choice Questions**

Que 1. The maximum and minimum temperatures displayed daily in the weather bulletin refer to the
  (a) highest day temperature and lowest night temperature of the day
  (b) highest day temperature and highest night temperature of the month
  (c) temperature recorded at 12 noon and at mid night (00.00 h).
  (d) average highest temperature of day and average lowest temperature of night

Ans. (a) This refers to the highest day temperature and lowest night temperature of the day.

Que 2. Out of the given definitions, which is the most appropriate definition of climate?
  (a) Changes in weather conditions in a year
  (b) Average weather pattern of many years
  (c) Change in weather pattern in a few years
  (d) Weather conditions during summer

Ans. (b) Climate is the average weather pattern of many years.

Que 3. Which of the following briefly describes the desert climate?
  (a) Hot and humid
  (b) Dry and humid
  (c) Hot and dry
  (d) Hot and wet

Ans. (c) Desert climate is hot and dry.

Que 4. Paheli went to a wildlife sanctuary, where she saw dense vegetation of trees, shrubs, herbs and also a variety of animals like monkeys, birds, elephants, snakes, frogs, etc. The most likely location of this sanctuary is in the
  (a) temperate region   (b) tropical region
  (c) polar region   (d) coastal region

Ans. (b) Wildlife sanctuary is situated in tropical region.

Que 5. Given below are some adaptive features of animals:
  (i) Layer of fat under the skin
  (ii) Long, curved and sharp claws
  (iii) Slippery body
  (iv) Thick white fur
  Which of them is/are the adaptive feature of a polar bear?
  (a) Only (i)   (b) (i) and (ii)
  (c) (i), (ii) and (iii)   (d) (i), (ii) and (iv)
Ans. (d) Adaptive features of a polar bear are
  (i) Layer of fat under the skin
  (ii) Long, curved and sharp claws
  (iv) Thick white fur

Que 6. Which of the following statements is incorrect for penguins?
  (a) They huddle together
  (b) They cannot swim
  (c) They have webbed feet
  (d) They have streamlined body
Ans. (b) They cannot swim. Penguins are good swimmer.

Que 7. Read the following environmental conditions of tropical rainforests.
  (i) Hot and humid climate
  (ii) Unequal lengths of day and night
  (iii) Abundant rainfall
  (iv) Abundant light and moisture

  Identify the conditions from the above list that are responsible for the presence of large number of plants and animals in tropical rainforests.
  (a) (i) and (ii)   (b) (i) and (iii)
  (c) (i), (iii) and (iv)   (d) (ii) and (iv)
Ans. (c) The conditions responsible for the presence of large number of plants and animals are
  (i) Hot and humid climate
  (iii) Abundant rainfall
  (iv) Abundant light and moisture.

Que 8. The coldest region on the earth is the
    (a) polar region   (b) tropical region
    (c) temperate region   (d) coastal region

Ans. (a) The coldest region on the earth is the polar region.

Que 9. Choose the odd one from the following options:
    (a) Thick layer of fat under the skin
    (b) White fur
    (c) Long grasping tail
    (d) Wide and large feet with sharp claws

Ans. (c) Long grasping tail is not an adaptive feature of polar bear.

> Very Short Answer Type Questions

Que 10. A fish dies when taken out of water, whereas a wall lizard will die if kept under water. Mention the term used to describe such abilities that allow fish and lizard to survive in their respective habitats.

Ans. **Adaptation** is the term used to describe such ability. Animals are adapted to survive in the conditions in which they live. So, fish dies when taken out of water while wall lizard dies if kept under water.

Que 11. Give one example of an animal that can live both in water and on land.

Ans. Those animals that can live both in water and an land are called **amphibian**, e.g. frog.

Que 12. State whether the following statements are True or False. Correct the False statements.
    (a) It is easy to predict weather rather than climate.
    (b) Since very few prey are available, polar bear does not need to have strong sense of smell.
    (c) Penguins stick together to fight the cold polar climate.
    (d) Tropical rainforests are cool and humid throughout the year because of heavy rains all the time.

Ans. (a) False, it is easy to predict the climate rather than the weather.
    (b) False, since very few prey are available polar bear need to have a strong sense of smell.
    (c) True
    (d) False, tropical rainforests are hot and humid throughout the year because of heavy rains all the time.

Que 13. Unscramble the following words using the hints given against them.

(i)	MATLICE	(Hint : weather pattern in a region over a period of time)
(ii)	AROPL	(Hint : coolest region on the earth)
(iii)	TREHMEOMRET	(Hint : used to measure temperature)
(iv)	UDHIDYTMI	(Hint : feature of weather)

Ans. (i) Climate   (ii) Polar
     (iii) Thermometer   (iv) Humidity

❯ Short Answer Type Questions

Que 14. Match the animals mentioned in Column I with their characteristic features given in Column II.

	Column I		Column II
(a)	Red eyed frog	(i)	Very sensitive hearing
(b)	Penguin	(ii)	Streamlined body
(c)	Tiger	(iii)	Silver-white mane
(d)	Lion-tailed macaque	(iv)	Sticky pads on feet

Ans.

	Column I		Column II
(a)	Red eyed frog	(iv)	Sticky pads on feet
(b)	Penguin	(ii)	Streamlined body
(c)	Tiger	(i)	Very sensitive hearing
(d)	Lion-tailed macaque	(iii)	Silver-white mane.

Que 15. Why is it difficult to predict the weather of a place while it is easy to predict its climate?

Ans. Weather is a complex phenomenon which can vary over a short period of time and thus is difficult to predict, while it is easier to predict climate as it is the average weather pattern taken over a long time.

Que 16. Name two animals each that live in polar region and tropical rainforests.

Ans. **Polar regions** Polar bear/penguin/reindeer/musk oxen/ any other.
   Tropical rainforests Red eyed frog /elephants /lion-tailed macaque/ any other.

Que 17. Write two common adaptive features of a polar bear which help in keeping it warm.

Ans. Adaptive features of a polar bear that help in keeping it warm are as follows:
  (i) They have two thick layers of white fur.
  (ii) They have layer of fat under their skin.

Que 18. Mention two adaptive features of penguin that help it in swimming.

Ans. Adaptive features of penguin that help it in are as follows:
  (i) It has streamlined body
  (ii) Webbed feet

Que 19. Differentiate between:
  (i) Weather and climate
  (ii) Humidity and rainfall
  (iii) Climates of polar region and tropical rainforest
  (iv) Maximum and minimum temperatures of the day

Ans. (i) Weather is the daily fluctuation in temperature, humidity, etc while climate is the average weather pattern of a place.
  (ii) Humidity indicates the wetness of a place due to amount of moisture in the atmosphere while rainfall is the drop of water that fall from clouds on the ground.
  (iii) Polar region remains very cold for most part of the year, whereas tropical rainforest is hot and humid.
  (iv) Maximum and minimum temperatures of the day indicate highest and lowest recorded temperatures respectively.

› Long Answer Type Questions

Que 20. Fill in the blanks in the paragraph given below.
  Weather of a place is the day-to-day condition of the ...(a)... with respect to ...(b)... , ...(c)..., ...(d)..., ...(e)... , at that place, while climate is the ...(f)... weather pattern taken over many years.

Ans. (a) atmosphere   (b) temperature
  (c) humidity   (d) rainfall
  (e) wind speed   (f) average

Chapter **8**

Winds, Storms *and* **Cyclones**

Important Points

- **Wind** Moving air is called wind. Air moves from high pressure region to the low pressure region. It is caused due to the difference in air pressures between two places.

- **Atmospheric pressure** It is the force per unit area exerted on a surface by the weight of air above that surface in the atmosphere of the earth (or that of another planet).

- **High speed winds** These are accompanied by reduced air pressure. Air moves from the region of higher pressure to the lower pressure. The greater the difference in pressures, the faster the air moves. It is due to the heat of the sun from which air becomes warm, producing a low pressure. So, the warm air rises up and the cool air from the surrounding moves towards that area.

- **Air expands on heating** On heating air expands and occupies more space. When the same thing occupies more space, it becomes lighter. The warm air is therefore lighter than the cold air. That is the reason that the smoke goes up.

- **Wind current** As we know air moves from high pressure to the lower pressure. The different reasons for wind currents are

  (i) **Uneven heating between the equator and the poles** due to the shape of earth and its inclination. The wind flows from the North and South towards the equator. The change in direction of wind is due to rotation of the earth.

(ii) **Uneven heating of land and water** In summer near the equator, the land warms up faster and most of the time, temperature of the land is higher than that of water in the oceans. The air over the land gets heated and rises. This causes the winds to blow from the oceans towards the land.

In winter, the direction of the wind flow gets reversed. It flows from the land to the ocean.

- **Monsoon winds** The seasonal winds bring rain between June and September in India and South Asia are known as monsoon winds.
- **Thunderstorm** It develops in hot, humid tropical areas very frequently. The rising temperature produces strong upward rising winds. These winds carry water droplets upward.

At a certain height, these tiny water droplets freeze and fall down again. Because of their swift movement, the water and ice particles rub against each other and build up a negative electric charge in the cloud. The electric charge is then released by the clouds by the stroke of **lightning** and thunder is produced.

The precautions in thunderstorms are as below:

(i) It is well advised not to take shelter under an isolated tree because an isolated tree is prone to lightning. While in a forest, it is advised to take shelter under a small tree.

(ii) Do not lie on ground.

(iii) Do not take shelter under an umbrella with a metallic rod, as pointed metallic materials are prone to lightning.

(iv) Do not sit near a window. Open garages, storage sheds, metal sheds are not safe places to take shelter.

(v) If one is in water, he should get out and go inside a building.

(vi) A bus or car is a safe place to take shelter.

- **Cyclone** Winds blow at a speed of 120 km per hour or above are known as cyclone.

  Note A cyclone is known by different names in different parts of the world. It is called **hurricane** in the American continent. It is called **typhoon** in Japan and Philippines.

- **Formation of cyclone** The formation of cyclone is a very complex process. Due to heat of the atmosphere, water gets evaporated and changes to water vapour.

- When water vapour changes back to water due to condensation, the heat is released to atmosphere and warms the air around. Then the hot air rises up causing a drop in pressure.

- More air from surrounding regions not only rushes in but also starts spiraling. This cycle is repeated. This chain of events ends with the formation of a very low pressure system with very high speed winds revolving around it. This weather condition is called a **cyclone**. Factors like wind speed, wind direction, temperature and humidity contribute to the development of cyclone.

- **Eye of a storm** The centre of a cyclone is calm area. It is called the eye of a storm. A large cyclone is a violently rotating mass of air in the atmosphere. The diameter of the eye varies from 10 to 30 km.

- Cyclones can be very destructive. Strong winds push water towards the shore even if the storm is hundreds of kilometers away. These are the first indications of an approaching cyclone.

  Note The whole coastline of India is vulnerable to cyclones particularly the east coast. The west coast of India in less vulnerable to cyclonic stoms both in terms of intensity and frequence of the cyclones.

- **Tornado** A tornado is a dark funnel shaped cloud that reaches from the sky to the ground. The neck of the funnel sucks up anything which comes in its way. The tornadoes may form within cyclone. The wind in a violent tornado can circle around at a speed of 300 km per hour.

- **Protection from Tornado** We can protect ourselves from tornado through tornado shelter, a room situated deep inside or underground having no windows. Otherwise, it is better to shut windows and take shelter under a table, workbench, where debris cannot reach. One has to know down on knees protecting head and neck using arms.

- **Anemometer** It is a device used for measuring wind speed and is a common weather station instrument.

- **Effective safety measures**
  - (i) With the help of satellite weather observation radars, the formation of cyclone and its direction and intensity is detected by the meteorological department.

(ii) The news of the formation of cyclone, its direction and intensity, etc is immediately telecasted and broadcasted at least 48 h before the arrival of the cyclone.

(iii) Cyclone warning is telecasted and broadcasted every hour or half an hour.

- **The action on the part of the people**
  (i) We should not ignore the warning issued by the meteorological department through television, radio or newspapers.

  (ii) We should make necessary arrangements to shift the essential household goods, domestic animals and vehicles, etc to safer places.

  (iii) Avoid driving on roads through standing water.

  (iv) Keep ready the phone numbers of all emergency services like police, fire brigade and medical centres.

- Some other precautions, if you are staying in a cyclone hit area:
  (i) Do not drink water that could be contaminate.

  (ii) Do not touch wet switches and fallen power lines.

  (iii) Do not go out just for the sake of fun.

  (iv) Do not pressurise the rescue force by making undue demands.

- A **cyclone alert** or **cyclone water** is issued 48 h in advance of any expected storm and a **cyclone warning** is issued 24 h in advance.

Intext Questions

Que 1. What are cyclones? How are they formed?   *(Pg 80)*

Ans. Cyclone is an area of closed circular fluid motion, rotating in the same direction as the earth. They are formed when water vapour changes back to liquid by the release of heat. This heat warms air around and it rises to move up and more air rushes to the vacant place. Thus, a cycle is formed which have very low pressure and very high speed of air.

Que 2. How are the pressure difference created in nature? *(Pg 83)*

Ans. Pressure difference created in nature by the heat of the sun. When it falls on the earth surface, the surface of the earth gets heated and air above it also gets warm and becomes light weight and moves upward. Thus, the pressure difference is created.

Que 3. Can you say why smoke always rises up? *(Pg 84)*

Ans. As we know that smoke is the combination of hot air and hot air becomes light weight with respect to cold air. Thus, it always rises up.

Que 4. Why winds are not exact from North pole to South pole? *(Pg 85)*

Ans. The winds would have blown in the North-South direction either from North to South or from South to North. A change in direction is however, caused by the rotation of the earth.

Que 5. What monsoon winds do for us? *(Pg 85)*

Ans. The monsoon winds carry water and it rains. Clouds bring rain and give us happiness. Farmers in our country depend mainly on rains for their harvests. There are many folk songs associated with clouds and rain.

Exercises

Que 1. Fill the missing word in the blank spaces in the following statements:

    (a) Wind is .... air.

    (b) Winds are generated due to .... heating on the earth.

    (c) Near the earth's surface, ... air rises up whereas, ... air comes down.

    (d) Air moves from a region of .... pressure to a region of .... pressure.

Ans. (a) Wind is **moving** air.

    (b) Winds are generated due to **uneven** heating on the earth.

    (c) Near the earth's surface, **warm** air rises up whereas, **cold** air comes down.

    (d) Air moves from a region of **high** pressure to a region of **low** pressure.

Que 2. Suggest two methods to find out wind direction at a given place.

Ans. Two methods to find out wind direction at a given place are

    (i) An instrument called anemometer can be used to find the direction and speed of the wind.

    (ii) Hold a strip of paper outside. The direction in which the paper is blowing, is the direction in which the wind blows.

Que 3. State two experiences that made you think that air exerts pressure (other than those given in the text).

Ans. Two experiences that made us think that air exerts pressure are

(i) Cycling against the direction of the wind, it is difficult to ride. It shows that the air exerts pressure.

(ii) While rowing a sailboat in the direction of the wind, it is always easier to row and while rowing a sailboat against the direction of the wind, it is very difficult to row. It also shows that the air exerts pressure.

Que 4. You want to buy a house. Would you like to buy a house having windows but no ventilators? Explain your answer.

Ans. No, I would not like to buy a house having windows but no ventilators, as warm air rises up and cool air comes downward. So, to make a stream of cool and fresh air to continuously flow to the house through the windows, there must be some ventilators in the upper part of the wall.

Que 5. Explain why holes are made in hanging banners and hoardings.

Ans. Holes are made in hanging banners and hoardings to allow air to pass through them as a result of which there will be less pressure of air on the banners or hoardings. Unless it is done, these may be uprooted or distorted due to the pressure of the air.

Que 6. How will you help your neighbours in case cyclone approaches your village/town?

Ans. I will help my neighbours in case cyclone approaches my village/town by the following ways:

(i) I will help in shifting their household articles, domestic animals, etc to safe place.

(ii) I will provide phone numbers of all emergency services like police, fire brigade and medical centres.

(iii) I will give them safety advice like avoid driving on roads through standing water, not to touch wet switches, etc.

Que 7. What planning is required in advance to deal with the situation created by a cyclone?

Ans. A good planning in advance will minimise the damages to be caused by a cyclone. Some of the plannings are as follows :

(i) The cyclone warning issued by the meteorological department through television, radio or newspapers must not be ignored and this instruction given should be followed carefully.

   (ii) The household articles, domestic animals, vehicles, etc should be shifted to safe places.

   (iii) The telephone numbers of essential services like police, fire brigade and medical centres, etc should be kept ready to meet the emergency situation.

Que 8. Which one of the following place is unlikely to be affected by a cyclone?

   (a) Chennai   (b) Mangaluru (Mangalore)

   (c) Amritsar   (d) Puri

Ans. (c) Amritsar is least likely to be affected by a cyclone because this city does not lie near to any coastal area.

Que 9. Which of the statements given below is correct?

   (a) In winter, the winds blow from the land to the ocean

   (b) In summer, the wind blow from the land towards the ocean

   (c) A cyclone is formed at a very high pressure system with very high speed winds revolving around it

   (d) The coastline of India is not vulnerable to cyclones

Ans. (a) The correct statement is, in winter, the winds blow from the land to the ocean.

Selected **NCERT Exemplar Problems**

❯ Multiple Choice Questions

Que 1. Four schematic diagrams are shown below to depict the direction of sea breeze. Which of them gives the correct direction?

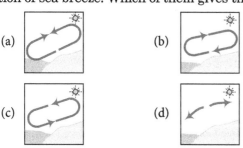

   (a)   (b)

   (c)   (d)

Ans. (c) In summer near the equator, the land becomes warm and the temperature of the air increases. This causes the air from the ocean to blow towards the land. These are known as summer monsoon winds.

Que 2. Figure shows a child blowing air with a straw near the opening of another straw which has its other end in a soft drink bottle. It was observed that the level of the soft drink in the straw

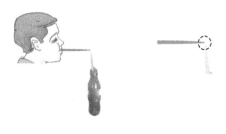

rises up as soon as air is blown over its open end. Which one of the following best explains the reason for rise in level of the drink?

    (a) Blowing of air decreases pressure over the opening of the straw

    (b) The straw of the soft drink bottle collapses when air is blown over its open end

    (c) Blowing of air warms up the air inside the straw

    (d) Blowing of air increases the pressure on the surface of soft drink in the bottle

Ans. (a) Blowing of air decreases pressure over the opening of the straw.

Que 3. Which of the following place is most likely to be affected by a cyclone?

    (a) Mumbai   (b) Puri

    (c) Goa   (d) Porbandar

Ans. (b) Puri is most likely to be affected by cyclone because this city lies near the coastal area.

Que 4. A curtain is hanging at the entrance of a room. A long corridor runs at right angles to the door, that is parallel to the curtain.

    If a strong wind blows along the corridor, the curtain will

    (a) get pushed inside the room

    (b) get pushed outside the room

    (c) get collected towards one end/ swirled

    (d) remain unaffected

Ans. (b) The air pressure increased along the corridor. Then, the curtain gets pushed outside the room.

> **Very Short Answer Type Questions**

Que 5. Why is Chandigarh unlikely to be affected by a cyclone?

Ans. Chandigarh is unlikely to be affected by a cyclone because it is not near to the sea or an ocean.

Que 6. Name the ocean which is mainly responsible to bring rain bearing monsoon winds to Kerala coast in June every year?

Ans. An Indian ocean is mainly responsible to bring rain bearing monsoon winds to Kerala coast in June every year.

Que 7. Fill in the blanks.

    (a) Air around us exerts ....

    (b) The moving air is called ....

    (c) The main cause of wind movement is uneven .... on the earth.

    (d) High speed wind can cause cyclone in regions of .... pressure.

Ans. (a) pressure   (b) wind

      (c) heating   (d) low

Que 8. State whether the following statements are true or false.

    (a) If wind blows from land to the ocean, then it is day time.

    (b) A very high pressure system with very high speed wind surrounding it, forms a cyclone.

    (c) The coastline of India is not vulnerable to cyclones.

    (d) Warm air is lighter than cool air.

Ans. (a) False, if wind blows from land to the ocean then, it is night time.

     (b) False, the formation of a very low pressure system with very high speed winds revolving around it.

     (c) False, the coastline of India is vulnerable to cyclones.

     (d) True

Que 9. To expel hot air out of the kitchen, *A* has an exhaust fan fitted on the window of her kitchen and *B* has a similar exhaust fan fitted on the wall near the ceiling of her kitchen. Which of the exhaust fan will expel the hot air more effectively? Explain why.

Ans. *B*'s exhaust fan will expel the hot air more effectively because hot air rises up and her fan is at greater height than *A*'s.

Que 10. Why is it advisable not to shut all the doors and windows during a storm?

Ans. To avoid the roof getting blown away due to the low pressure created by heavy wind.

Que 11. A flat in Mumbai with a balcony facing the sea has some clothes hung on a clothes line in the balcony. Towards which direction, the clothes will be blown in the afternoon? Explain it.

Ans. As during the afternoon, the land becomes hot which ultimately creates hot air above it and we know that hot air rises up and there is low pressure created. Thus, winds from sea start blowing towards the land and the clothes will be blown towards the house because sea breeze blowing towards the land.

Que 12. A flag mounted on a flag post near the sea coast flutters in the direction of sea. At what time of the day does this happen—at midnight or in the afternoon?

Ans. In the midnight, the wind blows from land to sea. So, in the midnight flag mounted on a flag post near the sea coast flutters in the direction of sea.

Que 13. Figure shows a diagrammatic representation of trees in the afternoon along a sea coast. State on which side is the sea, *A* or *B*? Give reasons for your choice.

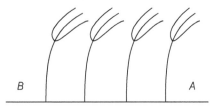

Ans. In the afternoon, the wind blows from **sea to land**. As pressure on the land is less than the pressure above sea, so the sea is on *B* side.

> **Short Answer Type Questions**

Que 14. Match Column I with Column II. There can be more than one match.

	Column I		Column II
(a)	On heating air	(i)	Descends
(b)	On cooling air	(ii)	Expands
		(iii)	Contracts
		(iv)	Rises

Ans. (a) (ii) and (iv)

(b) (i) and (iii)

On heating air, the air expands and rises because on heating its density decreases.

On cooling air, the air descends and contracts because on cooling its density increases.

Que 15. Paheli kept an empty bottle made of plastic inside a refrigerator. After few hours, when she opened the refrigerator, she found the bottle had collapsed. Explain the possible reason.

Ans. On cooling the air, contraction of air takes place. The air inside the bottle contracts due to low temperature. Hence, the bottle collapses due to the outside pressure.

Que 16. When strong/high speed wind blows, an umbrella held upright at times gets upturned. Explain the reason.

Ans. High speed wind passing over the umbrella creates low pressure above the umbrella with respect to below of it. Therefore, the umbrella upturns.

Que 17. Suggest some precautions to be taken to prevent the roof of a tin sheet from flying away during a fierce wind storm.

Ans. Some precautions are

(i) Put heavy stones on it.

(ii) Screw it tight.

❯ Long Answer Type Question

Que 18. Identify the names of six natural phenomena from the following word diagram given as figure.

G	C	H	T	H	T	E	N	M	R
R	C	Y	H	O	O	N	C	Z	P
V	L	O	U	E	R	O	E	R	T
A	N	C	N	A	N	N	L	C	L
H	T	H	D	B	A	D	A	P	I
L	U	N	E	K	D	C	Y	D	G
H	U	R	R	I	C	A	N	E	H
W	C	T	S	L	M	N	O	P	T
M	Y	O	T	Y	P	H	O	O	N
O	C	R	O	H	C	T	P	Q	I
C	L	N	R	U	A	Y	R	S	N
F	O	A	M	R	N	P	T	U	G
P	N	D	X	R	E	H	Y	E	N
Z	E	O	A	I	O	U	N	Y	B

Ans.

G	C	H	T	H	T	E	N	M	R
R	C	Y	H	O	O	N	C	Z	P
V	L	O	U	E	R	O	E	R	T
A	N	C	N	A	N	N	L	C	L
H	T	H	D	B	A	D	A	P	I
L	U	N	E	K	D	C	Y	D	G
H	U	R	R	I	C	A	N	E	H
W	C	T	S	L	M	N	O	P	T
M	Y	O	T	Y	P	H	O	O	N
O	C	R	O	H	C	T	P	Q	I
C	L	N	R	U	A	Y	R	S	N
F	O	A	M	R	N	P	T	U	G
P	N	D	X	R	E	H	Y	E	N
Z	E	O	A	I	O	U	N	Y	B

Chapter 9

Soil

Important Points

- **Soil** It is an inseparable part of our life. It supports the growth of plants by holding the roots firmly and supplying water and nutrients. It is the natural habitat for many organisms. It is essential for agriculture which provides food, clothing and shelter for all organisms.

- **Soil pollution** Polythene bags and plastics pollute the soil, they also kill the organisms living in the soil. So, there is a demand to ban the polythene bags and plastics. Some other substances like chemicals, water products and pecticides also pollute the soil. They should be treated before they are released into the soil.

- **Humus** The rotting dead matter in the soil is called humus. It makes the soil fertile and provide nutrients to growing plants.

- **Formation of soil** The soil is formed by the breaking down of rocks by the action of wind, water and climate. This process is called **weathering**. The nature of any soil depends upon the rocks from which it has been formed and the type of vegetation that grows in it.

- **Soil profile** A vertical section through different layers of the soil is called soil profile. Each layer differs in texture (feel), colour, depth and chemical composition.

  These layers are called **horizons** and can be described as follows :

  (i) **A-horizon** It is the uppermost layer or **topsoil** which is generally dark in colour as it is rich in humus and minerals. This layer is generally fertile, and can retain more water in it as it is soft and porous. This layer provides shelter for many living organisms. The roots of small plants are embedded entirely in the topsoil.

(ii) **B-horizon** This layer is next to A-horizon or middle layer, has a lesser amount of humus but has more minerals. This layer is generally harder and more compact.

(iii) **C-horizon** This layer is third layer of soil, made up of small lumps of rocks with cracks and crevices. It has partially weathered rocks and is below C-hrizon harder than A and B horizon.

(iv) **Bedrock** This layer is hard and difficult to dig with a spade.

- **Soil type** The mixture of rock particles and humus is called the soil. Soil can be classified into several types on the basis of the proportion of particles of various sizes as sandy, clayey and loamy.

(i) **Sandy soil** The soil with about 60% of sand (big) particles in it is called sandy soil. It has some clay also. It has least water holding capacity.

(ii) **Clayey soil** The soil with large amount of clay (fine) particles in it, is called clayey soil. Its water holding capacity is the highest among all soils. It is rich in minerals and is used to make pots, toys and statues.

(iii) **Loamy soil** The soil with approximately equal amount of large and fine particles in it is called loam or loamy soil. It is a mixture of sand, clay and silt.

The best topsoil for growing plants is loamy soil because of the following reasons :

(i) It is rich in humus.

(ii) It has good water-holding capacity.

(iii) It holds enough air for respiration of organisms.

- **Percolation rate of water in soil** Percolation means the amount of water (in mL) that passes from the surface into the soil (in unit time).

$$\text{Percolation rate (mL/min)} = \frac{\text{Amount of water (mL)}}{\text{Percolation time (min)}}$$

Note Percolation of water is highest in the sandy soil and least in clayey soil.

- **Moisture in soil** Soil absorbs water and also holds water in it, which is called soil moisture. The capacity of a soil to hold water is also called water retention capacity and is important for various crops.

▪ **Percentage of water absorbed** It can be calculated by using the following formula

Percentage of water absorbed

$$= \frac{\text{Amount of water absorbed (mL)}}{\text{Amount of soil (gm)}} \times 100$$

▪ **Soil and crops**

(i) Climatic factors as well as the components of soil determine the various types of vegetation and crops grown in any region.

(ii) Clayey and loamy soils are both suitable for growing cereals like wheat and gram. Such soils are good at retaining water.

(iii) For paddy, soils rich in clay and organic matter and having a good capacity to retain water are ideal.

(iv) For lentils (Masoor) and other pulses, loamy soils, which drain water easily, are required.

(v) For cotton, sandy-loam or loam, which drain water easily and can hold plenty of air, are more suitable.

(vi) Crops such as wheat are grown in the fine clayey soils because they are rich in humus and are very fertile.

▪ **Soil erosion** The removal of land surface by water, wind or ice is known as soil erosion, plant roots firmly bind the soil. In the absence of plants, soil becomes loose. Erosion of soil is more severe in areas of little or no surface vegetation such as desert or bare lands.

Intext Questions

Que 1. Why is it necessary to ban the use of polythene bags and plastics? *(Pg 97)*

Ans. Polythene bags and plastics pollute the soil as they kill the organisms living in the soil. That is why, it is necessary to ban the use of polythene bags and plastics.

Que 2. Can we make toys with the soil obtained from a field? *(Pg 97)*

Ans. No, soil from a field cannot be used to make toys. In order to make toys, the soil should be clayey.

Que 3. Name the substances which pollute the soil.   *(Pg 97)*

Ans. The substances which pollute the soil are polythene bags, plastics, waste products, chemicals, pesticides, etc.

Que 4.   *(Pg 97)*
    (a) Draw a diagram to show different layers of soil.
    (b) Define the term humus.

Ans. (a) A well labelled diagram of different layers of soil is given below :

    (b) The rotting dead matter in the soil is called **humus**.

Que 5. What kind of soil should be used for making matkas and surahis?   *(Pg 99)*

Ans. Clayey soil is used to make matkas and surahis.

Que 6. Do all the soils absorb water to the same extent?
                                                   (Pg 101)

Ans. No, different types of soil has different absorbing capacity of water.

Que 7. Which soil would have the highest and least percolation rate?   *(Pg 102)*

Ans. Percolation rate of water is highest in the sandy soil. While the lowest in the clayey soil.

Que 8. Which kind of soil would be most suitable for planting rice?   *(Pg 104)*

Ans. For planting paddy (rice), clayey soil that is rich in organic matter and have a good water retaining capacity is ideal.

Que 9. What is the difference between rate of percolation and the amount of water retained? *(Pg 104)*

Ans. Percolation property of any material is linked to its porosity. Different soils have different porosity. Therefore, water percolates differently through different soil.

$$\text{Percolation rate of water in the soil} = \frac{\text{Volume of water percolated}}{\text{Time taken for percolation}}$$

Whereas, water retaining capacity of a soil is described in terms of the amount of water absorbed by a particular type of soil. High water retaining capacity means higher water absorption.

Exercises

Que 1. In addition to the rock particles, the soil contains
  (a) air and water
  (b) water and plants
  (c) minerals, organic matter, air and water
  (d) water, air and plants

Ans. (c) In addition to the rock particles, the soil contains minerals, organic matter, air and water.

Que 2. The water holding capacity is the highest in
  (a) sandy soil
  (b) clayey soil
  (c) loamy soil
  (d) mixture of sand and loam

Ans. (b) The water holding capacity is the highest in clayey soil.

Que 3. Match the items in Column I with those in Column II.

Column I		Column II
(a) A home for living organisms	(i)	Large particles
(b) Upper layer of the soil	(ii)	All kinds of soil
(c) Sandy soil	(iii)	Dark in colour
(d) Middle layer of the soil	(iv)	Small particles and packed tight
(e) Clayey soil	(v)	Lesser amount of humus

Ans.

Column I	Column II
(a) A home for living organisms	(ii) All kinds of soil
(b) Upper layer of the soil	(iii) Dark in colour
(c) Sandy soil	(i) Large particles
(d) Middle layer of the soil	(v) Lesser amount of humus
(e) Clayey soil	(iv) Small particles and packed tight

Que 4. Explain how soil is formed.

Ans. Soil formation is a slow process which occurs in following two steps :

(i) **Weathering of rocks** It is the breakdown of rocks into small particles by the action of air, wind and water.

(ii) These small particles mix with humus (organic matter) and form soil.

Que 5. How is clayey soil useful for crops?

Ans. Clayey soil has an important characteristic. It can retain water and moisture and are rich in humus. Therefore, it is suitable for growing cereals like wheat, gram and paddy.

Que 6. List the differences between clayey soil and sandy soil.

Ans. Differences between clayey and sandy soil are

Clayey soil	Sandy soil
Particles are of very small size.	Particles are of quite large size.
Particles are tightly packed together.	Particles are not closely packed.
No air is present between particles	Well aerated
It can retain water for long time	It cannot hold water
Water does not drain easily	Water drains easily
It is fertile	It is not fertile

Que 7. Sketch the cross-section of soil and label the various layers.

Ans.

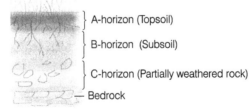

} A-horizon (Topsoil)

} B-horizon (Subsoil)

} C-horizon (Partially weathered rock)

— Bedrock

Que 8. Razia conducted an experiment in the field related to the rate of percolation. She observed that it took 40 min for 200 mL of water to percolate through the soil sample. Calculate the rate of percolation.

Ans. Given,

Time = 40 min

Volume of water = 200 mL

So, rate of percolation $= \dfrac{\text{Amount of water (mL)}}{\text{Percolation time (min)}}$

$= \dfrac{200}{40} = 5 \text{ mL/min}$

Therefore, percolation rate of water = 5 mL/min.

Que 9. Explain how soil pollution and soil erosion could be prevented.

Ans. Prevention of soil pollution can be done by

(i) use of manures instead of synthetic fertilisers.

(ii) use of natural pesticides.

(iii) avoid dumping of polythene and plastics in soil.

(iv) industrial waste should be treated before release in soil.

Prevention of soil erosion can be done by

(i) afforestation that is large scale planting in place of cut down forests.

(ii) avoiding overgrazing of grasslands.

(iii) terrace farming and other better farming methods in hilly areas.

Que 10. Solve the following crossword puzzle with the clues given:

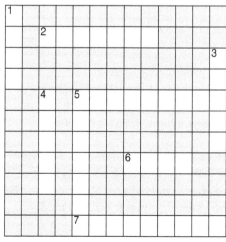

Across

   2. Plantation prevents it.

   5. Use should be banned to avoid soil pollution.

   6. Type of soil used for making pottery.

   7. Living organism in the soil.

Down

   1. In desert, soil erosion occurs through.

   3. Clay and loam are suitable for cereals like.

   4. This type of soil can hold very little water.

   5. Collective name for layers of soil.

Ans.

¹W										
I	²E	R	O	S	I	O	N			
N									³W	
D									H	
	⁴S		⁵P	O	L	Y	T	H	E	N	E
	A		R						A	
	N		O						T	
	D		F		⁶C	L	A	Y		
	Y		I							
			L							
			⁷E	A	R	T	H	W	O	R	M

Across

   2. Plantation prevents it (—) Erosion

   5. Use should be banned to avoid soil pollution (—) Polythene

   6. Type of soil used for making pottery (—) Clay

   7. Living organism in the soil (—) Earthworm

Down

   1. In desert, soil erosion occurs through (—) Wind

   3. Clay and loam are suitable for cereals like (—) Wheat

   4. This type of soil can hold very little water (—) Sandy

   5. Collective name for layers of soil (—) Profile

Selected **NCERT Exemplar Problems**

❯ **Multiple Choice Questions**

Que 1. The microorganisms present in the soil require moisture (water) and nutrients for growth and survival. Choose from the options below, the habitat (place) where the soil has plenty of water and nutrients.

(a) Desert   (b) Forest
(c) Open field   (d) Cricket ground

Ans. (b) The microorganisms present in the soil having plenty of water and nutrients are present in the habitat of forest.

Que 2. Availability of water and minerals in the soil for maximum absorption by roots is in the

(a) B-horizon   (b) C-horizon
(c) A-horizon   (d) surface of soil

Ans. (c) Availability of water and minerals in the soil for maximum absorption by roots is in A-horizon.

Que 3. Soil conservation measures are mainly aimed at protecting which of the following?

(a) Plants   (b) Topsoil
(c) Subsoil   (d) Soil organisms

Ans. (b) Soil conservation measures mainly aim at protecting topsoil which is rich in humus and nutrients making it fertile to grow plants.

Que 4. Read the following statements with reference to soil.

(i) Weathering is a very fast process of soil formation.

(ii) Percolation of water is faster in sandy soils.

(iii) Loamy soil contains only sand and clay.

(iv) Topsoil contains the maximum amount of humus.

Choose the correct statements from the above.

(a) (ii) and (iv)   (b) (i) and (iii)
(c) (ii) and (iii)   (d) (i) and (ii)

Ans. (a) Statements (ii) and (iv) are correct with reference to soil while (i) weathering is a slow process of soil formation and (iii) loamy soil consists of sand, clay and silt along with humus.

❯ Very Short Answer Type Questions

Que 5. Soil has particles of different sizes. Arrange the words given below in decreasing order of their particle size.

Rock, clay, sand, gravel, silt

Ans. The soil particles with the decreasing order of their particle sizes can be shown as :

Rock > gravel > sand > silt > clay

Que 6. The components of loamy soil are ...., ... and ....

Ans. The components of loamy soil are sand, silt and clay.

Que 7. Read the following statements and give the appropriate terms for each of them.

(a) The process of breakdown of rocks by the action of wind, water, sunlight.

(b) Removal of topsoil during heavy rains or strong winds.

(c) Accumulation of wastes in the soil generated by human activity which alter the features of soil.

(d) The process of movement of water into deeper layers of soil.

Ans. The terms for the above described statements are as follows :

(a) Weathering   (b) Soil erosion
(c) Soil pollution   (d) Percolation

Que 8. Unscramble the following jumbled words related to soil.

(a) S U H U M

(b) I L O S   F I P R O L E

(c) Z O I N O R H

(d) M O A L

(e) G I N R H E T W E A

(f) A T O N I E R P C L O

Ans. The words unscrambled to form the following words related to soil.

(a) HUMUS   (b) SOIL PROFILE
(c) HORIZON   (d) LOAM
(e) WEATHERING   (f) PERCOLATION

> Short Answer Type Questions

Que 9. How can a farmer convert acidic soil into neutral soil?

Ans. The farmer can convert acidic soil into neutral soil by adding a small quantity of quicklime or slaked lime solution to the soil.

Que 10. Is it a good practice to remove grass and small plants that are growing in an open, unused field? Give reason to support your answer.

Ans. No, it is not a good practice to remove grass and small plants growing in an open, unused field because the plants cover the soil surface. Their roots bind the soil particles, holding and adhering them in place. It helps in preventing the topsoil from being washed off during heavy rain, floods and winds. This way, soil erosion is prevented and topsoil layer is preserved for growing more plants.

Que 11. A man digging a pit found that he could dig with ease initially but digging became difficult as he went deeper. He could not dig beyond a depth of 5 feet. Provide a suitable scientific explanation.

Ans. The man digging a pit could dig with ease initially because of the presence of topsoil and subsoil (mainly comprising of humus and nutrients). But as he digs deeper, he finds it difficult to dig beyond a depth of 5 feet as lower layers is made up of small partially weathered rocks with cracks and crevices and with bedrock which makes it hard to dig.

Que 12. Rajasthan is a desert state in India. Once while travelling to Rajasthan by train, Boojho observed several streams and rivulets of rainwater during the journey but to his surprise, he did not see streams of water in the desert region even during rains. Help Boojho find a suitable explanation for this.

Ans. Deserts are made up of sand, thus when the rainwater falls on land, it percolates immediately downwards in the spaces between sand particles. So, the streams of water in desert region are not visible even during rainy season.

Que 13. Locate the following zones given as boxed items in figure which shows a diagram of soil profile.

Topsoil, subsoil, C-horizon, bedrock

Ans. The different layers/zones in the soil profile are labelled as :

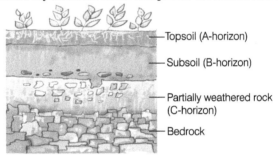

Que 14. Match the animals in Column I with their natural place of dwelling (habitat) in Column II.

	Column I		Column II
(a)	Earthworm	(i)	Sand and beaches
(b)	Garden lizard	(ii)	Burrows in soil
(c)	Crab	(iii)	Deep, narrow holes in dry soils
(d)	Rodents	(iv)	Surface of soil
(e)	Scorpion	(v)	Surface of shaded moist soils
(f)	Snails and slugs	(vi)	A-horizon of moist soils

Ans. The animals with their natural place of habitat are

Column I	Column II
(a) Earthworm	(vi) A-horizon of moist soils
(b) Garden lizard	(iv) Surface of soil
(c) Crab	(i) Sand and beaches
(d) Rodents	(ii) Burrows in soil
(e) Scorpion	(iii) Deep, narrow holes in dry soils
(f) Snails and slugs	(v) Surface of shaded moist soils

> Long Answer Type Questions

Que 15. Continuously water-logged soils are disadvantageous for plant growth. Why?

Ans. Roots, although underground, posseses living cells that require oxygen for respiration and production of energy. They absorb oxygen that is present in the spaces between soil particles. But in water-logged soils, water occupies spaces between soil particles and pushes the oxygen out into the atmosphere. Thus, roots are deprived of oxygen and this affects the plant growth.

Que 16. Why is soil erosion relatively less in dense forests as compared to barren, open fields?

Ans. In dense forests, the tree cover (canopy) prevents rainwater from directly falling on the ground/soil. Also roots of the vegetation bind the soil particles and hold them together. As a result, soil erosion is minimised.

But in barren, open fields, the soil is exposed to the falling rain. The soil particles become loose due to the impact of rain drops and the flow of water carries them away. The flowing water further erodes the soil surface aggravating erosion.

Que 17. Gardeners gently dig up the soil around the roots of garden herbs (plants) frequently. Give reasons.

Ans. A gardener often gently digs up the soil around the roots of garden plants or herbs for following reasons:
(i) It enables easy root growth.
(ii) For easier percolation of water.
(iii) For aerating the soil enabling air to get into deeper layers of soil.
(iv) For removing the weeds.

Que 18. In towns and cities, generally, the borewells have to be dug very deep to get water as compared to borewells dug in villages. Give suitable reasons.

Ans. The borewells have to be dug very deep to get water as compared to those in villages because
(i) excessive use of water depletes the groundwater.
(ii) towns and cities have asphalted roads and vast areas of soil are concreted. As a result, rainwater cannot percolate to recharge groundwater and the groundwater level further decrease. Villages have larger areas of open soil surface and fewer asphalted roads and concrete surfaces.
Thus, larger soil surface area is available for rainwater to percolate into the soil easily and recharge the groundwater. As a result, even shallow borewells yield water.

Que 19. Several terms related to soil are hidden in the squares given as figure, spot them and make a list. Two examples are given for you.

G	R	P	E	L	I	F	O	R	P
W	H	U	M	U	S	S	G	M	E
E	A	B	S	R	G	A	I	G	R
A	E	T	C	G	V	N	K	N	C
T	R	H	E	G	E	D	Z	C	O
H	O	E	D	R	O	C	K	S	L
E	S	P	A	A	A	K	P	C	A
R	I	L	D	V	R	S	I	L	T
I	O	A	K	E	G	Q	M	A	I
N	N	N	T	L	S	G	H	Y	O
G	K	T	H	O	R	I	Z	O	N

Ans. Humus, sand, water, clay, gravel, weathering, horizon, percolation, mineral, plant, erosion, profile, silt.

G	R	P	E	L	I	F	O	R	P
W	H	U	M	U	S	S	G	M	E
E	A	B	S	R	G	A	I	G	R
A	E	T	C	G	V	N	K	N	C
T	R	H	E	G	E	D	Z	C	O
H	O	E	D	R	O	C	K	S	L
E	S	P	A	A	A	K	P	C	A
R	I	L	D	V	R	S	I	L	T
I	O	A	K	E	G	Q	M	A	I
N	N	N	T	L	S	G	H	Y	O
G	K	T	H	O	R	I	Z	O	N

Chapter 10

Respiration
in Organisms

Important Points

- **Cell** All organisms are made up of small microscopic units called cells. It is the smallest structural and functional unit of an organism. Each cell of an organism performs certain functions, i.e. nutrition, transport, excretion and reproduction. To perform these functions, the cell needs energy.

- **Respiration** The biological process in which food is utilised to produce energy is called respiration. It is necessary for the survival of living beings. A living being cannot survive even for a few seconds without respiration.

- **Cellular respiration** The process of breakdown of food in the cell with the release of energy is called cellular respiration. It takes place in the **cells of all organisms**.

- **Site of respiration** Respiration takes place inside the cells. So, it is also called cellular respiration. A cell organelle, called **mitochondria** is the site of cellular respiration.

- **Aerobic respiration** It takes place in the presence of oxygen. Carbon dioxide and water are the end products of aerobic respiration. It occurs in most of the organisms.

$$\text{Glucose} \xrightarrow{\text{Presence of oxygen}} \text{Carbon dioxide} + \text{Water} + \text{Energy}$$

- **Anaerobic respiration** It takes place in the absence of oxygen. Alcohol and carbon dioxide are formed as the end products of anaerobic respiration. It usually occurs in most of the microbes (anaerobes) such as yeast.

$$\text{Glucose} \xrightarrow{\text{Absence of oxygen}} \text{Alcohol} + \text{Carbon dioxide} + \text{Energy}$$

- **Anaerobes** There are some organisms such as yeast that can survive in the absence of air. They are called anaerobes.

  Note Yeasts are single-celled organisms. They respire anaerobically and during this process yield alcohol. Therefore, they are used to make wine and beer.

- **Anaerobic respiration in humans** Anaerobic respiration also takes place in the muscle cell but only for a short time, when there is a temporary deficiency of oxygen. When someone runs or walks too fast, the demand for the energy is high but the supply of oxygen to produce the energy is limited. Then anaerobic respiration has taken place in the muscle cells to fulfil the demand of energy.

  $$\underset{\text{In muscle}}{\text{Glucose}} \xrightarrow{\text{Absence of oxygen}} \text{Lactic acid} + \text{Energy}$$

- **Muscle cramps** Sometimes after heavy exercise persons get muscle cramps. It happens due to anaerobic respiration in muscle cells. The partial breakdown of glucose produces lactic acid. The accumulation of lactic acid causes cramps. Muscle cramps can be relieved through a hot water bath or massage because it improves circulation of blood which increases the supply of oxygen to the muscle cells. Increase in the supply of oxygen results in the complete breakdown of lactic acid into carbon dioxide and water.

- **Breathing** It is the process of taking in air rich in oxygen, (i.e. **inhalation**) and giving out air rich in carbon dioxide, (i.e. **exhalation**) with the help of respiratory organs. It is a continuous process which goes on all the time and throughout the life of an organism.

- **Breathing rate** The number of times a person breathes in a minute is termed as the breathing rate. A **breath** means one inhalation plus one exhalation. When we are doing normal activities, the rate of breathing is normal. It increases when we do physical work such as running, swimming, jogging, etc. The rate of breathing decreases when we take rest or when we are sleeping.

Note On an average, an adult human being at rest breathes in and out 15-18 times in a minute.

- **Breathing in humans** The inhaled air first enters through the **nostrils**, then flows through the **nasal cavity**. From the nasal cavity, air reaches our **lungs** through **windpipe**.

- **Lungs** They are present in the chest cavity surrounded by ribs on the sides. Lung is a soft, spongy and cone-shaped structure. The right lung is larger (consists of three lobes) than the left lung (consists of two lobes).

- **Ribs** They are the long curved bones which form the cage. They surround the chest, enabling the lungs to expand and thus facilitate breathing by expanding the chest cavity. **Rib cage** is separated from the lower abdomen by the thoracic diaphragm.

- **Diaphragm** It is a large muscular sheet (membrane) present between the chest and abdomen. It forms the floor of the chest cavity. The process of breathing is controlled by the movement of the diaphragm and ribs.

    (i) When the diaphragm moves down, the rib cage expands. This leads to the expansion inside the lungs. As a result air moves into the lungs. This process is called **inspiration** or **inhalation**.

    (ii) When the diaphragm moves up, the rib cage contracts. This leads to contraction of the lungs. As a result, the air moves out of the lungs. This process is called **expiration** or **exhalation**.

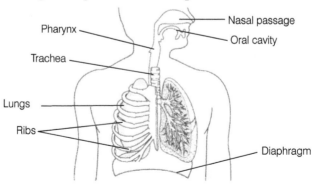

Human respiratory system

- **Sneezing** The air around us has various types of unwanted particles such as smoke, dust, pollens, etc. When we inhale, the particles get trapped in the hair present in the nasal cavity. Sometimes these particles may get past the hair in the nasal cavity. Then they irritate the lining of the cavity, as a result of which we sneeze, it expels these foreign particles from the inhaled air and clean air enters in our body. During sneezing, we should cover our nose so that expelled particles are not inhaled by others.

  Note Smoking damages lungs. It is also linked with cancer. It must be avoided.

- **Breathing in other animals** Animals such as elephants, lions, cows, goats, lizards, snakes, birds use lungs for breathing.

  (i) **Cockroach** Cockroach and other insects breathe through **spiracles and tracheae. Insects like coackroch have small openings on the sides of their body. These openings are called spiracles.** Insects also have a network of air tubes called tracheae for gas exchange.

  (ii) **Earthworm** They breathe through their skin which is moist and slimy.

  (iii) **Frog** They have a pair of lungs (for breath) like human being. In water they also breathe through their skin which is moist and slippery.

- **Breathing under water** Aquatic animals like fish have a pair of **gills** for breathing. Gills are projections of the skin that help fishes to use oxygen dissolved in water.

  Unicellular animals breathe through their cells membrane.

- **Respiration in plants** In plants, each part breathes independently through its external layer of cells. Roots breathe through root hairs. Stems breathe through epidermis. Leaves have numerous small pores called stomata for breathing.

Intext Questions

Que 1. What happens when breathe is released after holding it for sometime. Also, tell why it happens?

(Pg 110)

Ans. Releasing breathe after holding it for sometime results in rapid breathing. It happens to maintain a healthy balance between breathing in oxygen and breathing out carbon dioxide.

Que 2. How many times a person breathe in and breathe out in a minute? *(Pg 111)*

Ans. On an average, an adult human being at rest breathes in and out 15-18 times in a minute. During heavy exercise, the breathing rate can increase upto 25 times per minute.

Que 3. Why do you feel hungry after a physical activity? *(Pg 111)*

Ans. During physical activity, we require more energy. To fulfil this energy requirement, a person breathes faster. As a result, more oxygen is supplied to our cells. Due to this, rate of breakdown of food increases and more energy is released. Due to rapid breakdown of food, we feel hungry.

Que 4. Why we yawn when we are sleepy or drowsy? *(Pg 111)*

Ans. During drowsiness, our breathing rate slows down. The lungs do not get enough oxygen from the air resulting in yawning. Yawning brings extra oxygen into the lungs and helps us to keep awake. So, we yawn when we are sleepy or drowsy.

Que 5. Figure given adjacent shows various activities carried out by a person during normal day. Can you say in which activity, the rate of breathing will be slowest and in which it will be the fastest? *(Pg 111)*

Ans. Yes, we can say that the rate of breathing will be slowest and fastest and rate of breathing is given below :

	Activity	Rate of breathing
(i)	Washing clothes	Fast
(ii)	Sleeping	Normal (slowest)
(iii)	Studying	Normal (slow)
(iv)	Walking	Normal
(v)	Running	Fastest
(vi)	Working	Fast

Increasing order of rate of breathing will be
(ii) < (iii) < (iv) < (i) < (vi) < (v)

Que 6. Demonstrate that carbon dioxide is produced during respiration. *(Pg 114)*

Ans. Take a clean test-tube. Pour some freshly prepared lime water. Now, blow gently through the straw for a few times. Lime water will turn milky. This is because of carbon dioxide present in the breathed air.

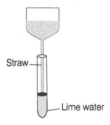

Straw

Lime water

Effect of exhaled air on lime water

Que 7. What is the percentage of oxygen and carbon dioxide in inhaled and exhaled air? *(Pg 115)*

Ans. The percentage of oxygen and carbon dioxide in inhaled and exhaled air is given below :

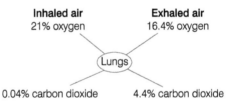

Inhaled air
21% oxygen

Exhaled air
16.4% oxygen

Lungs

0.04% carbon dioxide   4.4% carbon dioxide

Que 8. Whales and dolphins release a fountain of water sometimes while moving upwards. Why do they do so? *(Pg 116)*

Ans. Whales and dolphins breathe air through their lungs. Therefore, they have to come to the surface of water regularly.
The nostrils of whales and dolphins are located at the top of their heads and are called blowholes. They come to the surface or jump into the air regularly to inhale and exhale air through these blowholes.

Que 9. Roots which are underground also take in oxygen. If so, how? *(Pg 116)*

Ans. Like all other cells of the plants, the root cells of the plants, also need oxygen to generate energy. Roots take up air from the air spaces present between the soil particles with the help of root hairs.

Exercises

Que 1. Why does an athlete breathe faster and deeper than usual after finishing the race?

Ans. Our body needs energy for all activities, while doing heavy exercises like running, there is larger demand of energy to perform these activities. Hence, more oxygen is required to meet extra demand of energy. Therefore, an athlete breathes faster and deeper than usual after finishing the race.

> **Note** Also while running, due to lack of oxygen, some muscles may respire anaerobically and form lactic acid. Extra oxygen is also required to burn this lactic acid into carbon dioxide.

Que 2. List the similarities and differences between aerobic and anaerobic respiration.

Ans. Differences between aerobic and anaerobic respiration are as follows:

	Aerobic respiration	Anaerobic respiration
(i)	It uses oxygen.	It takes place in absence of oxygen.
(ii)	Glucose is completely broken down into CO_2, and water along with release of energy.	Glucose is broken into ethyl alcohol or lactic acid, CO_2 and energy.
(iii)	It occurs in all living organisms like mammals.	It occurs in lower organisms like yeast, fungi and bacteria.
(iv)	Glucose $+ O_2 \longrightarrow CO_2 + H_2O$ $+$ Energy	Glucose $\longrightarrow$ Ethyl alcohol $+ CO_2$ $+$ Energy

Similarities between aerobic and anaerobic respiration are as follows :
  (i) Both breakdown the glucose.
  (ii) Release of energy takes place in both.
  (iii) CO_2 is the common product in both.

Que 3. Why do we often sneeze when we inhale a lot of dust-laden air?

Ans. When we inhale dust-laden air, dirt-particles are captured within the nostrils. Sometimes, they get pass the nostril hair in the nasal cavity and irritate the lining of the cavity. As a result, we sneeze. Sneezing expels these foreign particles from the inhaled air and a dust free, clean air enters in our body.

Que 4. Take three test-tubes. Fill 3/4th of each with water. Label them *A, B* and *C.* Keep a snail in test-tube *A,* a water plant in test-tube *B* and in *C,* keep snail and plant both. Which test-tube would have the highest concentration of CO_2?

Ans.

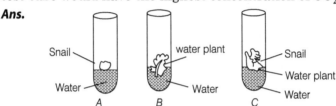

Test-tube *A* will have higher concentration of CO_2. This experiment shows the relationship between plants and animals. During breathing, snail inhales dissolved oxygen from water and releases CO_2.

Water-plant along with respiration performs another important function called photosynthesis. During photosynthesis, water-plant absorbs CO_2, prepares food and releases oxygen.

Therefore, test-tube *B* and *C* have less amount of CO_2 concentration as compared to test-tube *A.*

Que 5. Tick (✔) the correct answer.

(a) In cockroaches, air enters the body through
   (i) lungs   (ii) gills
   (iii) spiracles   (iv) skin

(b) During heavy exercise, we get cramps in the legs due to the accumulation of
   (i) carbon dioxide   (ii) lactic acid
   (iii) alcohol   (iv) water

(c) Normal range of breathing rate per minute in an average adult person at rest is
   (i) 9-12   (ii) 15-18
   (iii) 21-24   (iv) 22

(d) During exhalation, the ribs
   (i) move outwards   (ii) move downwards
   (iii) move upwards   (iv) do not move at all

Ans. (a) (iii) Spiracles
   (b) (ii) Lactic acid
   (c) (ii) 15-18
   (d) (ii) move downwards

Que 6. Match the items in Column I with those in Column II.

	Column I		Column II
(a)	Yeast	(i)	Earthworm
(b)	Diaphragm	(ii)	Gills
(c)	Skin	(iii)	Alcohol
(d)	Leaves	(iv)	Chest cavity
(e)	Fish	(v)	Stomata
(f)	Frog	(vi)	Lungs and skin
		(vii)	Tracheae

Ans. The correct match of both columns :

	Column I		Column II
(a)	Yeast	(iii)	Alcohol
(b)	Diaphragm	(iv)	Chest cavity
(c)	Skin	(i)	Earthworm
(d)	Leaves	(v)	Stomata
(e)	Fish	(ii)	Gills
(f)	Frog	(vi)	Lungs and skin

Que 7. Mark 'T' if the statement is True and 'F' if it is False.

(a) During heavy exercise, the breathing rate of a person slows down.

(b) Plants carry out photosynthesis only during the day and respiration only at night.

(c) Frogs breathe through their skins as well as their lungs.

(d) The fishes have lungs for respiration.

(e) The size of the chest cavity increases during inhalation.

Ans. (a) F, during heavy exercise, the breathing rate of a person increases.

(b) F, photosynthesis occurs in the presence of sunlight. Respiration is a continuous process and occurs all the time (day and night).

(c) T

(d) F, fishes breathe through gills.

(e) T

Que 8. Given below is a square of letters in which are hidden different words related to respiration in organisms. These words may be present in any direction — upwards, downwards, or along the diagonals. Find the words for your respiratory system. Clues about those words are given below the square.

S	V	M	P	L	U	N	G	S
C	Z	G	Q	W	X	N	T	L
R	M	A	T	I	D	O	T	C
I	Y	R	X	Y	M	S	R	A
B	R	H	I	A	N	T	A	Y
S	T	P	T	B	Z	R	C	E
M	I	A	M	T	S	I	H	A
S	P	I	R	A	C	L	E	S
N	E	D	K	J	N	S	A	T

  (i) The air tubes of insects

 (ii) Skeletal structures surrounding chest cavity

(iii) Muscular floor of chest cavity

(iv) Tiny pores on the surface of leaf

 (v) Small openings on the sides of the body of an insect

(vi) The respiratory organs of human beings

(vii) The openings through which we inhale

(viii) An anaerobic organism

(ix) An organism with tracheal system

Ans.

S	V	M	P	L	U	N	G	S
C	Z	G	Q	W	X	N	T	L
R	M	A	T	I	D	O	T	C
I	Y	R	X	Y	M	S	R	A
B	R	H	I	A	N	T	A	Y
S	T	P	T	B	Z	R	C	E
M	I	A	M	T	S	I	H	A
S	P	I	R	A	C	L	E	S
N	E	D	K	J	N	S	A	T

    (i) The air tubes of insects–Trachea.

   (ii) Skeletal structures surrounding chest cavity–Ribs

  (iii) Muscular floor of chest cavity–Diaphragm

  (iv) Tiny pores on the surface of leaf–Stomata

   (v) Small openings on the sides of the body of an insect–Spiracles

  (vi) The respiratory organs of human beings–Lungs

 (vii) The openings through which we inhale–Nostrils

(viii) An anaerobic organism–Yeast

  (ix) An organism with tracheal system–Ant

Que 9. The mountaineers carry oxygen with them because

    (a) at an altitude of more than 5 km, there is no air

    (b) the amount of air available to a person is less than that available on the ground

    (c) the temperature of air is higher than that on the ground

    (d) the pressure of air is higher than that on the ground

Ans. (b) The mountaineers carry oxygen with them because the amount of air available to a person is less than that available on the ground.

Selected **NCERT Exemplar Problems**

❯ **Multiple Choice Questions**

Que 1. Sometimes when we do heavy exercise, anaerobic respiration takes place in our muscle cells. What is produced during this process?

    (a) Alcohol and lactic acid

    (b) Alcohol and CO_2

    (c) Lactic acid and CO_2

    (d) Lactic acid only

Ans. (d) Sometimes when we do heavy exercise, anaerobic respiration takes place in our muscle cells and lactic acid is formed as end products.

$$\underset{\text{(in muscles)}}{\text{Glucose}} \xrightarrow{\text{Absence of oxygen}} \text{Lactic acid} + \text{Energy}$$

Que 2. Yeast is used in wine and beer industries because it respires
    (a) aerobically producing oxygen
    (b) aerobically producing alcohol
    (c) anaerobically producing alcohol
    (d) anaerobically producing CO_2

Ans. (c) Yeast is used in wine and beer industries because it respires anaerobically and during this process yield alochol.

Que 3. During the process of exhalation, the ribs move
    (a) down and inwards   (b) up and inwards
    (c) down and outwards   (d) up and outwards

Ans. (a) During the process of exhalation, the diaphragm moves up and the rib cage contracts, i.e. ribs move down and inwards.

Que 4. Breathing is a process that
    (i) provides O_2 to the body
    (ii) breaks down food to release energy
    (iii) helps the body to get rid of CO_2
    (iv) produces water in the cells

Which of the following gives the correct combination of functions of breathing?
    (a) (i) and (ii)   (b) (ii) and (iii)
    (c) (i) and (iii)   (d) (ii) and (iv)

Ans. (c) Breathing is the process of taking in air rich in oxygen, (i.e. inhalation) and giving out air rich in carbon dioxide, (i.e. exhalation) with the help of respiratory organs.

Que 5. Fish breathe with the help of gills which are richly supplied with blood vessels. The gills help the fish to
    (a) take in oxygen from air
    (b) take in oxygen dissolved in water
    (c) absorb nutrients present in water
    (d) release waste substances in water

Ans. (b) Fish breathe with the help of gills which are richly supplied with blood vessels. The gills help the fish to take in oxygen dissolved in water.

Que 6. Earthworms and frogs breathe through their skin because of which the skin of both the organisms is
    (a) moist and rough   (b) dry and rough
    (c) dry and slimy   (d) moist and slimy
Ans. (d) Earthworms and frogs breathe through their skin because the skin of both the organisms is moist and slimy.

> **Very Short Answer Type Questions**

Que 7. Mark the following statements as True or False. Correct the False statements.
    (a) Oxygen breaks down glucose outside the cells of organisms.
    (b) Frogs can breathe through their skin as well as lungs.
    (c) Insects have spiracles on the lower surface of the body.
    (d) Exhaled air has more percentage of CO_2 than inhaled air.
Ans. (a) False, correct statement – Oxygen breaks down glucose inside the cells of organisms.
    (b) True
    (c) False, correct statements – Insects have spiracles on the sides of the body.
    (d) True

Que 8. Fill in the blanks with suitable words.
    (a) The roots of a plant take up oxygen from the .... trapped between the .... particles.
    (b) Diaphragm forms the .... of the chest cavity.
    (c) Exchange of gases in the leaves take place with the help of ....
    (d) Cockroaches breathe with the help of air tubes called ....
Ans. (a) The roots of a plant take up oxygen from the **air** trapped between the **soil** particles.
    (b) Diaphragm forms the **floor** of the chest cavity.
    (c) Exchange of gases in the leaves take place with the help of **stomata**.
    (d) Cockroaches breathe with the help of air tubes called **tracheae**.

❯ Short Answer Type Questions

Que 9. Pick the odd-one out from each of the groups given below on the basis of respiratory organs. Give reason for your answer.

(a) Cockroach, grasshopper, snail, ant
(b) Lizard, cow, earthworm, snake
(c) Crocodile, whale, dolphin, fish
(d) Snake, tadpole, crow, goat

Ans. (a) Snail, as it does not breathe by means of trachea.
(b) Earthworm, because it breathes through its skin and it does not have lungs.
(c) Fish, as most fish breathe through their gills and do not have lungs.
(d) Tadpole, as it breathes through gills and does not have lungs.

Que 10. Which gas present in air is essential for aerobic respiration? What is the role of oxygen during respiration?

Ans. Oxygen present in air is essential for aerobic respiration.

Oxygen breaks down food and releases energy during respiration.

$$\text{Glucose} \xrightarrow{\text{Presence of oxygen}} \text{Carbon dioxide} + \text{Water} + \text{Energy}$$

Que 11. On an average, an adult human being at rest breathes 15-18 times per minute. The breathing rate, however, may differ under different conditions. Arrange the following activities given below in order of increasing breathing rates and give reason for your answer.

Sleeping, cycling, brisk walk, watching TV

Ans. The activities arranged in order of increasing breathing rates are as follows:

Sleeping < watching TV < brisk walk < cycling

Whenever a person does normal activities, the rate of breathing is normal. It increases when we do strenuous physical works such as cycling, running, etc. The rate of breathing decreases when we are sleeping.

Que 12. On a very cold morning, Boojho and Paheli were talking with each other as they walked down to their school. They observed that the air coming out of their mouth looked like smoke. They were amused and wondered how it happened. Help them to find the answer.

Ans. On a cold day, the warm and moist air exhaled by us condenses into mist when it comes in contact with the cold air of the atmosphere. This looks like white smoke.

Que 13. Insects and leaves of a plant have pores through which they exchange gases with the atmosphere. Can you write two points of differences between these pores with respect to their position, number and extension into the body?

Ans. Pores present on the sides of insects are called **spiracles** while pores present on the surface of leaves are called **stomata**. These structures are responsible for the exchange of gases with the atmosphere.

Differences between these two are as follows:

(i) Spiracles are fewer in number as compared to stomata.

(ii) Spiracles lead to an extensive network of tracheal system which is absent in the leaves.

> Long Answer Type Questions

Que 14. Paheli participated in a 400 m race competition held at her school and won the race. When she came home, she had mixed feelings of joy and pain as she had cramps in her leg muscles. After a massage, she was relieved of the pain.

Answer the following questions related to the situation.

(a) What can be the possible reasons for the pain in her legs?

(b) Why did she feel comfortable after a massage?

Ans. (a) The pain in her legs could be because of the accumulation of lactic acid in the muscles. During heavy exercise or running, etc the muscle cells respire anaerobically and produce lactic acid.

(b) The massage gave her relief because it improves the circulation of blood leading to increased supply of oxygen to the muscle cells which helps in complete breakdown of lactic acid into CO_2 and water.

Que 15. Observe the given figures carefully and answer the following questions.

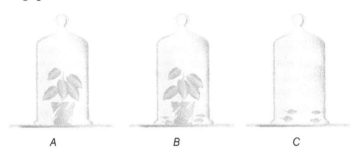

         A   B   C

    (a) In which jar, will the amount of CO_2 be the highest and why?

    (b) In which jar, will the amount of CO_2 be the lowest and why?

Ans. (a) The amount of CO_2 will be the highest in jar C. It is because the mice kept under the jar will breathe out CO_2 continuously increasing its amount in the jar.

    (b) The amount of CO_2 will be the lowest in jar A. It is because in jar A, CO_2 released during respiration is used by the plants, i.e. during the process of photosynthesis.

Que 16. Observe the figures carefully and answer the following questions.

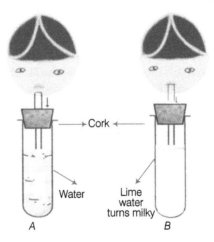

                      ——→ Cork ←——

                   Water   Lime
                             water
                         turns milky

           A   B

(a) Which process is being tested in the activity?

(b) What is the result of the activity? Give reasons.

Ans. (a) **Exhalation** process of respiration is being tested in the activity.

    (b) **Result of the activity** The lime water in test-tube *B* turns milky but water in test-tube *A* remains unchanged. Because CO_2 is present in the exhaled air, it mixes with lime water in test-tube *B* and turns it milky.

Que 17. A food stall owner was preparing dough for making *bhaturas*. He added a pinch of yeast and sugar to the dough and left it in a warm place. After few hours, the dough had risen. There was a sour smell too.

(a) Why did the dough rise?

(b) Why did the dough smell sour?

(c) Why was sugar added to the dough?

(d) What would have happened if the dough was kept in the refrigerator, soon after it was prepared?

Ans. (a) The CO_2 released during respiration by the yeast results in the rise of dough.

    (b) During anaerobic respiration, yeast produces alcohol resulting in sour smell.

    (c) Sugar was added to the dough because it acts as food for yeast.

    (d) If the dough will be kept in the refrigerator (at low temperatures), yeast will not multiply and respire because of which the dough will not rise or become sour.

Que 18. Observe the given figures as *A* and *B* and answer the following questions.

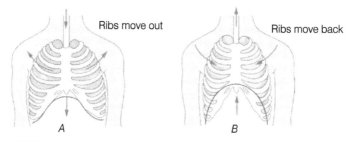

Ribs move out

Ribs move back

A   *B*

(a) Which of the figures *A* or *B* indicates the process of inhalation and which the process of exhalation?

(b) In the figure label the arrows and indicate the direction of
    (i) movement of air
    (ii) movement of diaphragm
    (iii) movement of ribs

Ans. (a) Figure *A* indicates inhalation and figure *B* indicates exhalation.

(b) Movement of air, diaphragm and ribs are indicated in below figure :

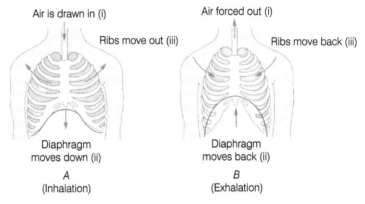

A	B
(Inhalation)	(Exhalation)

Que 19. Match the names of organisms in Column I with their organs of breathing given in Column II.

	Column I		Column II
(a)	Butterfly	(i)	Lungs
(b)	Earthworms	(ii)	Gills
(c)	Sparrow	(iii)	Spiracles
(d)	Fish	(iv)	Skin

Ans. The correct match of the both columns :

	Column I	Column II
(a)	Butterfly	(iii) Spiracles
(b)	Earthworms	(iv) Skin
(c)	Sparrow	(i) Lungs
(d)	Fish	(ii) Gills

Chapter 11

Transportation *in* Animals *and* Plants

Important Points

- **Transport** In biology, transport is a life process in which a material absorbed or made in one part of the body of an organism is carried to other parts in its body.

- **Circulatory system** The circulatory system is defined as the system that moves blood, oxygen and nutrients through the body. The human circulatory system consists of the heart, blood vessels (arteries, veins and capillaries) and blood.

  Note Animals such as sponges and *Hydra* do not posses any circulatory system. The water in which they live brings food and oxygen as it enters their bodies.

- **Blood** It is a red coloured liquid (connective tissue) which flows in blood vessels and circulate throughout the body.

- **Functions of blood**
    - (i) It transports substances like digested food from the small intestine to the other parts of the body.
    - (ii) It carries oxygen from the lungs to the cells of the body.
    - (iii) It also transports waste for removal from the body.

- **Plasma** The fluid part of the blood is called plasma. It is pale yellow, sticky liquid.

- **Red Blood Cells** (RBCs) The red blood cells also called **erythrocytes,** carry oxygen and contain a red pigment called haemoglobin.

- **Haemoglobin** It is a red protein that binds with oxygen and transports oxygen to all the parts of the body and ultimately to all the cells. It is the presence of haemoglobin which makes the blood appear red.

- **White Blood Cells** (WBCs) These are also called **leukocytes** which fight against germs that may enter our body.

- **Platelets** These are also called 'thrombocytes' are blood cells whose function (along with the coagulation factors) is to stop bleeding with the formation of a blood clot.

- **Blood vessels** These are a kind of tubes which carry blood through our body. Two types of blood vessels, arteries and veins are present in the body.

- **Arteries** These are the blood vessels which carry oxygen-rich blood from the heart to all parts of the body. Since, the blood flow is rapid and at a high pressure, the arteries have thick elastic walls.

- **Veins** These are the vessels which carry carbon dioxide-rich blood from all parts of the body back to the heart.

- **Capillaries** The arteries divide into branches which again divide into smaller branches called capillaries. These are the extremely thin tubes (blood vessels) which connect arteries to veins.

- **Pulmonary artery** It is the only artery which carries carbon dioxide rich blood away from the heart.

- **Pulmonary vein** It is the only vein which carries oxygen rich blood from the lungs of the heart.

- **Heart** It is an organ which beats continuously to act as a pump for the transport of blood, which carries other substances with it. Human heart has four chambers. The upper two chambers of heart are called **atria** and the lower two chambers of heart are called **ventricles**.

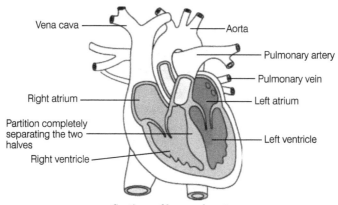

Vena cava

Aorta

Pulmonary artery

Pulmonary vein

Right atrium

Left atrium

Partition completely separating the two halves

Left ventricle

Right ventricle

Sections of human heart

- **Heartbeat** Muscles of the heart contract and relax rhythmically. This rhythmic contraction followed by its relaxation constitute a heartbeat.

- **Pulse** The expansion of an artery each time the blood is forced into it, is called pulse.

- **Pulse rate** The number of heart beats per minute is called the pulse rate. A resting person, usually has a pulse rate between 72 and 80 beat per minute.

- **Stethoscope** The doctor feels your heartbeats with the help of an instrument called a stethoscope. It is a device to amplify the sound of the heart. It consists of a chest piece that carries a sensitive diaphragm, two ear pieces and a tube joining the parts.

- **Excretion** The process of removal of wastes produced in the cells of the living organisms is called excretion.

- **Excretory system** The parts involved in excretion, forms the excretory system. Generally, kidneys along with other organs, e.g. ureters, urinary bladder and urethra form our excretory system.

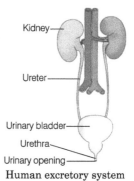

Kidney

Ureter

Urinary bladder

Urethra

Urinary opening

Human excretory system

- **Kidney** It is a bean-shaped, reddish brown, about four inches long structure that filters the blood to eliminate nitrogenous waste from it. The function of kidneys is to purify our body by removing waste and excess fluid.

- **Urine** The wastes dissolved in water are removed as urine. It is a yellowish liquid which consists of 95% water, 2.5% urea and 2.5% other waste products. An adult human being normally passes about 1-1.8 L of urine in 24 h.
- **Urinary bladder** It is the hollow organ that collects urine excreted by the kidneys before disposal by urination.
- **Ureters** These are the tubes that carry urine from the kidney to the urinary bladder.
- **Urethra** It is a tube that leads from the bladder and transports and discharges urine outside the body.
- **Sweat** It is a liquid waste of the body produced by sweat glands in our body. It contains water and salts.
- **Ammonia** It is a colourless gas. Aquatic animals like fishes excrete waste as ammonia which directly dissolves in water.
- **Uric acid** It is a nitrogenous waste and very less soluble in water. Some land animals like birds, lizards snakes excrete a semi- solid, white coloured compound (uric acid).
- **Urea** It is the major excretory product in humans. The urea and other unwanted salt dissolve in water in the body to form a yellowish liquid waste called urine. The way in which waste chemicals are removed from the body of the animals depends on the availability of water.
- **Dialysis** It is the treatment used for people whose kidneys do not work properly.

    Note In case of a major injury or an accident or an operation, there may be rapid loss of blood from the body. In such cases, blood obtained from another healthy person is given to the deficient person. This process is called blood transfusion.

- **Transport of substances in plants** The plants absorb water and minerals by the roots and transport it to leaves. In turn, leaves synthesise food which is transported to other parts of the plant.
- **Root hair** These are long tubular-shaped outgrowths from root epidermal cells. The root hair increase the surface area of the root for the absorption of water and mineral or nutrients dissolved in water.

- **Vessels** Plants have pipe-like structure is called vessels to transport water and nutrients from the soil. The vessels are made of special cells, forming the **vascular tissue**.
- **Tissue** It is a group of cells that perform specialised function in an organism.
- **Vascular tissue** Those tissues which transport water, minerals and food to different parts of a plant, are called vascular tissues.
  - (i) The vascular tissue for the transport of water and nutrients in the plant is called **xylem**.
  - (ii) The vascular tissue for the transport of food to all parts of the plant is called **phloem**.
- **Transpiration** The process of evaporation of water through the stomata present on the surface of the leaves is called transpiration.
- **Suction pull** The evaporation of water from leaves generates a suction pull which pulls water to great heights in the tall trees.

Intext Questions

Que 1. Which side of the heart will have oxygen-rich blood and which side will have carbon dioxide-rich blood? *(Pg 124)*

Ans. The left side of the heart will have oxygen-rich blood and the right side of the heart will have carbon dioxide-rich blood.

Que 2. How does the water move from root to leaves? *(Pg 128)*

Ans. The water moves from root to leaves with the help of specialised cells called vascular tissue. The vascular tissue for the transport of water and nutrients in the plant is called xylem.

Que 3. Paheli says her mother puts ladyfinger and other vegetables in water if they are somewhat dry. She wants to know how water enters into them. *(Pg 129)*

Ans. By soaking the ladyfinger and other vegetables in water, the skin of the vegetables becomes moist and water starts moving from one cell to another until the vegetables are fresh again.

Que 4. Why plants absorb a large quantity of water from the soil, then given it off by transpiration? *(Pg 129)*

Ans. Plants absorb a large quantity of water from the soil because plants need nutrients which are dissolved in water. The excess water evaporates through the stomata present on the surface of the leaves by the process of transpiration.

Exercises

Que 1. Match structures given in Column I with functions given in Column II.

Column I	Column II
(a) Stomata	(i) Absorption of water
(b) Xylem	(ii) Transpiration
(c) Root hairs	(iii) Transport of food
(d) Phloem	(iv) Transport of water
	(v) Synthesis of carbohydrates

Ans. The correct match of the both columns :

Column I	Column II
(a) Stomata	(ii) Transpiration
(b) Xylem	(iv) Transport of water
(c) Root hairs	(i) Absorption of water
(d) Phloem	(iii) Transport of food

Que 2. Fill in the blanks.

(a) The blood from the heart is transported to all parts of the body by the ....

(b) Haemoglobin is present in ....cells.

(c) Arteries and veins are joined by a network of ....

(d) The rhythmic expansion and contraction of the heart is called ....

(e) The main excretory product in human beings is ....

(f) Sweat contains water and ....

(g) Kidneys eliminate the waste materials in the liquid form called ....

(h) Water reaches great heights in the trees because of suction pull caused by ....

Ans. (a) arteries   (b) Red Blood Cells (RBCs)
      (c) capillaries   (d) heartbeats
      (e) urea   (f) salts
      (g) urine   (h) transpiration

Que 3. Choose the correct option.

(a) In plants, water is transported through
     (i) xylem   (ii) phloem
     (iii) stomata   (iv) root hair

(b) Water absorption through roots can be increased by keeping the plants
     (i) in the shade   (ii) in dim light
     (iii) under the fan   (iv) covered with a polythene bag

Ans. (a)   (i) In plants, water is transported through xylem.

      (b) (iii) Water absorption through roots can be increased by keeping the plants under the fan.

Que 4. Why is transport of materials necessary in a plant or in an animal? Explain.

Ans. All organisms (plants and animals) need food, water and oxygen for survival. They need to transport all these to various parts of their body. Further, animals need to transport wastes to the parts from where they can be removed or excreted. Thats why transportation is necessary in both plants and animals.

Que 5. What will happen if there are no platelets in the blood?

Ans. The blood clot is formed due to the presence of the cells called platelets in the blood. If there were no platelets in the blood, then bleeding caused by a cut from an injury would not stop. This may cause loss of too much blood from the body of a person leading to death.

Que 6. What are stomata? Give two functions of stomata.

Ans. The tiny pores present on the surface of leaves are called stomata. Functions of stomata are as follows :

(i) Stomata help in the exchange of gases.

(ii) The water evaporates through the stomata present on the surface of the leaves by the process of transpiration.

Que 7. Does transpiration serve any useful function in the plants? Explain.

Ans. Transpiration is the evaporation of water from the surface of plants. It is important for plants as

  (i) It generates a force which pulls up water absorbed by the roots from the soil, to reach the stem and leaves.

  (ii) It also helps in cooling in plants.

Que 8. What are the components of blood?

Ans. Blood is a liquid connective tissue. It has two components:

  (i) **Plasma** The fluid part of the blood is called plasma. It is pale yellow, sticky liquid.

  (ii) **Cells of blood** There are three kinds of blood cells suspended in the plasma (RBCs, WBCs and platelets).

    (a) **Red Blood Cells** (RBCs) These are also called erythrocytes, carry oxygen. They contain a red pigment called **haemoglobin** which is responsible for transport of O_2.

    (b) **White Blood Cells** (WBCs) These are also called leukocytes and lacks haemoglobin. These cells fight against germs that may enter our body.

    (c) **Platelets** These are also called thrombocytes, whose function (along with the coagulation factors) is to stop bleeding by the formation of blood clot.

Que 9. Why is blood needed by all the parts of a body?

Ans. Blood is needed by all parts of the body due to following reasons:

  (i) All the parts of the body need food and oxygen, which is carried to them by blood.

  (ii) It carries CO_2 also a waste product to the lungs, so that it can be exhaled easily.

  (iii) It fights against diseases and infection and also helps in the formation of blood clot at the time of a cut.

  (iv) It transmits heat, thus regulating the body temperature.

Que 10. What makes the blood look red?

Ans. The red pigment, (haemoglobin), present in the red blood cells of the blood makes the blood look red. The haemoglobin carries oxygen and transports it to all the parts of the body.

Que 11. Describe the function of the heart.

Ans. The heart acts as a pump for the transport of blood. The human heart is divided into four chambers. The upper two chambers are called right and left atrium and the lower two chambers are called the right and left ventricles. The right side of the heart, i.e. the right auricle and ventricle receive carbon dioxide rich blood from all parts of the body and transport it to the lungs. Its left side, i.e. the left auricle and ventricle, receive oxygen-rich blood from the lungs and transport it to all parts of the body.

Que 12. Why is it necessary to excrete waste products?

Ans. When our cells perform their functions, certain waste products are produced. These waste products are toxic and hence need to be removed from the body. The process of removing waste products produced in the cells of the living organisms is called **excretion.**

Que 13. Draw a diagram of the human excretory system and label the various parts.

Ans. Labelled diagram of human excretory system given below:

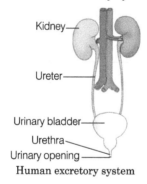

Kidney

Ureter

Urinary bladder

Urethra

Urinary opening

Human excretory system

Selected NCERT Exemplar Problems

⟩ Multiple Choice Questions

Que 1. The muscular tube through which   stored urine is passed out of the body is called

    (a) kidney   (b) ureter

    (c) urethra   (d) urinary bladder

Ans. (c) The muscular tube through which stored urine is passed out of the body is called urethra.

Que 2. They are pipe-like, consisting of a group of specialised cells. They transport substances and form a two-way traffic in plants. Which of the following terms qualify for the features mentioned above?

    (a) Xylem tissue
    (b) Vascular tissue
    (c) Root hairs
    (d) Phloem tissue

Ans. (d) Phloem tissue are pipe-like, consisting of a group of specialised cells. They transport substances and form a two-way traffic in plants.

Que 3. The absorption of nutrients and exchange of respiratory gases between blood and tissues takes place in

    (a) veins   (b) arteries
    (c) heart   (d) capillaries

Ans. (d) The absorption of nutrients and exchange of respiratory gases between blood and tissues takes place in capillaries.

Que 4. In which of the following parts of human body are sweat glands absent?

    (a) Scalp   (b) Armpits
    (c) Lips   (d) Palms

Ans. (c) Sweat glands are absent in **lips**.

Que 5. In a tall tree, which force is responsible for pulling water and minerals from the soil?

    (a) Gravitational force
    (b) Transportation force
    (c) Suction force
    (d) Conduction force

Ans. (c) In a tall tree, suction force is responsible for pulling water and minerals from the soil.

Que 6. Aquatic animals like fish excrete their wastes in gaseous form as

    (a) oxygen   (b) hydrogen
    (c) ammonia   (d) nitrogen

Ans. (c) Aquatic animals like fish excrete their wastes in gaseous form as ammonia.

❯ Very Short Answer Type Questions

Que 7. Veins have valves which allow blood to flow only in one direction. Arteries do not have valves. Yet the blood flows in one direction only. Can you explain why?

Ans. Veins have valves to prevent blood from flowing backwards and pooling, whereas arteries pump blood at very high pressures, which naturally prevents back flow.

Que 8. What is the special feature present in a human heart which does not allow mixing of blood when oxygen-rich and carbon dioxide-rich blood reach the heart?

Ans. In human, the heart has four chambers. The two upper chambers are called the atria and the two lower chambers are called the ventricles. The partition between the chambers helps to avoid mixing up of blood rich in oxygen with the blood rich in carbon dioxide.

Que 9. Name the organ which is located in the chest cavity with its lower tip slightly tilted towards the left.

Ans. The heart is located in the chest cavity with its lower tip slightly tilted towards the left.

❯ Short Answer Type Questions

Que 10. Arrange the following statements in the correct order in which they occur during the formation and removal of urine in human beings.

    (a) Ureters carry urine to the urinary bladder.

    (b) Wastes dissolved in water is filtered out as urine in the kidneys.

    (c) Urine stored in urinary bladder is passed out through the urinary opening at the end of the urethra.

    (d) Blood containing useful and harmful substances reaches the kidneys for filtration.

    (e) Useful substances are absorbed back into the blood.

Ans. The correct order of the formation and removal of urine in human beings is

    (d) Blood containing useful and harmful substances reaches the kidneys for filtration.

    (e) Useful substances are absorbed back into the blood.

    (b) Wastes dissolved in water is filtered out as urine in the kidneys.

    (a) Ureters carry urine to the urinary bladder.

    (c) Urine stored in urinary bladder is passed out through the urinary opening at the end of the urethra.

Que 11. Paheli uprooted a rose plant from the soil. Most of the root tips with root hairs got left behind in the soil. She planted it in a pot with new soil and watered it regularly. Will the plant grow or die? Give reason for your answer.

Ans. Possible answers are

  (i) Without the root hairs, the roots will not be able to absorb water and nutrients and the plant will die.

  (ii) The stem of the rose plant may grow new roots and the plant will live.

  (iii) The rose plant may not be able to survive in a different types of soil.

Que 12. (a) Name the only artery that carries carbon dioxide-rich blood.

  (b) Why is it called an artery if it does not carry oxygen-rich blood?

Ans. (a) **Pulmonary artery** carries carbon dioxide-rich blood.

  (b) It is called an artery because it carries blood away from the heart.

Que 13. Boojho's uncle was hospitalised and put on dialysis after a severe infection in both of his kidneys.

  (a) What is dialysis?

  (b) When does it become necessary to take such a treatment?

Ans. (a) The procedure used for cleaning the blood of a person by separating the waste product (urea) from blood it is called dialysis.

  (b) In the event of kidney failure, dialysis is necessary.

Que 14. Name the process and the organ which helps in removing the following wastes from the body.

  (a) Carbon dioxide   (b) Undigested food

  (c) Urine   (d) Sweat

Ans.

	Wastes	Process	Organ
(a)	Carbon dioxide	Exhalation	Lungs
(b)	Undigested food	Egestion	Large intestine and anus
(c)	Urine	Excretion	Kidneys
(d)	Sweat	Perspiration (sweating)	Sweat glands

Que 15. Observe given figure and answer the given questions

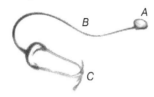

  (a) Name the instrument.
  (b) Label the parts *A*, *B* and *C*.

Ans. (a) The name of the given instrument is stethoscope.

  (b)

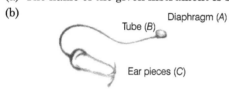

Que 16. Paheli noticed water being pulled up by a motor-pump to an overhead tank of a five-storeyed building. She wondered how water moves up to great heights in the tall trees standing next to the building. Can you tell why?

Ans. The evaporation of water from leaves (transpiration) generates a suction pull. This pull help the water to reach at great heights in the tall trees standing next to the building.

> Long Answer Type Questions

Que 17. Match the parts of the heart in Column I with the direction of flow of blood in Column II.

Column I	Column II
(a) Right ventricle	(i) Pushes blood into the pulmonary artery.
(b) Pulmonary veins	(ii) Take deoxygenated blood from the heart to lungs.
(c) Left atrium	(iii) Receives blood from different parts of the body.
(d) Pulmonary arteries	(iv) Bring oxygenated blood from lungs to the heart.
(e) Left ventricle	(v) Pushes blood into the aorta.
(f) Right auricle	(vi) Receives deoxygenated blood from the pulmonary veins.

Ans. The correct match of the both columns :

Column I		Column II
(a) Right ventricle	(i)	Pushes blood into the pulmonary artery.
(b) Pulmonary veins	(iv)	Bring oxygenated blood from lungs to the heart.
(c) Left atrium	(vi)	Receives deoxygenated blood from the pulmonary veins.
(d) Pulmonary arteries	(ii)	Take deoxygenated blood from the heart to lungs.
(e) Left ventricle	(v)	Pushes blood into the aorta.
(f) Right auricle	(iii)	Receives blood from different parts of the body.

Que 18. Fill in the blanks of the following paragraph using just two words-arteries and veins.

......(a)...... carry oxygen-rich blood from the heart to all parts of the body and ......(b)...... carry carbon dioxide-rich blood from all parts of the body back to the heart. ......(c)...... have thin walls and ......(d)...... have thick elastic walls. Blood flows at high pressure in ......(e)...... . Valves are present in ......(f)...... which allow blood to flow only towards the heart. ......(g)...... divide into smaller vessels. These vessels further divide into extremely thin tubes called capillaries. The capillaries join up to form ......(h)....... .

Ans.　(a) arteries　　(b) veins
　　　　(c) veins　　　(d) arteries
　　　　(e) arteries　　(f) veins
　　　　(g) arteries　　(h) veins

Que 19. While learning to ride a bicycle, Boojho lost his balance and fell. He got bruises on his knees and it started bleeding. However, the bleeding stopped after sometime.

(a) Why did the bleeding stop?

(b) What would be the colour of the wounded area and why?

(c) Which type of blood cells are responsible for clotting of blood?

Ans.　(a) When a cut or wound start bleeding after sometime, a clot is formed which plugs the cut and bleeding stops.

(b) Wounded area is dark red in colour due to clotting of blood.

(c) The blood clot is formed due to the presence of the cells called platelets in the blood.

Chapter 12

Reproduction in Plants

Important Points

- **Reproduction** The process of formation of new similar individuals or organisms from their parents is called reproduction. The reproduction increases the number of the organisms of a species.

- **Vegetative parts** The various parts of a plant such as roots, stems and leaves each with a specific function are called vegetative parts.

- **Reproductive parts** The parts of a plant that participate in the process of sexual reproduction are called reproductive parts or organs. In plants, the reproductive parts are flower which may have the male or female part or both the parts in same flower.

- **Modes of reproduction** There are several ways by which plants produce their offspring. These are categorised into two types: (i) asexual and (ii) sexual reproduction.

- **Asexual reproduction** Process of reproduction in which only one parent is involved to produce new individuals of same kind is called asexual reproduction. In plants, asexual reproduction results in the formation of offsprings or new plants without seeds or spores.

- **Vegetative propagation** A type of asexual reproduction in which new similar identical plants are formed from the older vegetative parts of plant such as roots, stem and leaves is called vegetative propagation.

Some of the common methods of vegetative propagation in plants are stem cutting in rose, eyes in potato, leaves of *Bryophyllum* (sprout leaf plant) and buds in yeast.

- **Vegetative buds** Apart from the flower buds, some buds also develops in the axil that consist of a short stem around which immature overlapping leaves are folded. These are called vegetative buds. These buds can give rise to a new plant.

- **Budding** Another type of asexual reproduction, in which a small bulb like portion called **bud** projects out from the body of an organism. This bud grows and gets detached from the parent cell to form a new identical individual such as in yeast. This process is known as budding. Sometimes, another bud arises from the bud forming a chain of buds.

- **Fragmentation** A method of asexual reproduction in which plant body breaks up into two or more fragments, each of which develops into new individual is called fragmentation. It is common in filamentous algae (*Spirogyra*).

- **Sporangium** The parts of plants such as fungus like *mucar* and yeast, which produce through spore formation under favourable conditions are celled sporangium.

- **Spore formation** The spores are asexual reproductive bodies. Each spore can withstand extremes of temperature and unfavourable climatic conditions due to its coverage by a hard protective coat. A spore germinate on the arrival of favourable conditions to develop into a new identical plant. Spore formation is commonly observed in fungus, mosses and ferns.

- **Hypha** It is a branched, long filamentous structure of mycelium to derive nutrition from the substratum, e.g. in bread mould.

- **Sexual reproduction** In plants, sexual reproduction refers to the process of formation of new individual from seeds, as it results by the participation of two parent plants or **gametes**. In a flower, the male reproductive parts are called **stamens** and the female reproductive parts are called **pistil**.

- **Unisexual flowers** The flowers which have either stamen or pistil are called unisexual flowers, e.g. corn, cucumber, papaya.

- **Bisexual flowers**   The flowers comprising of both male and female reproductive part, i.e. stamen and pistil are called bisexual flowers, e.g. mustard, *Petunia*, rose, etc.

- **Gametes**   The special reproductive cell formed by male and female individuals that takes part in sexual reproduction, is called gametes.

- **Male gametes** Anther produces **pollen grains** which form male gametes and take part in sexual reproduction.

- **Female gametes** Ovary comprises of one or more **ovules** where female gamete or **egg** is formed.

- **Zygote**   The single cell formed as a result of fusion of two gamete cells, i.e. male and female gametes is called zygote.

- **Pollination**   The process of transfer of pollen grains from anther to the stigma of flower is called pollination.

- **Self-pollination**   When pollen grains from the anther of a flower are transferred to the stigma of same flower, it is called self-pollination.

- **Cross-pollination**   When the pollen grains from the anther of a flower or of a plant are transferred to the stigma of a flower of the same plant, or that of a different plant of the same kind the process is called cross-pollination. This transfer to another plant is mediated by insects, wind, water, animals, birds, etc.

- **Pollen tube**   When pollen grain falls on the stigma of a flower, its outer covering ruptures and pollen grain germinates to form a long tube called pollen tube. Through this pollen tube, male gametes inside pollen grain reaches to female gamete or egg.

- **Fertilisation**   The process of **fusion** of male and female gametes is called fertilisation.

- **Embryo**   The zygote divides into a cluster of cells, called embryo which is present inside the seed in an inactive state. Embryo is capable of giving rise to a new plant.

- **Fruits**   After fertilisation, the ovary grows into a fruit and other parts of the flower fall off. So, the fruit is actually a **ripened ovary**. They may be **fleshy** like mango, orange, apple or **hard** like almonds and walnuts.

- **Seeds** The ovules present inside the ovary of a flower after fertilisation (fusion of male gamete with egg present inside ovule) develops into seeds. Seeds enclose developing embryo which is protected by a tough covering called **seed coat**.

- **Seed dispersal** Scattering of seeds over a wide area and to distant places in order to avoid overcrowding of plants and preventing competition among them is called seed dispersal.

  Various agents are responsible for seed or fruits dispersal such as wind (in winged seeds of drumstick, maple, small light seeds of grass, etc.), water (in floating fruit of coconut), animals (as in *Xanthium* seed having hooks to get attached to animal bodies) or explosion of fruits as in castor.

Intext Questions

Que 1. How do the plants of sugarcane, potato and rose reproduce when they cannot produce seeds?

(Pg 133)

Ans. Sugarcane and rose are propagated by stem cutting, a method of vegetative reproduction, in which stem is capable of growing into a mature independent plant that are identical to their parents.

Whereas, potato is an underground modified stem have buds called eyes, which sprouts and develops into a new identical plant.

Thus, the plants which cannot produce seeds, can be propagated vegetatively with the help of vegetative parts such as stem, roots, buds and leaves.

Que 2. What are the advantages of vegetative propagation? *(Pg 135)*

Ans. The method of producing plants by vegetative propagation requires less time to grow into a mature plants bearing flower and fruits as compared to plants produced from seeds. Besides the plants propagated vegetatively are identical to parent plant as only one parent is involved and no mixing of parental characters occur.

Que 3. How the male gametes present inside pollen grain reaches the female gamete present in the ovule? *(Pg 137)*

Ans. After pollination, the pollen grain falls on the surface of stigma and germinates to form a long tube, reaching the ovule inside the ovary, the egg or female gamete is present in the ovule. The outer surface (exine) of pollen grain ruptures and male gametes are released to fuse with egg.

Que 4. Why are flowers so colourful and fragrant? Is it to attract insects? *(Pg 138)*

Ans. Flowers are so colourful because of the light energy they reflect and absorb. And flowering plants produce volatile chemical in flowers which evaporate into the air and produce their fragrances. Petal is the colourful part of flower which attracts insects. Yes, it is too attract insects.

Exercises

Que 1. Fill in the blanks :

    (a) Production of new individuals from the vegetative part of parent is called ....

    (b) A flower may have either male or female reproductive parts. Such a flower is called ....

    (c) The transfer of pollen grains from the anther to the stigma of the same or of another flower of the same kind is known as ....

    (d) The fusion of male and female gametes is termed as ....

    (e) Seed dispersal takes place by means of ...., ... and ....

Ans. (a) Production of new individuals form the vegetative part of parent is called **vegetative propagation**.

    (b) A flower may have either male or female reproductive parts. Such a flower is called **unisexual flower**.

    (c) The transfer of pollen grains from the anther to the stigma of the same or of another flower of the same kind is known as **pollination**.

    (d) The fusion of male and female gametes is termed as **fertilisation**.

    (e) Seed dispersal takes place by means of **wind, water** and **animals**.

Que 2. Describe the different methods of asexual reproduction. Give examples.

Ans. Different methods of asexual reproduction are

(i) **Fragmentation** Parent body divides into distinct pieces or fragments, each of which grows into new individuals, e.g. *Spirogyra* (an alga).

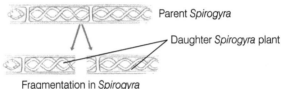

Fragmentation in *Spirogyra*
(filamentous alga)

(ii) **Budding** A small part of parent body grows out as a bud, which detaches and becomes a new individual. Sometimes, a chain of buds is also formed, e.g. yeast, corals, sponges, etc.

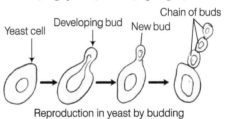

Reproduction in yeast by budding

(iii) **Spores formation** Parent plant develops and releases thousands of tiny, spherical and unicellular asexual spores, which are protected by cell wall. When these spores find favourable environment, they grow into identical new plants, e.g. mosses, ferns, bread, moulds, etc.

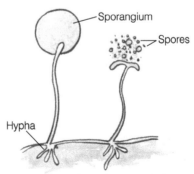

Reproduction through spore formation in fungus

(iv) **Vegetative propagation** Many plants like cacti, potato, rose, sugarcane, etc reproduce by this method. New plants are produced from vegetative parts of mother plant such as roots, stem, buds and leaves.

Que 3. Explain what do you understand by sexual reproduction.

Ans. Sexual reproduction is a process of formation of new individuals by involving two parents or gamete formation. In sexually reproducing plants, new plants are produced from seeds. In this method, gametes fuse to form **zygote** that gives rise to new individual.

Que 4. State the main differences between asexual and sexual reproduction.

Ans. The main differences between asexual and sexual reproduction are

Asexual reproduction	Sexual reproduction
Only one parent is needed.	Two parents male and female are required.
Offsprings are genetically identical to their parents.	Offsprings exhibit variation with respect to their parents.
No seed is formed. Fragmentation, budding, spore formation, vegetative propagation are its different types.	Seeds are formed due to fusion of male and female gametes.
Spirogyra, yeast, moulds and potato exhibit asexual reproduction.	Fruit bearing plants like mango and China rose, reproduce sexually.

Que 5. Sketch the reproductive parts of a flower.

Ans. The reproductive parts of a flower are stamen and pistil.

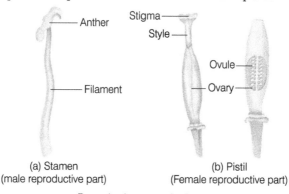

(a) Stamen
(male reproductive part)

(b) Pistil
(Female reproductive part)

Reproductive parts of a flower

Que 6. Explain the differences between self-pollination and cross-pollination.

Ans. The differences between self-pollination and cross-pollination are

Self-pollination	Cross-pollination
Pollens are transferred to the stigma of same flower.	Pollens are transferred to the stigma of different flower.
Do not require pollinating agents.	Requires pollinating agents.
Occurs in legumes, peanuts and sunflower.	Common in most of flowers like rose, China rose, etc.

Que 7. How does the process of fertilisation take place in flowers?

Ans. The steps involved in the process of fertilisation are

 (i) After pollination, pollen grains start growing into a pollen-tube on the stigma passing through pistil.

 (ii) The tube extends through the style and reaches to the ovules.

 (iii) The pollen-tube carries the male gametes called **pollen grains**.

 (iv) Male gametes fuse with the egg (female gamete) present inside ovule and forms a **zygote**. This process is called **fertilisation**.

 (v) Later zygote develops into an **embryo** and ovules develop into a seed.

 (vi) Thus, seed carries an embryo with stored food and is covered by a hard protective covering called **seed coat**.

Que 8. Describe the various ways by which seeds are dispersed.

Ans. Scattering of seeds or fruits to distant places by various agents is called **seed dispersal**.

Following are some agents of seeds dispersal:

 (i) **Wind** Seeds of cotton have hairs surrounding it, which is easily carried by wind. Similarly, seeds of maple has wings which help in its dispersal.

 (ii) **Water** Coconut seeds which have thick fibre that help it to float in water and reach at distant places.

 (iii) **Animals** Seeds like *Xanthium* have spines which help them to stick to fur or skin of the animals. Some seeds eaten by birds and animals along with fruit that pass out unharmed with their faecal matter. They germinate where they fall.

 (iv) **Explosion mechanism** Fruits of balsam, castor and pea burst on drying and spread the seeds in surroundings.

Que 9. Match items in Column I with those in Column II.

Column I	Column II
(a) Bud	(i) Maple
(b) Eyes	(ii) *Spirogyra*
(c) Fragmentation	(iii) Yeast
(d) Wings	(iv) Bread mould
(e) Spores	(v) Potato
	(vi) Rose

Ans. The correctly matched options of both the columns are

Column I	Column II
(a) Bud	(iii) Yeast
(b) Eyes	(v) Potato
(c) Fragmentation	(ii) *Spirogyra*
(d) Wings	(i) Maple
(e) Spores	(iv) Bread mould

Que 10. Tick (✓) the correct answer.
  (i) The reproductive part of a plant is the
      (a) leaf   (b) stem   (c) foot   (d) flower
 (ii) The process of fusion of the male and the female gametes
      is called
      (a) fertilisation   (b) pollination
      (c) reproduction   (d) seed formation
(iii) Mature ovary forms the
      (a) seed   (b) stamen
      (c) pistil   (d) fruit
 (iv) A spore producing plant is
      (a) rose   (b) bread mould
      (c) potato   (d) ginger
  (v) *Bryophyllum* can reproduce by its
      (a) stem   (b) leaves   (c) roots   (d) flower

Ans.   (i) (d) The reproductive part of a plant is the flower.
           (ii) (a) The process of fusion of the male and the female gametes
                is called fertilisation.
          (iii) (d) Mature ovary forms the fruit.
           (iv) (b) A spore producing plant is bread mould.
            (v) (b) *Bryophyllum* can reproduce by its leaves.

Selected **NCERT Exemplar Problems**

❯ **Multiple Choice Questions**

Que 1. Which of the following parts of a plant take part in sexual reproduction?

    (i) Flower   (ii) Seed

    (iii) Fruit   (iv) Branch

    Choose the correct answer from below:

    (a) (i) and (ii)   (b) (i), (ii) and (iii)

    (c) (iii) and (iv)   (d) (ii), (iii) and (iv)

Ans. (b) The reproductive part of plant is flower that takes part in sexual reproduction. The result of sexual reproduction is fruit, which contains seeds. Seeds in turn on germination give rise to another new similar plant.

Que 2. Lila observed that a pond with clear water was covered up with a green algae within a week. By which method of reproduction did the algae spread so rapidly?

    (a) Budding   (b) Sexual reproduction

    (c) Fragmentation   (d) Pollination

Ans. (c) The algae most probably reproduced by fragmentation (an asexual method) to spread, so rapidly to cover the surface of pond within a week.

Que 3. Seeds of drumstick and maple are carried to long distances by wind because they possess

    (a) winged seeds

    (b) large and hairy seeds

    (c) long and ridged fruits

    (d) spiny seeds

Ans. (a) Seeds of drumstick and maple are carried to long distances by wind because they possess winged seeds.

Que 4. The ovaries of different flowers may contain

    (a) only one ovule   (b) many ovules

    (c) one to many ovules   (d) only two ovules

Ans. (c) The ovaries of different flowers may contain one to many ovules.

Que 5. Which of the following statements is/are true for sexual reproduction in plants?

(i) Plants are obtained from seeds

(ii) Two plants are always essential

(iii) Fertilisation can occur only after pollination

(iv) Only insects are agents of pollination

Choose from the options given below:

(a) (i) and (iii)   (b) only (i)

(c) (ii) and (iii)   (d) (i) and (iv)

Ans. (a) Statements (i) and (iii) are true for sexual reproduction in plants. Two plants are not always essential for reproduction. Some plants bear bisexual flowers having both male and female reproductive parts required for sexual reproduction in the same flower.

Que 6. Pollination refers to the

(a) transfer of pollen from anther to ovary

(b) transfer of male gametes from anther to stigma

(c) transfer of pollen from anther to stigma

(d) transfer of pollen from anther to ovule

Ans. (c) Pollination refers to the transfer of pollen from anther to stigma.

❯ Very Short Answer Type Questions

Que 7. Fungus, moss and fern reproduce by a common method of asexual reproduction. Name the method.

Ans. Fungus, moss and fern reproduce by the common method of spore formation which is a type of asexual reproduction.

Que 8. Pick the odd one out from the following on the basis of mode of reproduction and give reason for it,

Sugarcane, Potato, Rice, Rose.

Ans. The odd one out is rice, in the above given pairs as rice reproduces by sexual reproduction and sugarcane, potato and rose reproduces vegetatively.

Que 9. Boojho had the following parts of a rose plant—a leaf, roots, a branch, a flower, a bud and pollen grains. Which of them can be used to grow a new rose plant?

Ans. Branch can be used to grow a new rose plant. As, rose reproduces by vegetative propagation, i.e. stem cutting method.

Que 10. Which type of pollination does the given figure indicate?

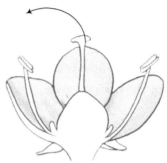

Ans. The given figure shows self pollination, as the pollen grains from anther of flower are transferred to the stigma of same flower.

Que 11. One morning as Paheli strolled in her garden she noticed many small plants, which were not there a week ago. She wondered, where they had come from as nobody had planted them there. Explain the reason for the growth of these plants.

Ans. The small plants which were not there in the garden a weak ago have grown up due to seed dispersal. The seeds from the tree may have fallen below or have been dispersed by wind or animals on the ground, which on germination developed into new small plants.

> Short Answer Type Questions

Que 12. In the figure given below label the part marked (i), (ii) and (iii).

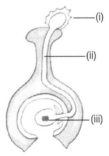

Ans. The parts in the given figure are labelled as follows:

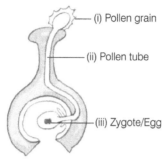

— (i) Pollen grain

— (ii) Pollen tube

— (iii) Zygote/Egg

Que 13. When you keep food items like bread and fruits outside for a long time especially during the rainy season, you will observe a cottony growth on them.

   (a) What is this growth called?

   (b) How does the growth take place?

Ans. (a) When food items like bread and fruits are kept outside for a long time especially during rainy season, a cottony growth of bread mould, a fungus is observed.

   (b) This growth of fungus takes place by spores present in air, which when comes in the contact with moisture in bread germinates and grow to produce spores.

Que 14. Group the seeds given in fig. (i)-(iii) according to their means of dispersion.

   (a) Seed dispersed by wind   (b) Seed dispersed by water

   (c) Seed dispersed by animal

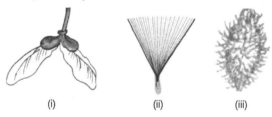

(i)   (ii)   (iii)

Ans. (a) Seed (i) is the seed of maple and is dispersed by wind as it has wings.

   (b) Seed of madar (aak) (ii) is dispersed by wind as it is light and hairy.

   (c) Seed of *Xanthium* (iii) is dispersed by animal as its has hooks and spines on it.

Que 15. Coconut is a large and heavy fruit. How is it adapted for dispersal by water?

Ans. The outer covering of coconut having spongy jute fibres, help it to float easily in water, thus it is adapted for dispersal by water.

› Long Answer Type Questions

Que 16. Fill in the blanks with correct terms.

The male and female gametes fuse to form a .... (a) .... during the process of ...(b)... . This grows into an .... (c) .... which is enclosed within a seed. After fertilisation the ovules develop into .... (d) .... and the ovary develops into a .... (e) ....

Ans. The male and female gametes fuse to form a **(a) zygote** during the process of **(b) fertilisation.** This grows into an **(c) embryo** which is enclosed within a seed. After fertilisation the ovules develop into **(d) seed** and the ovary develops into a **(e) fruit.**

Que 17. In the figure of a flower given below, label the parts whose functions are given below and give their names.

(a) The part which contains pollen grains.
(b) The part where the female gamete is formed.
(c) The female reproductive part, where pollen grains germinate.
(d) The colourful part of flower which attracts insects.

Ans. The various parts of a flower whose functions are mentioned above are labelled as follows :

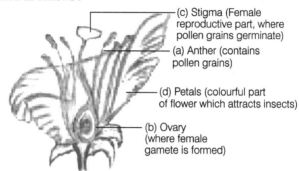

(c) Stigma (Female reproductive part, where pollen grains germinate)

(a) Anther (contains pollen grains)

(d) Petals (colourful part of flower which attracts insects)

(b) Ovary (where female gamete is formed)

Que 18. Write how the following seeds are dispersed.

(a) Seeds with wings.

(b) Small and light seeds.

(c) Seeds with spines/hooks.

Ans. (a) The seeds with wings are dispersed by wind as wings help it to carry to distant places.

(b) Small and light seeds with hairs often present on them are also dispersed by wind.

(c) Seeds with spines and hooks are dispersed by animals, which stuck to their body or fur and are carried to different places.

Que 19. In the figure of a bisexual flower given along side draw the missing part and label the parts marked (i), (ii) and (iii). Also, label the missing part that you draw.

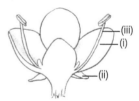

(iii)

(i)

(ii)

Ans. In the given figure, the missing part is pistil and all the parts of flower can be labelled as follows:

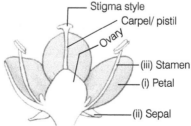

Stigma style

Carpel/ pistil

Ovary

(iii) Stamen

(i) Petal

(ii) Sepal

Chapter **13**

Motion *and* **Time**

Important Points

- **Motion** The process of moving or changing position of an object is called motion.

- The distance moved by objects in a given interval of time can help us to decide which object is faster or slower.

- **Speed** A higher speed indicates that a given distance has been covered in a shorter time interval. Speed is the distance covered by the body in a unit time.

  Average speed is the total distance covered by the body divided by the total time taken, i.e.

$$\text{Speed} = \frac{\text{Total distance covered}}{\text{Total time taken}}$$

- **Non-uniform motion** If the speed of an object moving along a straight line keeps changing, its motion is said to be non-uniform motion.

- **Uniform motion** An object moving along a straight line with a constant speed is said to be in uniform motion.

- **Measurement of time** Clocks or watches are the most common time measuring devices. The working of clocks is rather complex. But all of them make use of some periodic motion.

  One of the most well known periodic motions is that of a **simple pendulum** which consists of a small metallic ball or a piece of stone suspended from a rigid stand by a thread. The metallic ball is called the bob of the pendulum.

- **Oscillatory motion** When the bob of pendulum is released after taking it slightly to one side, it begins to move to and fro. The to and fro motion of a simple pendulum is an example of a periodic or an oscillatory motion.

- **Oscillation** The pendulum is said to have completed one oscillation when its bob moves from one extreme position *A* to the other extreme position *B* and comes back to *A*.

Different position of the bob
of an oscillating simple pendulum

- **Time period** The time taken by a pendulum to complete one oscillation is called time period.

- **Discovering of pendulum clock** Galileo found that a pendulum of a given length takes always the same time to complete one oscillation. This observation leads to the development of pendulum clocks. Winding clocks and wristwatches were refinements of the pendulum clocks.

- **Quartz clocks** Now-a-days, most clocks or watches have an electric circuit with one or more cells. These clocks are called quartz clocks. The time measured by quartz clock is much more accurate than that clocks available earlier.

- **Units of time and speed** The basic unit of time is a second. Its symbol is seconds (s) and the larger units of time are hours (h) and minutes (min).

  Since, the speed is distance/time, the basic unit of speed is m/s. It could also be expressed in other units such as m/min or km/h.

  Note The symbols of all units are written in singular.

- **Smaller unit of time** However, the most common unit of time is second. Now, some clocks are available that can measure time intervals smaller than a second. Some units of time smaller than second are microsecond (the one millionth part of a second is called microsecond) and nanosecond (the one billionth part of a second is called nanosecond).

- Distance covered is equal to speed multiplied by time.

  i.e. Distance = Speed × Time

- **Speedometer** It is the device used to measure speed of vehicle.
- **Odometer** It is the device used to measure distance covered by the vehicle.
- **Graph** It is the pictorial representation of the relation between two or more physical quantities.
- **Distance-time graph** If the distance-time graph is a straight line, it indicates that the object is moving with constant speed.

  If the speed-time graph is not a straight line, it indicates that object is moving with non-uniform velocity.

Intext Questions

Que 1. How will you decide which object is moving fast and which one is moving slow? *(Pg 143)*

Ans. If a body covers more distance in equal intervals of time with respect to other, then we can say that body is moving faster with respect to the other body.

Que 2. If you did not have a clock, how would you decide what time of the day it is? *(Pg 145)*

Ans. We can decide time of the day without clock by seeing shadow formed by the sun, e.g. At noon shadow formed by the sun is shorter than at evening.

Que 3. How do we measure time interval of a month? *(Pg 145)*

Ans. Time interval of a month is measured by one new moon to the next.

Que 4. What would be the basic unit of speed? *(Pg 147)*

Ans. As we know that speed is the distance travelled per unit time, so the basic unit of speed is metre/second, i.e. m/s.

Que 5. How many seconds are there in a day? *(Pg 147)*

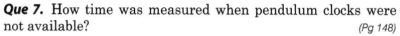

Ans. In a day, we have 24 h
We know that 1 h = 3600 s
So, 24 h = 3600 × 24 = 86400 s

Que 6. How many hours are there in a year? *(Pg 147)*

Ans. In a year, we have 365 days
and 1 day = 24 h
So, for 365 days, we have 24 × 365 h
= 8760 h

Que 7. How time was measured when pendulum clocks were not available? *(Pg 148)*

Ans. Before the discovery of pendulum clocks, sundials, water clocks and sand clocks were used.

Exercises

Que 1. Classify the following as motion along a straight line, circular or oscillatory motion.
  (a) Motion of your hands while running.
  (b) Motion of a horse pulling a cart on a straight road.
  (c) Motion of a child in a merry-go-round.
  (d) Motion of a child on a see-saw.
  (e) Motion of the hammer of an electric bell.
  (f) Motion of a train on a straight bridge.

Ans. (a) Oscillatory   (b) Straight line
  (c) Circular   (d) Oscillatory
  (e) Oscillatory   (f) Straight line

Que 2. Which of the following are not correct?
  (a) The basic unit of time is second.
  (b) Every object moves with a constant speed.
  (c) Distances between two cities are measured in kilometres.
  (d) The time period of a given pendulum is not constant.
  (e) The speed of a train is expressed in m/h.

Ans. (b), (d) and (e) are not correct.

Que 3. A simple pendulum takes 32 s to complete 20 oscillations. What is the time period of the pendulum?

Ans.   Time period of simple pendulum is given by

$$\frac{\text{Total number of oscillations}}{\text{Total time}} = \frac{20}{32} = \frac{5}{8}$$

(i.e. the time to complete one cycle)

Que 4. The distance between two stations is 240 km. A train takes 4 h to cover this distance. Calculate the speed of the train.

Ans.   As, we know that the speed of a body is given by

$$\text{Speed} = \frac{\text{Distance travelled}}{\text{Time taken}}$$

$$\therefore \qquad = \frac{240}{4} = 60 \text{ km/h}$$

Que 5. The odometer of a car reads 57321 km when the clock shows the time 08:30 AM. What is the distance moved by the car, if at 08:50 AM, the odometer reading has changed to 57336 km? Calculate the speed of the car in km/min during this time. Express the speed in km/h also.

Ans.   As, we know that

$$\text{Speed} = \frac{\text{Distance covered}}{\text{Time taken}}$$

Given,   distance covered = $57336 - 57321 = 15$ km

Time taken = $8{:}50$ AM $- 8{:}30$ AM $= 20$ min

So, $\qquad$ speed $= \dfrac{15}{20} = \dfrac{3}{4}$ km/min

Now, speed in km/h is given by $\dfrac{3}{4} \times 60 = 45$ km/h $\quad \left[\because \ 1\,\text{min} = \dfrac{1}{60}\,\text{h} \right]$

Que 6. Salma takes 15 min from her house to reach her school on a bicycle. If the bicycle has a speed of 2 m/s, calculate the distance between her house and the school.

Ans.   As, we know that

Distance covered by the body = Speed × Time

Given,   speed $= 2$ m/s

Time $= 15$ min $= 15 \times 60 = 900$ s

So,   distance $= 900 \times 2 = 1800$ m $=$ **1.8 km**

Que 7. Show the shape of the distance-time graph for the motion in the following cases:

(a) A car moving with a constant speed.

(b) A car parked on a side road.

Ans.

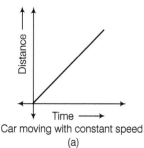

Car moving with constant speed	Car parking on a side road
(a)	(b)

Que 8. Which of the following relations is correct?

(a) Speed = Distance × Time

(b) Speed = $\dfrac{\text{Distance}}{\text{Time}}$

(c) Speed = $\dfrac{\text{Time}}{\text{Distance}}$

(d) Speed = $\dfrac{1}{\text{Distance} \times \text{Time}}$

Ans. Relation (b) is correct as speed is given by total distance covered by total time taken.

Que 9. The basic unit of speed is

(a) km/min (b) m/min (c) km/h (d) m/s

Ans. The basic unit of speed is metre/second or m/s. So, option (d) is correct.

Que 10. A car moves with a speed of 40 km/h for 15 min and then with a speed of 60 km/h for the next 15 min. The total distance covered by the car is

(a) 100 km (b) 25 km (c) 15 km (d) 10 km

Ans. Given, speed for first 15 min = 40 km/h

Speed for next 15 min = 60 km/h

As, we know that distance = Speed × Time

So, for first 15 min, distance travelled

$$= 40 \times \frac{15}{60} = 10 \text{ km} \qquad \left(\because 1 \text{ min} = \frac{1}{60} \text{ h} \right)$$

For second 15 min, distance travelled

$$= 60 \times \frac{15}{60} = 15 \text{ km} \qquad \left(\because 1 \text{ min} = \frac{1}{60} \text{ h} \right)$$

So, total distance = 15 + 10 = 25 km

Que 11. Figure shows the distance-time graph for the motion of two vehicles A and B. Which one of them is moving faster?

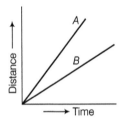

Ans. As from the given graph, slope of A is greater than B, i.e. distance covered by A in same time with respect to B is greater. So, A is moving with faster speed than B.

Que 12. Suppose the two photographs shown in two figures had been taken at an interval of 10 s. If a distance of 100 m is shown by 1 cm in these photographs, then calculate the speed of the circled car.

Ans. Speed of the circled car is given by

$$= \frac{\text{Distance covered}}{\text{Time taken}}$$

$$= \frac{100}{10 \times 100} \qquad \left(\because 1 \text{ cm} = \frac{1}{100} \text{ m} \right)$$

So, $\qquad\qquad = \frac{1}{10} \text{ m/s}$

Que 13. Which of the following distance-time graphs shows a truck moving with speed which is not constant?

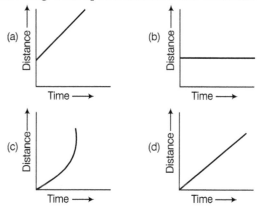

Ans. As we know that if the distance-time graph is straight line, then the motion is said to be uniform motion and if the graph between distance-time graph is not straight line, then the motion is said to be non-uniform. So, option (c) is correct.

Selected **NCERT Exemplar Problems**

> **Multiple Choice Questions**

Que 1. Which of the following cannot be used for measurement of time?
    (a) A leaking tap
    (b) Simple pendulum
    (c) Shadow of an object during the day
    (d) Blinking of eyes

Ans. (d) Blinking of eyes is not a periodic phenomenon, so we cannot measure the time.

Que 2. Two clocks A and B are shown in figure. Clock A has an hour and a minute hand, whereas clock B has an hour hand, minute hand as well as a second hand. Which of the following statements is correct for these clocks?

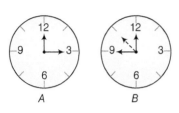

(a) A time interval of 30 s can be measured by clock A
(b) A time interval of 30 s cannot be measured by clock B
(c) Time interval of 5 min can be measured by both A and B
(d) Time interval of 4 min 10 s can be measured by clock A.

Ans. (c) The time interval of 5 minutes can be measured by both A and B.

Que 3. Two students were asked to plot a distance-time graph for the motion described by Table A and Table B.

Table A

Distance moved (m)	0	10	20	30	40	50
Time (min)	0	2	4	6	8	10

Table B

Distance moved (m)	0	5	10	15	20	25
Time (min)	0	1	2	3	4	5

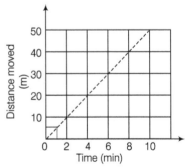

The graph given in figure is true for
(a) Both A and B (b) Only A
(c) Only B (d) Neither A nor B

Ans. (a) Since, speed is constant for A and B, so graph for A and B will be a straight line.

Que 4. A bus travels 54 km in 90 min. The speed of the bus is

    (a) 0.6 m/s   (b) 10 m/s

    (c) 5.4 m/s   (d) 3.6 m/s

Ans. (b) As, we know that

$$\text{Speed} = \frac{\text{Distance}}{\text{Time}} = \frac{54 \times 1000}{90 \times 60} \quad \left[\begin{array}{l} \because 1 \text{ km} = 1000 \text{ m} \\ \because 1 \text{ min} = 60 \text{ s} \end{array} \right]$$

$$= 10 \text{ m/s}$$

Que 5. If we denote speed by S, distance by D and time by T, the relationship between these quantities is

    (a) $S = D \times T$ (b) $T = \dfrac{S}{D}$

    (c) $S = \dfrac{1}{T} \times D$ (d) $S = \dfrac{T}{D}$

Ans. (c) $\text{Speed} = \dfrac{\text{Distance}}{\text{Time}}$

Que 6. Observe figure

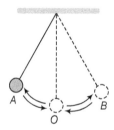

The time period of a simple pendulum is the time taken by it to travel from

    (a) A to B and back to A (b) O to A, A to B and B to A

    (c) B to A, A to B and B to O (d) A to B

Ans. (a) Time period of a simple pendulum is the total time taken to complete one full cycle.

Que 7. Figure shows an oscillating pendulum.

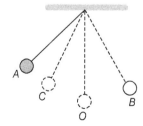

Time taken by the bob to move from A to C is t_1 and from C to O is t_2. The time period of this simple pendulum is

(a) $(t_1 + t_2)$ (b) $2 (t_1 + t_2)$
(c) $3 (t_1 + t_2)$ (d) $4 (t_1 + t_2)$

Ans.   (d) As from A to O, $\frac{1}{4}$th time of one full cycle of time is required, so time period will be $4 (t_1 + t_2)$.

Que 8. The correct symbol to represent the speed of an object is

(a) 5 m/s   (b) 5 mp
(c) $5 \text{ m}/\text{s}^{-1}$ (d) 5 s/m

Ans.   (a) 5 m/s is the correct symbol to represent the speed of an object.

Que 9. Boojho walks to his school which is at a distance of 3 km from his home in 30 min. On reaching, he finds that the school is closed and comes back by a bicycle with his friend and reaches home in 20 min. His average speed in km/h is

(a) 8.3   (b) 7.2
(c) 5   (d) 3.6

Ans.   (b) Given, total distance $= 3 + 3 = 6$ km

$$\text{Total time} = 30 + 20 = 50 \text{ min}$$

$$\text{Average speed} = \frac{\text{Total distance covered}}{\text{Total time taken}}$$

$$= \frac{6}{50} \times 60$$

$$= 7.2 \text{ km/h}$$

❯ **Very Short Answer Type Questions**

Que 10. A simple pendulum is oscillating between two points A and B as shown in figure. Is the motion of the bob uniform or non-uniform?

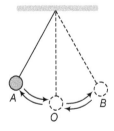

Ans.   The motion of bob is non-uniform, as it does not cover equal distance in equal intervals of time.

Que 11. Paheli and Boojho have to cover different distances to reach their school but they take the same time to reach the school. What can you say about their speed?

Ans. They do not have equal speed because they cover unequal distance in equal intervals of time. One of them has higher speed whom has to cover larger distance with respect to other.

Que 12. If Boojho covers a certain distance in one hour and Paheli covers the same distance in two hours, who travels with a higher speed?

Ans. Boojho travels with a higher speed as he has covered same distance in lesser time with respect to Paheli.

❯ Short Answer Type Questions

Que 13. Complete the data of the table given below with the help of the distance-time graph given in figure.

Distance (m)	0	4	?	12	?	20
Time (s)	0	2	4	?	8	10

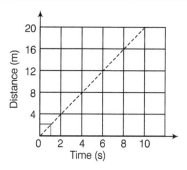

Ans. It is a uniform motion, so

Distance (m)	0	4	8	12	16	20
Time (s)	0	2	4	6	8	10

Que 14. The average age of children of Class VII is 12 years and 3 months. Express this age in seconds.

Ans. Given, 12 years and 3 months

$$\because \qquad 1 \text{ year} = 365 \text{ days}$$
$$= 365 \times 24 \text{ h} \qquad [\because 1 \text{ day} = 24 \text{ h}]$$
$$= 365 \times 24 \times 3600 \text{ s} \qquad [\because 1 \text{ h} = 3600 \text{ s}]$$
$$= 31536000 \text{ s}$$

and $\qquad 3 \text{ months} = 3 \times 30 \text{ days} \qquad [\because 1 \text{month} = 30\text{days}]$

$$= 3 \times 30 \times 24 \text{ h}$$
$$= 3 \times 30 \times 24 \times 3600 \text{ s}$$
$$= 7776000 \text{ s}$$

So, total age in seconds $= 31536000 + 7776000 = 39312000 \text{ s}$

Que 15. A spaceship travels 36000 km in one hour. Express its speed in km/s.

Ans. As, $\qquad \text{Speed} = \dfrac{\text{Distance}}{\text{Time}}$

$$= \dfrac{36000}{1 \times 3600} \qquad [\because 1 \text{ h} = 3600 \text{ s }]$$
$$= 10 \text{ km/s}$$

Que 16. Plot a distance-time graph of the tip of the second hand of a clock by selecting 4 points on X-axis and Y-axis respectively. The circumference of the circle traced by the second hand is 64 cm.

Ans.

Time (s)	X	15	30	45	60
Distance (cm)	Y	16	32	48	64

As, here equal distance is covered in equal intervals of time .
So, graph will be straight line.

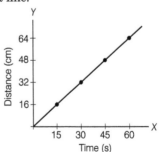

> Long Answer Type Questions

Que 17. Given below as figure is the distance-time graph of the motion of an object.

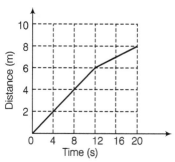

(a) What will be the position of the object at 20 s?
(b) What will be the distance travelled by the object in 12 s?
(c) What is the average speed of the object?

Ans.

(a) From the graph, it is clear that the distance at 20 s is 8 m.
(b) Distance travelled by the body object in 12 s is 6 m.
(c) As, average speed $= \dfrac{\text{Total distance}}{\text{Total time}}$

$$= \dfrac{8}{20} = 0.4 \text{ m/s}$$

Que 18. Boojho goes to the football ground to play football. The distance-time graph of his journey from his home to the ground is given as figure.

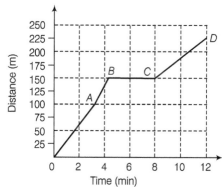

(a) What does the graph between points B and C indicate about the motion of Boojho?

(b) Is the motion between 0 to 4 min uniform or non-uniform?

(c) What is his speed between 8 to 12 min of his journey?

Ans. (a) Since, the graph between B and C is parallel to time axis, so it indicates that Boojho is at rest.

(b) Since, the graph is not straight line, so it is non-uniform motion.

(c) As, $\text{speed} = \dfrac{\text{Distance}}{\text{Time}} = \dfrac{225 - 150}{12 - 8}$

$= \dfrac{75}{4} = 18.75 \text{ m/min}$

Que 19. Distance between Bholu's and Golu's house is 9 km. Bholu has to attend Golu's birthday party at 7 o'clock. He started his journey from his home at 6 o'clock on his bicycle and covered a distance of 6 km in 40 min. At that point, he met Chintu and he spoke to him for 5 min and reached Golu's birthday party at 7 o'clock. With what speed, did he cover the second part of the journey? Calculate his average speed for the entire journey.

Ans. From the question, Bholu covers 3 km distance in 15 min.

So, speed of Bholu $= \dfrac{3}{15} \times 60$ $\left(\because 1 \text{ min} = \dfrac{1}{60} \text{ h} \right)$

$= 12 \text{ km/h}$

Now, average speed is given by

$= \dfrac{\text{Total distance travelled}}{\text{Total time taken}}$

$= \dfrac{9}{1} = 9 \text{ km/h}$

Chapter 14

Electric Current
and its Effects

Important Points

- **Electric current** It is defined as the rate of flow of electric charge through a conductor.
- **Electric cell** It maintains the constant flow of current across an electric circuit. An electric cell has a positive terminal and a negative terminal.
- Some of the electric components and their symbols given below :

	Electric component	Symbol
1.	Electric cell	⊣⊢
2.	Electric bulb	
3.	Switch in ON position	
4.	Switch in OFF position	
5.	Battery	⊣⊢--⊣⊢
6.	Wire	___

- **Electric circuit** For obtaining electric current in a conductor, an arrangement is used which is called electric circuit.
- **Battery** Combination of two or more cells with the positive terminal to negative terminal is called battery. Cell is the unit of battery. Many devices such as torches, transistors, toys, TV remote controls, use batteries.
- There is usually a thick wire or a metal strip connecting the positive terminal of one cell to the negative terminal of the next cell.
- In order to help you to place the cells correctly in the battery compartment, '+' and '−' symbols are usually printed.
    (i) Key or switch can be placed anywhere in the circuit.
    (ii) When switch is ON, the circuit is complete and it is said to be closed.
    (iii) When it is OFF, the circuit is incomplete and it is said to be open.
- **Bulb** In the bulb, there is a thin wire, called filament which glows when an electric current passes through it. When the bulb gets **fused,** its filament is broken.

    Note Never touch a lighted electric bulb connected to the mains. It may be very hot and can damage your hands.

- **Heating effect of current** When electric current is passes through a wire, it becomes hot, this is called heating effect of current.

    Note Do not keep the switch in the ON position for a long time, otherwise the cell may become weak very quickly.

- **Element** All electrical heating devices contain a coil of wire called an element. When these appliances are switched ON after connecting to the electric supply, their elements become red hot and give out heat. Electric appliances such as immersion heaters, hotplates, irons, geysers, electric kettles, hair dryers have elements inside them.
- The amount of heat produced in a wire depends on its material, length and thickness. Thus, for different requirements, the wires of different materials and different lengths and thickness are used. The wires used for making electric circuits do not normally become hot.

- **Compact Fluorescent Lamps** (CFLs) The wastage of electricity can be reduced by using fluorescent tubelights in place of the bulbs. An electric bulb is used for light but it also gives heat which is not desirable.

- Before buying bulbs or tubes or CFLs, look for the ISI mark of the **Bureau of Indian Standards** which ensures that the appliance is safe and wastage of energy is minimum.

- **Electric fuses** A fuse is a safety device made from some special materials melt quickly and breaks electric circuit when large electric currents passes through it. Fuse melts due to over heating of it when excessive current flows through it. One reason for excessive current in electrical circuits is the direct touching of wires. This may happen if the insulation on the wire has come off due to wear and tear, it may cause a short circuit. Fuses of different kinds are used for different purposes.

  Another reason for excessive current is connection of many devices to a single socket. It may cause overload in the circuit.

  Note Never try to investigate electric fuse connected to mains circuit on your own.

- **Miniature Circuit Breakers** (MCBs) These are used in place of fuse wire. It has an automatic switch which breaks the circuit for very high current.

- **Magnetic effect of current** When electric current is passed through a coil, it behaves like a magnet called magnetic effect of current. Hans Christian Oersted discovered the magnetic effect of current.

  Note An electric current can be used to make magnets.

- **Electromagnets** These are the temporary magnet, it has magnetic property till the current passes through it. Electromagnets can be made very strong and can lift very heavy loads. It looses its magnetism when current goes OFF. The electromagnets are used in many devices and also used to separate magnetic material from the junk.

  Note Doctors use tiny electromagnets to take out small pieces of magnetic material that have accidentally fallen in the eye.

- **Electric bell** It consists of a coil of wire wound on an iron piece. The coil acts as an electromagnet.

- An iron strip with a hammer at one end is kept close to the electromagnet. There is a contact screw near the iron strip. When the iron strip is in contact with the screw, the current flows through the coil which becomes an electromagnet. It then pulls the iron strip. In the process, the hammer at the end of the strip strikes the gong of the bell to produce a sound.

- However, when the electromagnet pulls the iron strip, it also breaks the circuit, the current through the coil stops flowing. The coil is no longer an electromagnet, so it does not attract the iron strip. The iron strip comes back to its original position and touches the contact screw again. So the current flows in the coil and the hammer strikes the gong again. This process is repeated in quick succession.

Intext Questions

Que 1. If cells are placed side by side. Then, how are the terminals of the cells connected?   *(Pg 161)*

Ans. If cells are placed side by side, then with the help of some connecting wires, the positive terminal of one cell is connected to the negative terminal of other to produce a combined power of all cells, which can be called a battery.

Que 2. Batteries used in tractors, trucks and inverters are also made from cells. Then, why it is called a battery?   *(Pg 162)*

Ans. As we know the cell is the unit of battery when more than one cell are combined together, it forms a battery. In trucks, tractors and inverters, cells are internally arranged and we need not to connect it externally, so we called it as batteries.

Que 3. If the filament of the bulb is broken, would the circuit be complete? Would the bulb still glow?   *(Pg 163)*

Ans. If the filament of the bulb is broken, the circuit will not be complete as the current from one side does not flow to other side. So, the bulb will not glow.

Que 4. Name some electric appliances where the heating effect of the electric current is used.   *(Pg 164)*

Ans. Some of the electric appliances where the heating effect of the electric current is used are electric heater, geyser, micro-oven, room heater, boiler, etc.

Que 5. Does the electric current have other effect except heating? Name it. *(Pg 166)*

Ans. Yes, electric current have other effect except heating, i.e. magnetic effect of current. When electric current is passed through a coil, there is a magnetic field developed around the coil or wire, if magnetic compass is placed near by, it deflects the magnetic needle.

Que 6. When the current flows through wire, does the wire behave like a magnet? *(Pg 168)*

Ans. When the current flows through any wire, a magnetic field is developed around that wire or coil and it behaves like a magnet. It can be analysed by placing a magnetic compass around the wire, it will show deflection of the needle.

Que 7. When current is passed through a coil, does the pins cling to the coil? *(Pg 168)*

Ans. When an electric current is passed through a coil, it gets magnetised due to phenomena of magnetic effect of current.

When magnetic materials such as pins are placed near to it. It gets attracted by the coil or we can say that pins cling to the coil.

Que 8. When the current through the coil stops flowing. Will the coil remain an electromagnet? *(Pg 169)*

Ans. When the current through the coil stops flowing, the coil does not remain an electromagnet.

As, from the concept of magnetic effect of current, magnetisation of the coil only persists till the current flows through it. As soon as circuit breaks the magnetic property of the coil disappears and the coils do not remain an electromagnet.

Exercises

Que 1. Draw the symbols in your notebook to represent the following components of electrical circuits: connecting wires, switch in the OFF position, bulb, cell, switch in the ON position and battery.

Ans.

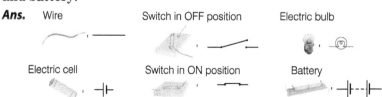

Wire   Switch in OFF position   Electric bulb

Electric cell   Switch in ON position   Battery

Que 2. Draw the circuit diagram to represents the circuit shown in figure.

Ans. Complete circuit is shown as below :

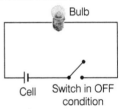

Que 3. Figure shows four cells fixed on a board. Draw lines to indicate how will you connect their terminals with wires to make a battery of four cells?

Ans. To connect all the cells, we should join negative terminal of one cell to positive terminal of other.

Que 4. The bulb in the circuit shown in figure does not glow. Can you identify the problem? Make necessary changes in the circuit to make the bulb glow.

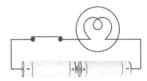

Ans. Since the two cells are connected with the positive terminal in one side. This can be corrected by joining the negative terminal of one cell to the positive terminal of other cell as shown in figure.

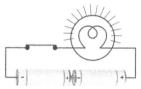

Que 5. Name any two effects of electric current.

Ans. The two effects of electric current are
(i) Heating effect   (ii) Magnetic effect

Que 6. When the current is switched ON through a wire, a compass needle kept nearby gets deflected from its North-South position. Explain.

Ans. When the current is switched ON through a wire or a coil, there is a magnetic field created around the coil or wire and we can say that the wire or coil gets magnetised. Thus, a compass needle kept nearby gets deflected from its North-South position due to other magnet formed by current carrying wire or coil.

Que 7. Will the compass needle show deflection, when the switch in the circuit shown by figure is closed?

Ans. Yes, the compass needle shows the deflection, when switch is closed or circuit is complete. On closing the circuit, current flows through the coil and it gets magnetised. Thus, due to this magnetic effect of current, compass needle shows deflection.

Que 8. Fill in the blanks:
(a) Longer line in the symbol for a cell represents its .... terminal.
(b) The combination of two or more cells is called a ....
(c) When current is switched ON in a room heater, it ....
(d) The safety device based on the heating effect of electric current is called a ....

Ans. (a) positive   (b) battery
(c) gets heated   (d) fuse wire

Que 9. Mark 'T', if the statement is True and 'F', if it is False:

(a) To make a battery of two cells, the negative terminal of one cell is connected to the negative terminal of the other cell.

(b) When the electric current through the fuse exceeds a certain limit, the fuse wire melts and breaks.

(c) An electromagnet does not attract a piece of iron.

(d) An electric bell has an electromagnet.

Ans. (a) False (F), to make a battery of two cells, the negative terminal of one cell is connected to the positive terminal of the other cell.

(b) True (T)

(c) False (F), as an electromagnet attracts magnetic material.

(d) True (T)

Que 10. Do you think an electromagnet can be used for separating plastic bags from a garbage heap? Explain.

Ans. No, an electromagnet cannot be used for separating plastic bags from a garbage heap because plastic bags are not magnetic materials. Only magnetic materials can be attracted by the magnet, so plastic bags do not get attracted by the magnet.

Que 11. An electrician is carrying out some repairs in your house. He wants to replace a fuse by a piece of wire. Would you agree? Give reasons for your response.

Ans. No, we should not agree for replacing a fuse by a piece of wire. As we know that fuse wire is made up of special material which can be melt on passing high amount of current or during any short circuit. If it is replaced by some other wire, melting of fuse may not take place on short circuiting or excessive current flow and it may cause fire.

Que 12. Zubeda made an electric circuit using a cell holder shown in figure, a switch and a bulb. When she put the switch in the ON position, the bulb did not glow. Help Zubeda in identifying the possible defects in the circuit.

Ans. These may be the reasons by which bulb will not glow :

(i) Zubeda may have arranged the cells not in a particular manner, i.e. terminals of cell may not be in alternate form.

(ii) May be the bulb used by Zubeda is fused one.

(iii) May be the connecting wire in cell holder is not attached properly.

Que 13. In the circuit shown in figure:

(a) Would any of the bulb glow, when the switch is in the OFF position?

(b) What will be the order in which the bulbs *A*, *B* and *C* will glow, when the switch is moved to the ON position?

Ans. (a) Any of the bulb will not glow when the switch is in the OFF position because circuit is not complete.

(b) All the bulbs glow simultaneously as the switch is moved to the ON position.

Selected **NCERT Exemplar Problems**

> **Multiple Choice Questions**

Que 1. When an electric current flows through a copper wire *AB* as shown in figure, the wire

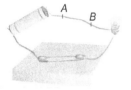

(a) deflects a magnetic needle placed near it

(b) becomes red hot

(c) gives electric shock

(d) behaves like a fuse

Ans. (a) It deflects a magnetic needle placed near it because a magnetic field is created near the current carrying wire.

Que 2. Three bulbs *A*, *B* and *C* are connected in a circuit as shown in figure. When the switch is ON

(a) bulb *C* will glow first

(b) bulbs *B* and *C* will glow simultaneously and bulb *A* will glow after sometime

(c) all the bulbs *A*, *B* and *C* will glow at the same time

(d) the bulbs will glow in the order *A*, *B* and *C*

Ans. (c) All the bulbs glow simultaneously because there is no time lag in the flow of current as soon as circuit is complete.

Que 3. When a switch is in OFF position,
  (i) circuit starting from the positive terminal of the cell stops at the switch
  (ii) circuit is open
  (iii) no current flows through it
  (iv) current flows after sometime

  Choose the combination of correct answer from the following.

  (a) All are correct   (b) (ii) and (iii) are correct
  (c) Only (iv) is correct   (d) (i) and (ii) are correct

Ans. (b) When switch is in OFF position, circuit is open and no current flows through it.

Que 4. Which of the following precautions need not be taken while using electric gadgets/ appliances/circuit?

  (a) We should never touch a lighted electric bulb connected to the mains
  (b) We should never experiment with the electric supply from the mains or a generator or an inverter
  (c) We should never use just any wire or strip of metal in place of a fuse
  (d) We should never turn the switch in ON position

Ans. (d) We should never turn the switch in ON position

> Very Short Answer Type Questions

Que 5. Which property of a conducting wire is utilised in making electric fuse?

Ans. Electric fuse wire is made up of special material which has low melting point. As if high amount of current is passed, it melts to disconnect the electric circuit and prevent us from causing any damage.

Que 6. Name the device used these days in place of electric fuses in electrical circuits.

Ans. The device used in these days in place of electric fuse is MCB (Miniature Circuit Breaker). It auto disconnects the circuit, when there is a short circuit or excess current flow.

Que 7. Fill in the blanks:
(a) Our body is a .... of electricity.
(b) An electric cell produces electricity from the .... in it.
(c) In an electric circuit, a fuse is a .... to prevent possible fire.
(d) A combination of two or more cells is called a ....

Ans. (a) good conductor   (b) chemicals stored
(c) safety device   (d) battery

Que 8. Unscramble the following words:
(a) TBTAYER   (b) SFEU
(c) HTRCO   (d) HICWTS

Ans. (a) BATTERY   (b) FUSE
(c) TORCH   (d) SWITCH

Que 9. Paheli does not have a night lamp in her room. She covered the bulb of her room with a towel in the night to get dim light. Has she taken the right step? Give one reason to justify your answer.

Ans. No, she has not taken the right step. Because due to excessive heat of bulb, the towel may burn and it also results in the wastage of electrical energy.

Que 10. Why are CFLs (Compact Fluorescent Lamps) preferred over electric bulbs?

Ans. Compact fluorescent lamps are preferred over electric bulbs because electric bulbs use more power of electricity and it also losses electrical energy in the form of heat but it is not so in compact fluorescent lamps.

Que 11. Why is an electric fuse required in all electrical appliances?

Ans. Electric fuse is required in all electrical appliances to prevent damage from excessive current flow and during short circuit.

› Short Answer Type Questions

Que 12. Can we use the same fuse in a geyser and a television set? Explain.

Ans. No, we cannot use same fuse in a geyser and in a television set because the fuse used in every appliances has some limit to withstand the current flows through it. So, different appliances have different fuses.

Que 13. Name two electric devices for each where
   (a) heating effect of current is used and
   (b) magnetic effect of current is used.

Ans. (a) Heating effect of current is used in electric heater and geyser.
   (b) Magnetic effect of current is used in electric bell and cranes to lift heavy magnetic materials from one place to other.

Que 14. Why do we cover plug pinholes which are within the reach of children with cellotape or a plastic cover when not in use?

Ans. We do cover plug pinholes which are within the reach of children with cellotape or plastic cover to avoid electric shocks. If unconsciously, a child puts his finger in the electric socket, the shock may be fatal.

Que 15. Boojho made an electromagnet by winding 50 turns of wire over an iron screw. Paheli also made an electromagnet by winding 100 turns over a similar iron screw. Which electromagnet will attract more pins? Given reason.

Ans. Since the magnetic effect directly depends on the number of turns of the coil. As, Paheli's coil has more number of turns than Boojho. So, her electromagnet is stronger than Boojho. So, electromagnet of Paheli attracts more pins as compared to Boojho.

> Long Answer Type Questions

Que 16. Your teacher has shown you the following activity.

Activity Teacher has wound a long insulated piece of wire around an iron nail in the form of a coil. Free ends of the wire are connected to a cell through a switch as shown in the figure. The current is switched on and some pins are placed near the ends of the nail.

Write down any three questions that come to your mind about this activity.

Ans. Some of the questions which rise are as follows:
   (i) On disconnecting circuit, why pin gets detached from the nails?
   (ii) What will happen, if we use some other materials accept nails like wood?
   (iii) If more number of turns of wire is wounded over nails, what will happen?

Que 17. Paheli took a wire of length 10 cm. Boojho took a wire of 5 cm of the same material and thickness. Both of them connected with wires as shown in the circuit given in figure. The current flowing in both the circuits is the same.

    (a) Will the heat produced in both the cases be equal? Explain.

    (b) Will the heat produced be the same, if the wires taken by them are of equal lengths but of different thickness? Explain.

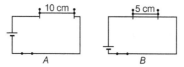

Ans. (a) No, the amount of heat produced in both the wires will be different because amount of heat produced in a wire on passing electric current depends on the length of wire and here length is different for both the wires.

    (b) No, the amount of heat produced in the wire of same length but different thickness cannot be same because amount of heat produced in a wire also depends on the thickness of the wire.

Que 18. How does the magnetic effect of electric current help in the working of an electric bell? Explain with the help of a diagram.

Ans. As, in the diagram when electric current is passed through the coil or solenoid. By the phenomenon of magnetic effect of current, the coil or solenoid gets magnetised which attracts nearby soft iron armature and the hammer strikes gong repeatedly. Thus, electric bell starts ringing and as soon as switch is OFF, no current flows through the coil and its magnetisation stops. So, bell will not work.

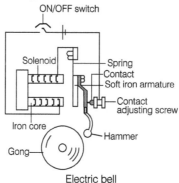

Electric bell

Chapter **15**

Light

Important Points

- **Light** It is a form of energy which enables us to see the colourful world around us. Light travels in a straight line, i.e. also called as rectilinear propagation of light.

- **Reflection of light** The change in direction of light by a mirror is called reflection of light. Reflection of light follows laws of reflection for every spherical surface or plane surface.

- **Image** The object which appears behind the mirror, is the image of the object formed by the mirror. An image formed by a plane mirror is always virtual, behind the mirror, of same size and always erect.

  The image formed by a plane mirror is laterally inverted, i.e. left is right and right is left, also the image is at the same distance behind the mirror as the object is in front of it.

- **Spherical mirror** It is the part of a sphere in which one side is silvered or polished. Spherical mirrors are of two types as below:

  (i) **Concave mirror** If the reflecting surface of a spherical mirror is concave, it is called a concave mirror.

   e.g. Curved shining surface of a spoon which is pushed inward acts as a concave mirror.

   Concave mirror can form real and virtual, inverted and erect, magnified and diminished images depending upon the position of object.

   Concave mirrors are used in examining eyes, ears, nose and throat by doctors. It is also used by dentist. The reflectors of torches, headlights of cars and scooters are concave in the shape.

(ii) **Convex mirror** If the reflecting surface of a spherical mirror is convex, it is called convex mirror, e.g. The pulled outward shining surface of a spoon acts as convex mirror.

Convex mirror can form only virtual, erect and diminished image inspite of the position of object.

Convex mirrors are used in **rear view mirror** in car and vehicle to have a wide view of traffic.

▪ **Real image** can be obtained on a screen but **virtual image** cannot be obtained on a screen.

▪ **Lens** It is a transparent glass bounded by two curved surfaces which allow the light to pass through it either by converging or diverging. Lenses are of two types as below:

(i) **Convex lens** It is also called converging lens because it converges light at a point called focus of lens.

It is thicker in the middle and thinner at the edges. It can form real or virtual, magnified and diminished image.

Convex lens can be used as magnifying glass when object is placed between its focus and centre of curvature.

Note It is advised not to look through convex lens at the sunlight or a bright light because it may damage your eyes.

(ii) **Concave lens** It is also called diverging lens because it spreads out the light after passing through it. It is thinner in the middle and thicker at the edge. It can only form virtual and diminished image of an object.

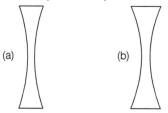

(a) A convex lens and   (b) a concave lens

▪ **Sunlight : White or Coloured** The sunlight is a mixture of different colours, i.e. when you blow soap bubbles, they appear colourful. Similarly, when light is reflected from the surface of a CD (compact disk).

- **Rainbow** It is the dispersion or spreading of white light when passed through tiny droplets of water during the rainy season in the sky. A white light can be dispersed into its seven constituent colours when passed through a prism.

  Note A white light of the sun is composed of seven constituent colours. These are red, orange, yellow, green, blue, indigo and violet. **Prism** is a piece of solid glass which breaks up the sunlight into its colours.

Intext Questions

Que 1. Does the mirror change the direction of light that falls on it? *(Pg 176)*

Ans. Yes, when a light ray falls on a mirror it changes the direction of reflecting light, i.e. bounces back the light in the same medium by changing its direction.

Que 2. What makes things visible to us? *(Pg 176)*

Ans. When a light ray falls on an object, then reflected light ray which comes from the object when falls on our eyes, allows us to see things around us.

Que 3. Is the image formed by a plane mirror is always upright? *(Pg 177)*

Ans. Yes, the image formed by the plane mirror is always upright. The image formed by the plane mirror is virtual, erect, same size as that of object and at the same distance from the mirror as the distance of object from the mirror.

Que 4. Why in ambulance words are written laterally inverted? *(Pg 178)*

Ans. In case of mirror, the image formed by it is laterally inverted, i.e. left seems to be right and right seems to be left. So, in ambulance there is emergency for patients to reach hospital and by viewing in rear mirror, it can be easily identified of a vehicle and everyone give him a way.

Que 5. Why are concave and convex mirrors called spherical mirrors? *(Pg 180)*

Ans. Concave and convex mirrors are the parts of sphere whose one side is polished or silvered. So, they are called spherical mirrors.

Que 6. Is it possible to obtain the image on the screen when the candle is too close to the concave mirror? *(Pg 181)*

Ans. When the candle is too close to the concave mirror, it means that object is in between focus and centre of curvature. Thus, at this position, image formed will be virtual and cannot be obtained on the screen.

Que 7. Can you get a real image at any distance of the object from the convex mirror? *(Pg 182)*

Ans. No, we cannot get a real image for any position of an object from the mirror because convex mirror always forms virtual, erect and diminished image inspite of the position of object.

Que 8. Can you name the mirrors used as side mirrors in scooters? *(Pg 183)*

Ans. In the side mirror of scooters, convex mirror is used to have a wider field of view of the traffic.

Exercises

Que 1. Fill in the blanks.

(a) An image that cannot be obtained on a screen is called ....

(b) Image formed by a convex .... is always virtual and smaller in size.

(c) An image formed by a .... mirror is always of the same size as that of the object.

(d) An image which can be obtained on a screen is called a .... image.

(e) An image formed by a concave .... cannot be obtained on a screen.

Ans. (a) virtual image

(b) mirror

(c) plane

(d) real

(e) lens

Que 2. Mark T if the statement is true and F if it is false.

(a) We can obtain an enlarged and erect image by a convex mirror.

(b) A concave lens always form a virtual image.

(c) We can obtain a real, enlarged and inverted image by a concave mirror.

(d) A real image cannot be obtained on a screen.

(e) A concave mirror always form a real image.

Ans. (a) F   (b) T   (c) T   (d) F   (e) F

Que 3. Match the items given in Column I with one or more items of Column II.

Column I	Column II
(a) A plane mirror	(i) Used as a magnifying glass.
(b) A convex mirror	(ii) Can form image of objects spread over a large area.
(c) A convex lens	(iii) Used by dentists to see enlarged image of teeth.
(d) A concave mirror	(iv) The image is always inverted and magnified.
(e) A concave lens	(v) The image is erect and of the same size as the object.
	(vi) The image is erect and smaller in size than the object.

Ans. (a) → (v),   (b) → (ii),(vi),   (c) → (i),   (d) → (iii),   (e) → (vi)

Que 4. State the characteristics of the image formed by a plane mirror.

Ans. Characteristics of the image formed by the plane mirror are as follows :

(i) It is virtual.

(ii) It is erect.

(iii) It is same in size.

(iv) It is at same distance from the mirror as the distance of an object from the mirror.

Que 5. Find out the letters of English alphabet or any other language known to you in which the image formed in a plane mirror appears exactly like the letter itself. Discuss your findings.

Ans. Image formed by the plane mirror shows lateral inversion, i.e. left seems to be right and *vice-versa*.

In case of alphabetic letters A, H, I, M, O, T, U, V, W, X, Y show same image in the plane mirror.

Que 6. What is a virtual image? Give one situation, where a virtual image is formed.

Ans. An image that cannot be obtained on a screen is called virtual image. In case of plane mirror, virtual image is formed.

Que 7. State two differences between a convex and concave lens.

Ans. Convex lens
   (i) It can form real and virtual image both.
   (ii) It can form inverted image of an object.
   Concave lens
   (i) It always form virtual image.
   (ii) Image formed by concave lens is always diminished.

Que 8. Give two uses each of a concave and a convex mirror.

Ans. Concave mirror
   (i) It is used by doctors to examine eyes, ears, etc.
   (ii) It is also used by dentists to see an enlarged image of the teeth.
   Convex mirror
   (i) It is used in side mirrors of vehicles.
   (ii) It is used in reflector of torch.

Que 9. Which type of mirror can form a real image?

Ans. A concave mirror can form a real image of an object.

Que 10. Which type of lens forms always a virtual image?

Ans. A concave lens always forms a virtual image.

Que 11. A virtual image larger than the object can be produced by a
   (a) concave lens   (b) concave mirror
   (c) convex mirror   (d) plane mirror

Ans. (b) Concave mirror can form real image and virtual image of larger size than the object.

Que 12. David is observing his image in a plane mirror. The distance between the mirror and his image is 4 m. If he moves 1m towards the mirror, then the distance between David and his image will be
   (a) 3 m   (b) 5 m   (c) 6 m   (d) 8 m

Ans. (a) As we know that in case of plane mirror, an image distance is equal to the object distance, so his image will be at $4 - 1 = 3$ m.

Que 13. The rear view mirror of a car is a plane mirror. A driver is reversing his car at a speed of 2 m/s. The driver sees in his rear view mirror, the image of a truck parked behind his car. The speed at which the image of the truck appears to approach the driver will be

    (a) 1 m/s   (b) 2 m/s

    (c) 4 m/s   (d) 8 m/s

Ans. (b) The speed at which the image of the truck appears to approach the driver will be same as that the reverse speed of the car, i.e. 2 m/s.

Selected **NCERT Exemplar Problems**

⟩ **Multiple Choice Questions**

Que 1. Boojho and Paheli were given one mirror each by their teacher. Boojho found his image to be erect and of the same size, whereas Paheli found her image erect and smaller in size. This means that the mirrors of Boojho and Paheli respectively are

    (a) plane mirror and concave mirror

    (b) concave mirror and convex mirror

    (c) plane mirror and convex mirror

    (d) convex mirror and plane mirror

Ans. (c) As in case of plane mirror image is virtual, erect and of same size and in case of convex mirror is smaller, virtual and erect.

Que 2. Which of the following can be used to form a real image?

    (a) Only concave mirror

    (b) Only plane mirror

    (c) Only convex mirror

    (d) Both concave and convex mirrors

Ans. (a) Only concave mirror can form a real image

Que 3. If an object is placed at a distance of 0.5 m in front of a plane mirror, the distance between the object and the image formed by the mirror will be

    (a) 2 m   (b) 1 m

    (c) 0.5 m   (d) 0.25 m

Ans. (b) The distance between object and mirror is given by 0.5 + 0.5 = 1 m.

Que 4. You are provided with a concave mirror, a convex mirror, a concave lens and a convex lens. To obtain an enlarged image of an object, you can use either

 (a) concave mirror or convex mirror
 (b) concave mirror or convex lens
 (c) concave mirror or concave lens
 (d) concave lens or convex lens

Ans. (b) Concave mirrors and convex lens can only form enlarged image.

Que 5. A rainbow can be seen in the sky

 (a) when the sun is in front of you
 (b) when the sun is behind you
 (c) when the sun is overhead
 (d) only at the time of sunrise

Ans. (b) A rainbow can only be seen in the sky when the sun is behind you in rainy season.

Que 6. An erect and enlarged image can be formed by

 (a) only a convex mirror
 (b) only a concave mirror
 (c) only a plane mirror
 (d) both convex and concave mirrors

Ans. (b) An erect and enlarged image can only be formed by concave mirror and it is virtual in nature.

Que 7. You are provided with a convex mirror, a concave mirror, a convex lens and a concave lens. You can get an inverted image from

 (a) both concave lens and convex lens
 (b) both concave mirror and convex mirror
 (c) both concave mirror and convex lens
 (d) both convex mirror and concave lens

Ans. (c) A real and inverted image can only be formed by concave mirror and convex lens.

Que 8. An image formed by a lens is erect. Such an image could be formed by a

 (a) convex lens provided the image is smaller than object
 (b) concave lens provided the image is smaller than object
 (c) concave lens provided the image is larger than object
 (d) concave lens provided the image is of the same size

Ans. (b) Image formed by a concave lens is erect provided the image is smaller than object.

❯ Very Short Answer Type Questions

Que 9. The image formed by a lens is always virtual, erect and smaller in size for an object kept at different positions in front of it. Identify the nature of the lens.

Ans. Such types of lenses which always form virtual, erect and smaller image inspite of the different positions of an object are called concave lens.

Que 10. Fill in the blanks.

   (a) The inner surface of a steel spoon acts as a .... mirror.

   (b) The outer surface of a flat steel plate acts as a .... mirror.

   (c) The outer shining surface of a round bottom steel bowl acts as a .... mirror.

   (d) The inner surface of the reflector of a torch acts as a .... mirror.

Ans. (a) concave　　　　(b) plane　　(c) convex　　(d) concave

Que 11. State whether the following statements are True or False.

   (a) A concave lens can be used to produce an enlarged and erect image.

   (b) A convex lens always produces a real image.

   (c) The sides of an object and its image formed by a concave mirror are always interchanged.

   (d) An object can be seen only if it emits light.

Ans. (a) False　　(b) False　　(c) True　　(d) False

❯ Short Answer Type Questions

Que 12. What type of mirror is used as a side mirror in a scooter? Why is this type of mirror chosen?

Ans. Convex mirror is used as a side mirror in a scooter because it can form images of objects spread over a larger area. So, this helps the driver to view the traffic over a large area behind them.

Que 13. Observe the figures given as figure carefully.

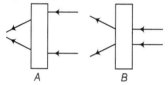

A   B

The given figures show the path of light through lenses of two different types, represented by rectangular boxes *A* and *B*. What is the nature of lenses *A* and *B*?

Ans. Since, in first case light rays are converging towards a point, so the lens *A* will be convex and in case of lens *B*, light rays diverge or spread out. So, the lens will be concave lens.

Que 14. Boojho made light from a laser torch to fall on a prism. Will he be able to observe a band of seven colours? Explain with a reason.

Ans. No, he will not observe band of seven colours because laser light consists of monochromatic light of single colour.

But seven colours of bands are only observed, when a white light is passed through a prism and dispersion takes place.

Que 15. State the correct sequence (1-7) of colours in the spectrum formed by the prisms *A* and *B* shown in figure.

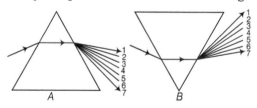

A   B

Ans. When a white light is passed through a prism, it disperses into its seven constituent colours.

For *A*	For *B*
1. ⟶ Red	1. ⟶ Violet
2. ⟶ Orange	2. ⟶ Indigo
3. ⟶ Yellow	3. ⟶ Blue
4. ⟶ Green	4. ⟶ Green
5. ⟶ Blue	5. ⟶ Yellow
6. ⟶ Indigo	6. ⟶ Orange
7. ⟶ Violet	7. ⟶ Red

Que 16. The side mirror of a scooter got broken. The mechanic replaced it with a plane mirror. Mention any inconvenience that the driver of the scooter will face while using it?

Ans. As we know that the side mirror of a scooter must be of convex mirror so that we can view a wide range of traffic spread over a large area.

But if plane mirror is used, we are not able to see large area of traffic which may be difficult for driving vehicle and can cause accident.

Que 17. The concave reflecting surface of a torch got rusted. What effect would this have on the beam of light from the torch?

Ans. If the reflecting surface of a torch got rusted, it produces diffused light with lower intensity and the objects are not clearly visible in this diffused and lower intensity of light.

Que 18. An erect and enlarged image of an object is formed on a screen. Explain how this could be possible.

Ans. An erect and enlarged image of an object is formed only by the concave mirror or convex lens when object is inverted and placed between F and $2F$.

Que 19. Two different types of lenses are placed on a sheet of newspaper. How will you identify them without touching?

Ans. On identifying the letters of newspaper, we can differentiate the two types of lenses.

If image is large or magnified, then the lens is a convex lens and if the image is smaller or diminished in size for all the positions of object, then the lens is concave .

Que 20. A shopkeeper wanted to fix a mirror which will give a maximum view of his shop. What type of mirror should he use? Give reason.

Ans. If a shopkeeper wanted to fix a mirror which will give him maximum view of his shop, he should use convex mirror.

In case of convex mirror, it will give a wider field of view, i.e. it can collect light from a large area spread over them.

Que 21. The distance between an object and a convex lens is changing. It is noticed that the size of the image formed on a screen is decreasing. Is the object moving in a direction towards the lens or away from it?

Ans. In case of convex lens, when we move the object far away from the lens, the size of image decreases and ultimately, when object is at infinity, it will form a point image at focus.

> Long Answer Type Questions

Que 22. Suppose we wish to obtain the real image of a distant tree. Explain two possible ways in which we can do it.

Ans. In first case, we will use a concave mirror, as we know that concave mirror can form real image, i.e. image on screen. The image of distant tree will be at focus in case of concave mirror.

In second case, we can use a convex lens, as it forms real image of a distant object at focus, i.e. image of distant tree in case of convex lens will be formed at focus.

Que 23. It was observed that when the distance between an object and a lens decreases, the size of the image increases. What is the nature of this lens? If you keep on decreasing the distance between the object and the lens, will you still able to obtain the image on the screen? Explain.

Ans. On decreasing distance between the object and lens, the size of the image increases, the nature of the lens will be convex type.

If the distance between object and lens is less than the focus of the lens, then it forms a virtual image and this image cannot be obtained on a screen but formed on the same side of the object.

Que 24. You are given three mirrors of different types. How will you identify each one of them?

Ans. We can identify the mirrors by forming image of an object.

(i) **Plane mirror** In case of plane mirror, image will be virtual, erect and of same size as that of object.

(ii) **Concave mirror** In case of concave mirror, image may be real, virtual and magnified or diminished.

(iii) **Convex mirror** In case of convex mirror, image formed will always be virtual, erect and diminished.

Chapter 16

Water : A Precious Resource

Important Points

- **Water** It is an essential, most common and useful substance around us.
- **World Water Day** 22 March is celebrated as World Water Day every year to attract the attention of everybody towards the importance of conserving water.
- United Nation has recommended a minimum of 50 litre of water for drinking, washing, cooking and maintaining proper hygiene per person per day.

  Note Year 2003 was observed as International year of freshwater.
- **Availability of water** About 71% of the earth's surface is covered with water. Out of this 97.4% is present in seas and oceans.

  The water which is fit for human use is called **freshwater**. Only 2.6% of total water on the earth is freshwater. Water present as snow is not readily used, i.e. only 0.014% is available for use. Out of this percent only 0.006% of freshwater is fit to be used.
- **Water cycle** The cyclic movement of water between land and sea is called water cycle. Supply of freshwater is maintained by water cycle.
- **Forms of water** When water circulates through the water cycle, it can be found in all the three forms, i.e. solid, liquid and gas.
  - (i) The **solid** form (snow and ice) is present as ice caps at the poles of the earth, snow covered mountains and glaciers.

(ii) **Liquid** form (water) is present in oceans, lakes, rivers and even underground.

(iii) The **gaseous** form is the water vapour in the air around us.

▪ **Water table** The upper level of water under the ground which occupies all the spaces in the soil and rocks is called water table. The water table varies from place to place and it may even change at a given place.

▪ **Groundwater** The water found below water table is called groundwater. This water serves as source of wells, lakes, ponds, etc. The moisture in the soil indicates the presence of water underground.

▪ **Infiltration** The rainwater and water from other sources such as rivers and ponds seeps through the soil and fills the empty spaces and cranks deep below the ground. The process of seeping of water into the ground is called infiltration.

▪ **Aquifer** The place where the groundwater is stored between the layers of hard rock below the water table is called aquifer. Water in the aquifers can be usually pumped out with the help of tube wells or handpumps.

▪ **Deflection of water table** When the water is not sufficiently replenished by natural processes and water table goes down, it is called depletion of water table. Factors affecting the depletion in water table are increase in population, industrial and agricultural activities, scanty rainfall, deforestation and decrease in effective area for seepage of water.

(i) **Increasing population** Increasing population creates demand for construction of houses, shops offices, roads and pavements. This decreases the open areas like parks and playgrounds. This, in turn, decreases the seepage of rainwater into the ground.

(ii) **Increasing industries** The number of industries is increasing continuously. Water used by most of the industries is drawn from the ground.

(iii) **Agriculture activities** Irrigation systems such as canals are there only in a few places. These systems may suffer from lack of water due to erratic rainfall. Therefore, farmers have to use groundwater for irrigation. Population pressure on agriculture forces increasing use of groundwater day by day resulting in depletion of groundwater.

- **Distribution of water** The distribution of water over the globe is quite uneven due to a number of factors. Some places have good amount of rain. On the other hand, these are deserts which have scanty rainfall. Some regions have excessive rains which cause floods while some others have very little rainfall which cause drought. India is a vast country and the rainfall is not same everywhere. Therefore some regions in our country may have floods while others may suffer from droughts at the same time.

- **Water management** It is the activity of planning developing, distribution and managing the optimum use of water resources. It is a subset of water cycle management. Water supply pipes leaking and a lot of water gushing out of the pipes are the responsibilities of the civic authorities to prevent such wastage of precious water. Mismanagement or wastage may also take place at the level of individuals also. All of us knowingly or unknowingly waste water, we should also take care for it.

- **Water conservation** To preserve water, some steps should be taken for its conservation:

  (i) **Rainwater harvesting** The rainwater is made to seep in the ground more efficiently by constructing percolation pits and recharge wells. It is also called as **water harvesting**.

  (ii) An old age practice of water storage and water recharge like the **bawris** which was the traditional way of collecting water. With time the bawris fell into disuse and garbage started piling in these reservoirs.

  (iii) **Drip irrigation** It is a technique of watering plants by making use of narrow tubings which deliver water directly at the base of the plant.

- **Bhujpur** in Kutch area of Gujarat has erratic rainfall, therefore villagers along with NGOs harvest rainwater. Eighteen check-dams were built on Rukmawati river and its tributaries where water percolates through the soil and recharge the aquifers.

- We can also conserve water by using following practices:

  (i) Turn off taps while brushing.

  (ii) Mop the floor instead of washing.

- Plants need water to get nutrients from the soil to prepare their food. If water is not available to plants, the green characters of the planet shall be lost. This may lead to the end of all life that mean no food, no oxygen, not enough rain, and innumerable other problems.

▪ **A successful initiative** Rajasthan is a hot and dry place. A band of social workers has transformed a dry area in the Alwar district into a green place. They have revived five dried-up rivers, i.e. Arveri, Ruparel, Sarsa, Bhagani and Jahazwali by constructing water-harvesting structures.

Intext Questions

Que 1. What problems are faced due to shortage of water? *(Pg 193)*

Ans. The problems that can be faced due to shortage of water are as follow:
  (i) Less amount of pure drinking water will be available
  (ii) Equal distribution of water lacks
  (iii) Drought

Que 2. What is the actual amount of water available for human use? *(Pg 195)*

Ans. The actual amount of water available for human use is very little, i.e. approx 0.006% of all water found on the earth.

Que 3. Match the numbers with the processes labelled in jumbled. *(Pg 196)*

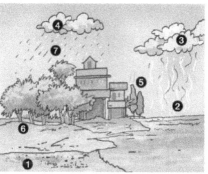

  1. rudgonrawet   2. atooniaervp
  3. acestoonnnid   4. duclos
  5. tspratniaoinr   6. aitfinlronit
  7. ntciepirtaipo

Ans. (i) Groundwater (1)   (ii) Evaporation (2)
  (iii) Condensation (3)   (iv) Clouds (4)
  (v) Transpiration (5)   (vi) Infilteration (6)
  (vii) Precipitation (7)

Que 5. What is the source of groundwater?   *(Pg 197)*

Ans. Rainwater and water from the other sources like rivers, ponds, etc are the sources of groundwater.

Que 6. From where do the workers get water for construction?
                                                          (Pg 198)

Ans. Workers get water for construction from the underground water.

Que 7. Can we keep on drawing water from under the ground? How will it affect the water table?   *(Pg 198)*

Ans. No, we cannot keep on drawing water from under the ground. It may cause of depletion of water table.

Que 8. Name some industries familiar to you. Make a list of the products obtained from these and used in our daily life. Discuss how the growing industrial activity is responsible for depletion of water table.   *(Pg 199)*

Ans. Following industries and their product pollute the water :
   (i) Leather industries, e.g. shoes and other products.
   (ii) Chemical factories, e.g. fertilisers, different insect repellant sprays, etc.
   (iii) Petrochemical industries, e.g. petroleum and different fuels.
   (iv) Oil industries.

All the above industries, release pollutants such as asbestos, lead, mercury, nitrates, sulphur, etc in different rivers, lakes and ponds which are polluting the water and hence is responsible for depletion of water table.

Exercises

Que 1. Mark 'T' if the statement is True and 'F' if it is False.
   (a) The freshwater stored in the ground is much more than that present in the rivers and lakes of the world.
   (b) Water shortage is a problem faced only by people living in rural areas.
   (c) Water from rivers is the only source for irrigation in the fields.
   (d) Rain is the ultimate source of water.

Ans. (a) T – True

(b) F – False, people living in both rural and urban areas, face the problem of shortage of water.

(c) F – False, irrigation also depends on the rainfall, wells , tanks, tubewells, etc.

(d) F – False, the groundwater and rivers, along with rainfall are considered as the natural source of water.

Que 2. Explain how groundwater is recharged.

Ans. The groundwater is recharged in the following manner :

(i) Rainwater and the water from waterbodies on the earth surface pass through the soil by the process of **infiltration**.

(ii) The infiltrated water then gets accumulated in the **aquifer** deep under the ground.

Que 3. There are 10 tubewells in a lane of 50 houses, what could be the long term impact on the water table?

Ans. If these tubewells are used for long time continuously, then the groundwater level would be reduced. Thus, we can say that population increase is one of the major cause for depletion of water table.

Que 4. You have been asked to maintain a garden. How will you minimise the use of water?

Ans. To maintain a garden, water is necessary. Therefore, to minimise the use of water, we can apply the drip irrigation method. In this method, water is supplied directly to the base of the plants using narrow pipes, thereby reducing the loss of water.

Que 5. Explain the factors responsible for the depletion of water table.

Ans. The factors responsible for depletion of water table are as follows :

(i) **Increasing population** It decreases the open area for seepage of water into the grounds.

(ii) **Increasing industries** Most of the stages of manufacturing processes in industries require water. If the number of industries increases, then the water required by them will also increase and will lead to the depletion of water table.

(iii) **Agricultural activities** The water for agriculture is mainly utilised from groundwater, rainwater and canal water. The increased population causes pressure on agricultural practices. This inturn causes increase the use of groundwater and leads to the depletion of water table.

Que 6. Fill in the blanks with appropriate answer.

    (a) People obtain groundwater through .... and ....

    (b) Three forms of water are ...., ... and ....

    (c) The water bearing layer of the earth is ....

Ans. (a) tubewells and handpumps   (b) solid, liquid, gas

    (c) aquifer   (d) infiltration

Que 7. Which one of the following is not responsible for water shortage?

    (a) Rapid growth industries

    (b) Heavy rainfall

    (c) Increasing population

    (d) Mismanagement of water resources

Ans. (b) Heavy rainfall is not responsible for water shortage, rather it increases water table.

Que 8. Choose the correct option. The total water

    (a) in the lakes and rivers of the world remains constant

    (b) under the ground remains constant

    (c) in the seas and oceans of the world remains constant

    (d) of the world remains constant

Ans. (d) The total water of the world remains constant.

Que 9. Make a sketch showing groundwater and water table. Label it.

Ans.

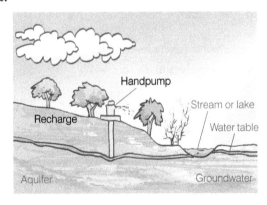

Selected **NCERT Exemplar Problems**

❯ **Multiple Choice Questions**

Que 1. Which of the following does not show water shortage?
   (a) Taps running dry
   (b) Long queues for getting water
   (c) Marches and protests for demand of water
   (d) A family gets three buckets of water per person per day

Ans. (d) A family gets three buckets of water per person per day, shows no shortage of water.

Que 2. Seas and oceans are full of water on the earth. However, a very small percentage of water present on the earth is available for use. This percentage is roughly
   (a) 0.006%   (b) 0.06%
   (c) 0.6%   (d) 6%

Ans. (a) However, the seas and oceans are full of water on the earth but only a small percentage of water is available for use. This is roughly 0.006%.

Que 3. Which of the following are not the liquid forms of water?
   (i) Snow   (ii) Lake water
   (iii) River water   (iv) Water vapour
   (v) Ice

   Choose the correct combination from the options below :
   (a) (i), (iv) and (v)   (b) (i) and (ii)
   (c) (ii) and (iii)   (d) Only (iv)

Ans. (a) Among the given options, snow and ice are solid forms and water vapour is gaseous form of water.

Que 4. A man digging the ground near a water body found that the soil was moist. As he kept digging deeper, and deeper he reached a level, where all the spaces between particles of soil and gaps between rocks were filled with water. The upper limit of this layer is called
   (a) water level   (b) water table
   (c) groundwater   (d) water limit

Ans. (b) The upper limit of this layer where all the spaces between particles of soil and gaps of rocks are filled with water is called water table.

Que 5. Which of the following is a way to use water economically?
  (a) Construction of bawris
  (b) Rainwater harvesting
  (c) Drip irrigation
  (d) Infiltration

Ans. (c) Among the given options, drip irrigation is a way to use water economically because the installation of drip irrigation techniques require less amount of water.

Que 6. On which of the following day is World Water Day observed?
  (a) 22 March   (b) 14 November
  (c) 2 October   (d) 21 December

Ans. (a) The World Water Day is observed on 22 March every year.

Que 7. The amount of water recommended by the United Nations for drinking, washing, cooking and maintaining proper hygiene per person per day is a minimum of
  (a) 5 L   (b) 15 L
  (c) 30 L   (d) 50 L

Ans. (d) The amount of water recommended by the United Nations for drinking, washing, cooking and maintaining proper hygiene per person per day is 50 L, i.e. approx. 2 and half buckets daily.

Que 8. 'Every Drop Counts' is a slogan related to
  (a) counting of drops of any liquid (b) counting of water drops
  (c) importance of water   (d) importance of counting

Ans. (c) "Every Drop Counts" is a slogan related to importance of water.

Que 9. Water cycle does not involve which of the following?
  (a) Evaporation   (b) Condensation
  (c) Formation of clouds   (d) Rainwater harvesting

Ans. (d) Water cycle does not involve rainwater harvesting. Rainwater harvesting is the technique to conserve water.

Que 10. Which of the following inhibits the seepage of rainwater into ground?
  (a) A pukka floor   (b) Playground
  (c) Grass lawn   (d) Forest land

Ans. (a) A pukka floor inhibits the seepage of rainwater into the ground because it is made up of hard impermeable rocks or rock materials.

› **Very Short Answer Type Questions**

Que 11. State whether the following statements are True or False. If False, write the correct statement.

(a) Water vapour is the gaseous form of water.

(b) Ice is solid, whereas snow is the semi-solid form of water.

(c) Ocean water cannot be used for domestic purposes.

(d) Rapid growth of industries is one of the causes for water shortage.

Ans. (a) True

(b) False, ice and snow both are solid forms of water.

(c) True

(d) True

Que 12. What is the source of water in each of the following?

(a) Wells

(b) Ground

(c) Atmosphere

Ans. (a) The source of water in wells is groundwater.

(b) The source of water on ground is rain.

(c) The source of water in atmosphere is evaporation.

› **Short Answer Type Questions**

Que 13. Fill in the blanks.

Cold, demand, leaders, dry, hot, scarcity, workers, wet, oceans, harvesting, rivers

Rajasthan is a .... and dry place. The challenge of natural .... of water was met by a successful experiment. A band of social .... had transformed a .... area into a green place. They have revived five dried-up .... by constructing water .... structures.

Ans. Rajasthan is a **hot** and dry place. The challenge of natural **scarcity** of water was met by a successful experiment. A band of social **workers** had transformed a **dry** area into a green place. They have revived five dried-up **rivers** by constructing water **harvesting** structures.

Que 14. Place the following statements in a proper order to form a meaningful paragraph.

(a) Which inturn decreases the seepage of rainwater into the ground.

(b) This decreases the open areas like parks and playgrounds.

(c) Increasing population create demand for construction of houses, shops, offices, roads and pavements.

(d) This results in depletion of water table and creates scarcity of more water.

Ans. Increasing population create demand for construction of houses, shops, offices, roads and pavements (c). This decreases the open areas like parks, and playgrounds (b), which inturn decreases the seepage of rainwater into the ground (a). This results in depletion of water table and creates scarcity of more water (d).

Que 15. How can you observe the three forms of water in (a) nature and (b) at home?

Ans. The three forms of water in

(a) nature are snow (solid), water (liquid) and water vapour (gas).

(b) at home ice (solid), water (liquid) and steam (gas).

Que 16. Complete the given table.

	Form of water	Process by which formed	Location where found
(a)	Liquid		
(b)	Solid		
(c)	Gaseous		

Ans. The complete table is given below :

	Form of water	Process by which formed	Location where found
(a)	Liquid	Condensation and Melting	Water bodies like rivers, lakes, etc.
(b)	Solid	Freezing	Cold regions like high mountains, poles, etc.
(c)	Gaseous	Evaporation	Atmosphere

Que 17. Match Column I with Column II.

Column I	Column II
(a) Ground water	(i) Solid form of water
(b) Bawris	(ii) Wastage of water
(c) Snow	(iii) Water management
(d) Drip irrigation	(iv) Small water body
(e) Leaking taps	(v) Water table

Ans. The correct matching is

Column I	Column II
(a) Ground water	(v) Water table
(b) Bawris	(iv) Small water body
(c) Snow	(i) Solid form of water
(d) Drip irrigation	(iii) Water management
(e) Leaking taps	(ii) Wastage of water

Que 18. A list of jumbled words are given here. Write the correct form of each word.

(a) WASHFERRET   (b) CHARREGE

(c) QUIFERA   (d) WOSN

Ans. The correct form of each world is given below:

(a) Freshwater   (b) Recharge

(c) Aquifer   (d) Snow

Que 19. From where do the following usually get water? In which form is water present in them?

(a) Clouds   (b) Plants

(c) Mountain tops   (d) Aquifer

(e) Animals

Ans.

		Source of water	Form of water
(a)	Clouds	Land	Liquid (droplets of water)
(b)	Plants	Soil	Liquid
(c)	Mountain tops	Atmosphere	Solid
(d)	Aquifer	Rain	Underground water
(e)	Animals	Water bodies	Liquid

❯ Long Answer Type Questions

Que 20. Complete the following chart by writing appropriate words in the boxes marked (a) to (e).

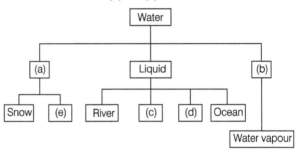

Ans. The complete flowchart is given below :

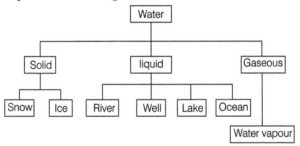

Que 21. Water is very precious for all the living beings. What will happen in future, if we do not save water now?

Ans. Water is needed for various life activities. If we continue the misuse of water and do not conserve it, the groundwater level will be depleted. This may result various consequences like :

Lowering of the water table Excessive pumping can lower the groundwater table.

Reduced surface water supplies Groundwater and surface water are connected. When groundwater is overused, the lakes, streams and rivers connected to groundwater, can also have little supply.

Loss of plants from land We fully depend on the plants for food directly or indirectly. Plants need water to prepare their food. If there will be scarcity of water on earth, the plants will be unable to prepare their food. This inturn will lead to the end of the life because world without plants means, no food, no oxygen, not enough rain and other innumerable problems.

Therefore, it is true that water is a precious resource .

Chapter 17

Forests : Our Lifeline

Important Points

- **Forests** They serve as green lungs and water purifying systems of nature. It is a large area covered mainly with trees, small plants and serve as home for many animals.

  There are several other trees, shrubs, herbs and grasses in the forests. The trees were also covered with different types of creepers and climbers. The sun was barely visible through the leaves of the trees, making it quite dark inside the forests.

- **Crown** It is the branchy part of a tree above the stem. It may be of different shapes and sizes.

- **Canopy** It is the uppermost branches of the trees in a forest, forming a more or less continuous layer of roof over plants in the forest.

- **Understorey** The different horizontal layers formed due to different types of crown in the forest is called understorey.

  An understorey constitutes of
  - (i) trees forming the top layer.
  - (ii) shrubs and tall grasses form the second understorey.
  - (iii) herbs form the lowest layer.
  - (iv) the forest floor remains covered with dead and decaying leaves, fruits, seeds, etc.

- Due to different climatic conditions, these are variations in the types of trees and other plants. The types of animals also differ from forest to forest.

- **Autotrophs** These are the organisms which make food themselves from simple substances and **heterotrophs** are the organisms which take in readymade food by the plants. **Saprotrophs** are the organisms which take in nutrients in solution form from dead and decaying matter.

- **Food chain** It is a chain formed in which one organisms dependent on the next organism as a source of food.

  The forest contains autotrophs (green plants) which produces food and release oxygen by photosynthesis. Other organism like herbivores or carnivores depend ultimately on plants and other animals for food.

$$\underset{\text{(autotroph)}}{\text{Grass}} \xrightarrow[\text{by}]{\text{Eaten}} \underset{\text{(herbivore)}}{\text{Insects}} \xrightarrow[\text{by}]{\text{Eaten}} \text{Frogs} \xrightarrow[\text{by}]{\text{Eaten}} \text{Snake} \xrightarrow[\text{by}]{\text{Eaten}} \text{Eagle}$$

- **Food web** All food chains are linked together and thus form a food web.

- **Humus** Different microorganisms found on the floor of forest in the soil feed upon dead plant and animal tissues and convert them into a dark coloured substance called humus.

- **Decomposers** The microorganisms which convert the dead plants and animals to humus are called decomposers. The decomposers release essential nutrients which get absorbed into the soil and thus increases the fertility of the soil.

  The dead animals become food for vultures, crows, jackals and insects. In this way, the nutrients are cycled. So, nothing goes waste in a forests.

- **Green lungs** Forests are called green lungs because plants in forests release oxygen through the process of **photosynthesis** and help in providing oxygen to animals for respiration. They also help in maintaining the balance of oxygen and carbon dioxide.

  Note Trees take in water from their roots and release water vapour in the air through **evaporation**.

- The forest is not just home to plants and animals. Many people also live in the forest. Some of them may belong to different tribes. The forests provide them food, shelter, water and medicines. They have traditional knowledge about many medicinal plants in the forests. The forest officers could recognise the presence of some animals in the forest by their droppings and footprints.

- **Soil** It helps the forest to grow and regenerate and in return forest prevents soil erosion. **Soil erosion** is the washing away of topmost fertile layer of soil by wind or water which makes the soil infertile.

- **Regeneration** It is an act of renewing forest by planting more and more trees and taking care of young growing trees.

- **Seed dispersal** It is the transport of seed away from the parent plant to a new place, which under favourable conditions grows into a new plant. We see in a forest different types of plants growing on different area. This takes place due to seed dispersal by animals, insects, birds, etc.

- **Dynamic living entity** By harbouring greater variety of plants, the forest provides great opportunities for food and habitat for the herbivores. Larger number of herbivores means increased availability of food for a variety of carnivores. The wide variety of animals helps the forest to regenerate and grow. Decomposers help in maintaining the supply of nutrients to the growing plants in the forest. Therefore, the forest is a dynamic living entity.

  There is a continuous interaction between soil, water, air, plants and animals in a forest.

- **Deforestation** It is the destruction of the forests by cutting down the forest trees. We are facing a serious threat of floods, global warming, extinction of species due to human activity of deforestation.

- **Importance of forests**
    (i) If forests disappear, the amount of carbon dioxide in air will increase, resulting in the increase of earth's temperature.
    (ii) In the absence of trees and plants, the animals will not get food and shelter.
    (iii) In the absence of trees, the soil will not hold water which will cause floods.
    (iv) Deforestation will endanger our life and environment.
    (v) We should protect our forests because forests influence climate, water cycle and air quality.
    (vi) They also provide timber, bamboo, medicines, fruits, gum and many other useful things to us.

Intext Questions

Que 1. Is there similar kind of trees in every forests? *(Pg 209)*

Ans. No, due to different climatic conditions, there are variations in the types of trees and other plants. The types of animals also differ from forest to forest.

Que 2. What is photosynthesis? *(Pg 212)*

Ans. The process by which green plants synthesise their own food and release oxygen in the environment is known as photosynthesis.

Que 3. How can a pipal sapling would have grown on a sidewall of some old buildings? *(Pg 213)*

Ans. Animals disperse the seeds of certain plants with the help of their droppings. Therefore, pipal seed would have come to the wall by a bird dropping. On coming in contact with water and suitable nutrient medium, it would have grown into pipal sapling.

Que 4. What would happen if forests disappear? *(Pg 215)*

Ans. If forests would disappear, then
   (i) carbon dioxide level will increase while oxygen level will decrease in the environment.
   (ii) plants and animals will lose their food and shelter.
   (iii) temperature of the earth will increase.
   (iv) floods would be common.
   (v) water table would be disturbed.
   (vi) soil erosion would occur.

Exercises

Que 1. Explain how animals dwelling in the forest help it to grow and regenerate.

Ans. The animals in forests are of various types. These could be herbivores, carnivores, microorganisms, etc. These play an important role in maintaining the food chains.
   (i) Microorganisms convert the dead plants and animals into humus. This humus helps in returning the nutrients back to the soil. These are absorbed by plants.

(ii) The animals also help in dispersing the seeds of certain plants.

(iii) The decaying animal dung provides nutrients.

All these activities of animals dwelling in the forest help it to grow and regenerate.

Que 2. Explain how forests prevent floods.

Ans. Forests provide floods in the following ways:

   (i) Forests act as a natural absorber of water. It allows rainwater to seep through.

 (ii) In the absence of trees, the rainwater would hit the ground directly, resulting in flood.

(iii) Because of presence of trees, rainwater does not hit the ground directly.

(iv) It rather hits the ground slowly. Hence, before flooding, all the rainwater seeps through ground.

Que 3. What are decomposers? Name any two of them. What do they do in the forest?

Ans. Decomposers are the microorganisms that convert the dead plants and animals into humus. Bacteria and mushroom are the two types of decomposers.

They help in the process of recycling of nutrients by decomposing various dead organisms such as plants and animals to form humus. Therefore, decomposers are helpful for the environment.

Que 4. Explain the role of forests in maintaining the balance between oxygen and carbon dioxide in the atmosphere.

Ans. Forests are called the green lungs. This is because plants in forests release oxygen through the process of photosynthesis and help in providing oxygen to animals for respiration. They consume carbon dioxide released by the animals. In this way, plants help in maintaining a balance of oxygen and carbon dioxide in atmosphere.

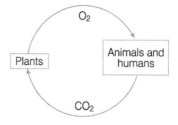

Que 5. Explain why there is no waste in a forest.

Ans. There is no waste in a forest because microorganisms act on the wastes and convert them into humus. The humus ensures that nutrients are returned back to the soil.

Que 6. List five products we get from forests.

Ans. The five products we get from forests are given below:

(i) Fruits   (ii) Vegetables

(iii) Medicines   (iv) Oxygen

(v) Cereals

Que 7. Fill in the blanks.

(a) The insects, butterflies, honeybees and birds help flowering plants in ....

(b) A forest is a purifier of .... and ....

(c) Herbs form the .... layer in the forest.

(d) The decaying leaves and animal droppings in a forest enrich the ....

Ans. (a) pollination   (b) air, water

(c) lowest   (d) soil as human

Que 8. Why should we worry about the conditions and issues related to forest far from us?

Ans. There are various reasons for which we should be vigilant about matters related to forests:

(i) A decrease in forest area would lead to an increase in carbon dioxide in air. This will lead to an increase of earth's temperature.

(ii) Soil erosion would occur if there are no forests.

(iii) Floods would occur if there are no forests.

(iv) Forests provide shelter and food to the living organisms.

> **Note** When forests are affected the habitat of wild animals and all living organisms are adversely affected. Therefore, we need to conserve our forests.

Que 9. Explain why there is a need of variety of animals and plants in a forests.

Ans. A greater variety of plants and animals in the forests help it to regenerate and grow. Greater variety of plants means more food and habitat for the herbivores. An increase in herbivores means more food for carnivores.

Que 10. In figure, the artist has forgotten to put the labels and directions on the arrows. Mark the directions on the arrows and label the diagram using the labels:
clouds, rain, atmosphere, carbon dioxide, oxygen, plants, animals, soil, roots, water table.

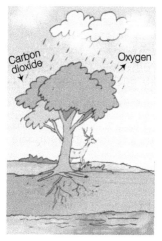

Ans. The given figure completely explains the exchange of gases between plants and animals.

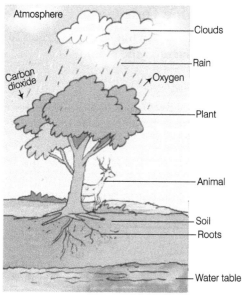

Que 11. Which of the following is not a forest product?
  (a) Gum   (b) Plywood
  (c) Sealing wax   (d) Kerosene
Ans. (d) Kerosene is a fossil fuel, it is not a forest product.

Que 12. Which of the following statements is incorrect?
  (a) Forests protect the soil from erosion
  (b) Plants and animals in a forest are not dependent on one another
  (c) Forests influence the climate and water cycle
  (d) Soil helps forest to grow and regenerate
Ans. (b) Plants and animals in a forest are not dependent on one another.

Que 13. Microorganisms act upon the dead plant to produce
  (a) sand   (b) mushroom
  (c) humus   (d) wood
Ans. (c) Microorganisms act upon the dead plant to produce humus. It forms the fertile layer of the soil.

Selected **NCERT Exemplar Problems**

> **Multiple Choice Questions**

Que 1. Which of the following serve as green lungs?
  (a) Green pigment of the plants
  (b) Forests
  (c) Kitchen gardens
  (d) Greenhouse gases
Ans. (b) Forests serve as green lungs as they produce oxygen and help in maintaining oxygen and carbon dioxide balance.

Que 2. Boojho visited a forest near his town with his classmates and his teacher. As they were entering the forest, their class teacher told them not to make noise in the forest as noise could disturb the
  (a) birds   (b) animals
  (c) Both (a) and (b)   (d) plants
Ans. (c) As Boojho was entering the forest, his class teacher told him not to make noise in the forest because it could disturb both birds and animals.

Que 3. Which among the following forests animals is the smallest?

(a) Fox   (b) Boar

(c) Bison   (d) Porcupine

Ans. (d) Porcupine is the smallest forest animal among the following given in the question.

Que 4. Which of the following has the strongest stem?

(a) A tree   (b) A creeper

(c) A climber   (d) A bush

Ans. (a) A tree has the strongest stem.

Que 5. Which of the following is not prepared from the wood obtained from forest?

(a) Paper   (b) Thermocol

(c) Matchsticks   (d) Plywood

Ans. (b) Thermocol is not prepared from the wood obtained from the forest. Paper, matchsticks and plywood are prepared from the wood.

Que 6. Which of the following is not the name of a tree?

(a) Teak   (b) Sal

(c) Porcupine   (d) Kachnar

Ans. (c) Porcupine is not the name of a tree rather it is an animal. Teak, sal and kachnar are names of trees.

Que 7. Pick the option which gives the names of a tree and an animal, respectively from the following.

(a) Semal and hornbill   (b) Sal and khair

(c) Chinkara and blue bull   (d) Neem and palash

Ans. (a) From the above given options, semal and hornbill are the names of a tree and an animal respectively.

Que 8. Which of the products is not obtained from a forest?

(a) Honey   (b) Catechu

(c) Gum   (d) Ginger

Ans. (d) Ginger is not a forest product.

Que 9. The branchy part of a tree above the stem is known as

(a) crown   (b) canopy

(c) sapling   (d) humus

Ans. (a) The branchy part of a tree above the stem is known as crown.

Que 10. Forests are not responsible for
    (a) providing medicinal plants
    (b) maintaining the flow of water into the streams
    (c) creating flood conditions
    (d) absorbing rainwater and maintaining water table

Ans. (c) Forests are not responsible for creating flood conditions, as they protect from flood condition.

❯ Very Short Answer Type Questions

Que 11. Paheli while moving in a forest observed that there was no noise pollution, though lots of heavy vehicles were passing from the nearby highway. Explain why.

Ans. Paheli observed that there is no noise pollution in a forest even though there is lots of heavy vehicles passing from the nearby highway because trees present in the forest absorb the noise.

Que 12. State whether the following statements are True or False. If False, give the correct statement.
    (a) Forests influence climate, water cycle and air quality.
    (b) In a forest, trees form the uppermost layer, followed by herbs. The shrubs form the lowest layer of vegetation.
    (c) The forest keeps on growing and changing and can regenerate.
    (d) Forests protect the soil from erosion.

Ans. (a) True
    (b) False, in a forest, trees form the uppermost layer followed by shrubs. The herbs form the lowest layer of vegetation.
    (c) True
    (d) True

Que 13. Paheli wrote a food chain in the following way:
        Frog → Eagle → Insects → Grass → Snake
The chain is not in the correct order. Help her to write the food chain correctly.

Ans. The correct food chain is
        Grass → Insects → Frog → Snake → Eagle

❯ Short Answer Type Questions

Que 14. Give names of any four birds which you expect to see in a forest.

Ans. The four birds which we expect to see in a forest are jungle crow, hornbill, myna and koel.

Que 15. Two friends shared their experiences of their vacation trip to two different forests. Do you think they would have seen the same type of plants and animals during their respective trips? Give reason.

Ans. No, they would not have seen the same type of plants and animals. This is so because climatic conditions in the two forests would vary leading to variations in the types of plants and animals.

Que 16. A bunch of seedlings were seen sprouting on a heap of animal dropping in a forest. How do you think is the seedling benefited from the animal dung?

Ans. The seedling was being benefited from the animal dung as the decaying animal dung provided nutrients to the growing seedlings.

Que 17. Match Column I with Column II

Column I	Column II
(a) Decomposers	(i) Dead plant and animal tissues
(b) Canopy	(ii) Habitats for wildlife
(c) Porcupine	(iii) Microorganisms
(d) Humus	(iv) Wild animal
(e) Forest	(v) Branches of tall trees

Ans. The correctly matched Column I with Column II is given below:

Column I	Column II
(a) Decomposers	(iii) Microorganisms
(b) Canopy	(v) Branches of tall trees
(c) Porcupine	(iv) Wild animal
(d) Humus	(i) Dead plant and animal tissues
(e) Forest	(ii) Habitats for wildlife

Que 18. Deforestation may lead to floods. Why?

Ans. Deforestation leads to floods as lesser number of trees will be available due to deforestation. In the absence of trees, the soil will not hold water leading to floods.

Que 19. Name any four useful products other than wood, which we get from forests.

Ans. Four useful products other than wood which we get from forests are gum, spices, fodder for animals and medicinal plants.

› **Long Answer Type Questions**

Que 20. Figure shows a part of a forest.

Write any three activities going on in the forest on the basis of this figure.

Ans. The three activities going on in the forest on the basis of the given figure are

    (i) Oxygen is given out by plant leaves.

    (ii) Carbon dioxide is consumed by the plants to prepare their food by the process of photosynthesis.

    (iii) Nutrients are being added to the soil by the action of decomposers.

Que 21. Give any four factors which are responsible for the destruction of forests.

Ans. The four factors which are responsible for the destruction of forests are

    (i) Construction of roads

    (ii) Construction of buildings

    (iii) Industrial development

    (iv) Increasing demand of wood

Que 22. All the needs of animals living in a forest are fulfilled. Justify this statement in a few sentences.

Ans. Forest provides home (shelter), food and water to the animals living there. Thus, all the needs of animals living in a forest are fulfilled.

Chapter 18

Wastewater Story

Important Points

- **Wastewater** It is the water containing waste from residential, commercial and industrial processes. It is obtained from kitchen, laundries toilets, etc. This used water should not be wasted. We must clean it up by removing pollutants.

- **Clean water** This is a basic need of human being. Water that is fit for use is unfortunately unavailable. More than one billion of our fellow human beings have no access to safe drinking water. This accounts for a large number of water-borne diseases and even deaths.

- **Water for life** On the World Water Day, i.e. 22 March 2005, the General Assembly of the United Nations proclaimed the period 2005-2015 as the International Decade for action on **Water for Life**. All efforts made during this decade aim to reduce by half the number of people who do not have access to safe drinking water.

- **Cleaning of water** It is a process of removing pollutants before it enters a water body or is reused. This process of wastewater treatment is commonly known as **sewage treatment**. Treatment of water is done in several stages.

- **Sewage** It is wastewater released by homes, industries, agricultural fields and other human activities. It also includes rainwater that has run down the street during a storm or heavy rain and it is a liquid waste.

- **Contaminants** There are unwanted constituents in material or impurities that are dissolved or suspended in wastewater.

- Sewage contains the following impurities :
  - (i) Organic impurities like human faeces, animal waste, oil, urea (urine), pesticides, herbicides, fruit, vegetable waste, etc.
  - (ii) Inorganic impurities like nitrates, phosphates and metals.
  - (iii) Nutrients like phosphorus and nitrogen.
  - (iv) Disease causing bacteria for cholera, typhoid, etc.
  - (v) Microbes causing dysentery.
- **Sewers** These are pipes which carry sewage.
- **Sewerage** It is a network of sewage carrying pipes from the point of being produced to the point of disposal, i.e. treatment plant. It is like a transport system.
- **Wastewater Treatment Plant** (WWTP) It reduces pollutants/contaminants from wastewater to a level which is not harmful for consumption. It takes place in the following steps:
  - (i) **Physical process** The wastewater is passed through bar screens to remove large objects and then passed to grit and sand removal tanks. Here, the water is allowed to settle and sludge is removed by a scraper. This cleared water is **clarified water.**

    Sludge is wastewater solid like faeces which settle at the bottom of large tank and are removed by scapers.
  - (ii) **Biological process** Sludge removed by physical process is decomposed by anaerobic bacteria to produce biogas and then air is pumped into clarified water for aerobic bacteria to grow, i.e. **aeration** is done.
    - (a) **Aerobic bacteria** are those which require oxygen to grow and multiply.
    - (b) **Anaerobic bacteria** are those which do not require oxygen to grow and multiply.
    - (c) **Biogas** is a gaseous fuel produced by breakdown of organic matter by the action of anaerobic bacteria.
    - (d) The suspended microbes settle at the bottom of the tank as **activated sludge** and the water is removed from the top.
  - (iii) **Chemical process** The treated water before discharging into distribution system is disinfected by chemicals like chlorine and ozone.

  Note The water in a river is cleaned naturally by processes that are similar to those adopted in a wastewater treatment plant.

- Being an active citizen, we can limit the type of waste and quantity of waste produced. We should be an enlightened citizen and approach the municipality or the gram panchayat. Insist that the open drains be covered. If the sewage of any particular house makes the neighbourhood dirty, we should request them to be more considerate about others' health.

   Note We should plant *Eucalyptus* trees all along sewage ponds. These trees absorb all surplus wastewater rapidly and release pure water vapour into the atmosphere.

- **Better house keeping practices** These points should be followed to minimise/eliminate waste and pollutants at their source:
   (i) One should throw oils and fats into the dustbin.
   (ii) Chemicals like paints, solvent medicines, etc should not be thrown into drain.
   (iii) Used tea leaves, solid food remains, soft toys, cotton, etc should be thrown in dustbin because these may choke the drain.

   Blocking of drains will not allow free flow of oxygen and thus hampers degradation process.

- **Sanitation** It is the adaptation of hygienic means for prevention of diseases by proper disposal of sewage and garbage. A very large fraction of our people defeats in the open on dry riverbeds, on railway tracks, near fields and many a time directly in water. Untreated human excreta is a health hazard. It may cause water pollution and soil pollution. Thus, it becomes the most common route for water-borne diseases. They include cholera, typhoid, polio, meningitis, hepatitis and dysentery.

- **Vermi-processing toilet** It is low water use toilet designed for safe processing of human waste. In this method, human excreta is treated by earthworm. The operation of the toilet is very simple and hygienic. The human excreta is completely converted into vermi cakes (a resource much needed for soil).

- **On-site sewage** disposal system like septic tanks, chemical toilets, composting pits are being encouraged to improve sanitation. These are low cost alternative arrangement for sewage disposal. Some organisation offer hygienic on-site human waste disposal technology. These toilets do not require scavenging.

Excreta from the toilet seats flow through covered drains into a biogas plant. The biogas produced is used as a source of energy.

■ **Sanitation at public places**

  (i) Railway stations, bus depots, airports, hospitals are very busy places. Thousands of people visit them daily which generate large amount of waste. It must be disposed of properly otherwise epidemics could break out.

  (ii) The government has laid down certain standards of sanitation but unfortunately, they are not strictly enforced.

  (iii) We should not scatter litter anywhere. If there is no dustbin in sight, we should carry the litter at home and throw it in the dustbin.

■ We all have a role to play in keeping our environment clean and healthy. We must realise our responsibility in maintaining the water sources in a healthy state.

> **Note** Mahatma Gandhi said, "No one need to wait for anyone else to adopt a humane and enlightened course of action".

Intext Questions

Que 1.   Add the uses of water in the blank bubbles.

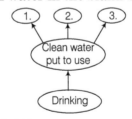

Ans.   Uses of water in the bubbles:

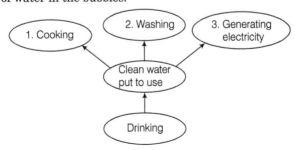

Que 2. Complete the table given below of the contaminant survey. *(Pg 220)*

Types of sewage	Point of origin	Substances which contaminate	Any other remark
1. Sullage water	Kitchen		
2. Foul waste	Toilets		
3. Trade waste	Industrial and commercial organisations		

Ans. Given below is the table of contaminant survey explaining types of sewage with their point of origin and contaminate in them.

Contaminant survey

Type of sewage	Point of origin	Substances which contaminate	Any other remark
1. Sullage water	Kitchen	Cooking oils and fats, etc	May chocks drains
2. Foul waste	Toilets	Faeces and cirine	Causes diseases like dysentery, cholera, etc.
3. Trade waste	Industrial and commercial organisations	Chemicals like paints, solvents, motor oil, etc.	Causes water and soil pollution

Que 3. With reference to the treatment of polluted water at home by aeration, filteration, chlorination processes answer the following questions. *(Pg 223)*

    (a) What changes did we observe in the appearance of liquid after aeration? Did aeration change the odour?

    (b) What is removed by the sand filter?

    (c) Does chlorine change the colour of treated water?

    (d) Do chlorine have an odour?

Ans. (a) Aerated water contains some suspended impurities and the foul odour of the polluted water disappears completely after aeration.

    (b) Sand filter removes tiny suspended impurities.

    (c) Chlorine makes the water clear and colourless.

    (d) Yes, chlorine have a peculiar odour which is not worse than wastewater.

Que 4. How is water in a river is cleaned naturally?   *(Pg 224)*

Ans. River water is cleaned naturally by a process that is similar to wastewater treatment plant.

As muddy water when flows through grass or weeds on its way to a stream, mud and solid particles get filtered out.

At the bottom of a lake or stream, microorganism brings chemical changes in the water. The natural filtration process removes pollution from the groundwater throughout the process making it clean and fit for drinking.

Que 5. Why the *Eucalyptus* trees are planted along sewage ponds?   *(Pg 224)*

Ans. The *Eucalyptus* trees are planted along sewage ponds because these trees absorb all surplus wastewater rapidly and release pure water vapour into the atmosphere.

Que 6. How one can avoid the addition of the load in WWTP?   *(Pg 225)*

Ans. By following proper sanitation and house-keeping practices by creating less waste at an individual level, we can avoid the addition of the load in wastewater treatment plant.

Que 7. How sewage is disposed of in an aeroplane?   *(Pg 226)*

Ans. Aeroplanes have their closed waste sewage tanks, which suck the wastewater and collect it in their tanks. Once the aeroplane lands on the ground, the crew disposed of the sewage properly into airport sewage facility.

Exercises

Que 1. Fill in the blanks.

(a) Cleaning of water is a process of removing ....

(b) Wastewater released by houses is called ....

(c) Dried .... is used as manure.

(d) Drains get blocked by .... and ....

Ans. (a) Cleaning of water is a process of removing **pollutants**.

(b) Wastewater released by houses is called **sewage**.

(c) Dried **sludge** is used as manure.

(d) Drains get blocked by **solid food remains** and **oil and fats**.

Que 2. What is sewage? Explain why it is harmful to discharge untreated sewage into rivers or sea.

Ans. **Sewage** is the wastewater containing both liquid and solid wastes (suspended solid) produced by human activities from homes, industries, hospitals, offices, etc. Sewage contains various contaminants including disease causing bacteria and other microbes. If an untreated sewage is discharged into rivers or sea then the water in the rivers or sea would get contaminated.

If this contaminated water is used for drinking, it can cause diseases such as cholera, typhoid, dysentery, etc which may lead to death. That is why, it is harmful to discharge untreated sewage into rivers or sea.

Que 3. Why should oils and fats not be released in the drain? Explain.

Ans. Oil and fats hardens and block the sewage pipes. In an open drain also, fats block porosity of soil which affects its water filtering efficiency. Therefore, it should not be released in the drain.

Que 4. Describe the steps involved in getting clarified water from wastewater.

Ans. The steps involved in getting clarified water from wastewater are as follows:

(i) Use of an aerator to bubble air through wastewater. A mechanical stirrer or a mixer can also be used in place of the aerator. It helps in reducing bad odour of the wastewater.

(ii) Then, the water is filtered through the layers of sand, find grains and medium gravel. This filtration makes the wastewater clean from various types of pollutants. The water is filtered continuously until it becomes clear.

(iii) Then, disinfectant such as chlorine tablet is added to the filterate and stirred to obtain completely clear and purified water.

The water in a river is cleaned naturally by processes that are similar to those adopted in a wastewater treatment plant.

Que 5. What is sludge? Explain how it is treated.

Ans. Collected semi-solid wastes such as faeces that settle down during wastewater treatment are called **sludge**. The sludge is removed by using a scraper and then transferred to a tank where it is decomposed by anaerobic bacteria to produce biogas. This biogas is used as a low cost fuel for heating, cooking, etc. Activated sludge produced by decomposition of bacteria is used as manure.

Que 6. Untreated human excreta is a health hazard. Explain.

Ans. Human excreta may cause water pollution and soil pollution which can lead to a lot of health related problems. Water polluted with it contains disease causing bacteria which can spread epidemics and becomes the most common route for water-borne diseases like cholera, dysentery, typhoid, etc.

Que 7. Name two chemicals used to disinfect water.

Ans. Two chemicals used to disinfect water are chlorine and ozone.

Que 8. Explain the function of bar screens in a wastewater treatment plant.

Ans. In wastewater treatment plant, bar screen removes large solid objects from water. The wastewater is allowed to pass through bar screens so that large solid objects such as rags, napkins, cans, plastic bags, polythene, etc present in wastewater can be removed under filtration process.

Que 9. Explain the relationship between sanitation and disease.

Ans. Sanitation and disease are related to each other. As lack of sanitation can cause diseases. In our country, a large number of people even today do not have sewerage facilities and thus defecate in open fields, railway tracks, etc. The untreated human excreta thus pollute soil and water resources (including underground water). When this contaminated water is used for drinking, it can cause diseases such as cholera, typhoid, hepatitis, dysentery, etc which may even lead to death.

Que 10. Outline your role as an active citizen in relation to sanitation.

Ans. As an active citizen, we have many responsibilities regarding sanitation. These can be listed as follows:

(i) To ensure that our surroundings are cleaned.

(ii) To ensure that the sewerage system in our house is properly managed.

(iii) If any leakage or any open drain in the sewerage system is present, then it should be reported to the municipality or the gram panchayats to insist that the open drain must be covered properly and several air and water-borne diseases can be prevented.

Que 11. Complete the crossword.

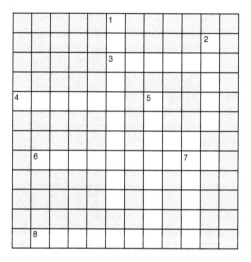

Across

3. Liquid waste products
4. Solid waste extracted in sewage treatment
6. A word related to hygiene
8. Waste matter discharged from human body

Down

1. Used water
2. A pipe carrying sewage
5. Microorganism which causes cholera
7. A chemical to disinfect water

Ans.

					[1]W					
					A					[2]S
					[3]S	E	W	A	G	E
					T					W
[4]S	L	U	D	G	E		[5]B			E
					W		A			R
					A		C			
	[6]S	A	N	I	T	A	T	I	[7]O	N
					E		E		Z	
					R		R		O	
							I		N	
	[8]E	X	C	R	E	T	A		E	

Across

3. Liquid waste product — Sewage
4. Solid waste extracted in sewage treatment — Sludge
6. A word related to hygiene — Sanitation
8. Waste matter discharged from human body — Excreta

Down

1. Used water — Wastewater
2. A pipe carrying sewage — Sewer
5. Microorganism which causes cholera — Bacteria
7. A chemical to disinfect water — Ozone

Que 12. Study the following statements about ozone.

   (i) It is essential for breathing of living organisms.

  (ii) It is used to disinfect water.

 (iii) It absorbs ultraviolet rays.

 (iv) Its proportion in air is about 3%.

Which of these statements are correct?

(a) (i), (ii) and (iii)   (b) (ii) and (iii)

(c) (i) and (iv)   (d) All of these

Ans. (b) Ozone is used as a water disinfectant. It absorbs harmful ultraviolet rays of the sun.

Selected **NCERT Exemplar Problems**

❯ **Multiple Choice Questions**

Que 1. Which of the following is wastewater?
(a) Water trickling from a damaged tap
(b) Water coming out of a shower
(c) Water flowing in a river
(d) Water coming out of a laundry

Ans. (d) Water coming out of a laundry is wastewater.

Que 2. Sewage is mainly a
    (a) liquid waste   (b) solid waste
    (c) gaseous waste   (d) mixture of solid and gas

Ans. (a) Sewage is mainly a liquid waste.

Que 3. Which of the following is/are products of wastewater treatment?
    (a) Biogas   (b) Sludge
    (c) Both biogas and sludge   (d) Aerator

Ans. (c) Biogas and sludge both are the products of wastewater treatment.

Que 4. Open drain system is a breeding place for which of the following?
(a) Flies
(b) Mosquitoes
(c) Organisms which cause diseases
(d) All of the above

Ans. (d) Open drain system is a breeding place for flies, mosquitoes and organisms which cause diseases.

Que 5. Water polluted by various human activities causes a number of water-borne diseases. Which of the following is not a water-borne disease?
    (a) Cholera   (b) Typhoid
    (c) Asthma   (d) Dysentery

Ans. (c) Asthma is not a water-borne disease. It is caused by polluted air.

Que 6. Pick from the following one chemical used to disinfect water.

    (a) Chlorine   (b) Washing soda

    (c) Silica   (d) Coal

Ans. (a) Chlorine is the chemical used as water disinfectant.

Que 7. The system of a network of pipes used for taking away wastewater from homes or public buildings to the treatment plant is known as

    (a) sewers

    (b) sewerage

    (c) transport system

    (d) treatment plant

Ans. (b) The system of a network of pipes used for taking away wastewater from homes or public buildings to the treatment plant is known as sewerage.

Que 8. Which of the following is a part of inorganic impurities of the sewage?

    (a) Pesticides   (b) Urea

    (c) Phosphates   (d) Vegetable waste

Ans. (c) Phosphate is an inorganic impurity of the sewage.

Que 9. In a filtration plant, water is filtered using layers of

    (a) sand and clay

    (b) clay and fine gravel

    (c) sand and fine gravel

    (d) sand, fine gravel and medium gravel

Ans. (d) In a filtration plant, water is filtered using layers of sand, fine gravel and medium gravel.

Que 10. Which of the following are not a source of wastewater?

    (a) Sewers   (b) Homes

    (c) Industries   (d) Hospitals

Ans. (a) Sewers are not considered as sources of wastewater. Homes, industries and hospitals are considered as a source of wastewater.

> **Very Short Answer Type Questions**

Que 11. Why is open drain a concern?

Ans. Open drain is a big concern for the society because they create unhygienic conditions and flies, mosquitoes and other insects breed can spread a number of diseases.

Que 12. State whether the following statements are True or False. In case a statement is false, write the correct statement.

(a) Sewage is a solid waste which causes water pollution and soil pollution.

(b) Used water is wastewater.

(c) Wastewater could be reused.

(d) Where underground sewerage systems and refuse disposal systems are not available, the high cost on-site sanitation system can be adopted.

Ans. (a) False, sewage is a liquid waste which causes water pollution and soil pollution.

(b) True

(c) True

(d) False, where underground sewerage systems and refuse disposal systems are not available, the low cost on-site sanitation system can be adopted.

> Short Answer Type Questions

Que 13. Name two inorganic impurities present in sewage.

Ans. Inorganic impurities present in sewage are nitrates and phosphates.

Que 14. Animal waste, oil and urea are some of the organic impurities present in sewage. Name two more organic impurities present in sewage.

Ans. Fruits and vegetable wastes, pesticides and herbicides are organic impurities present in sewage other than animal waste, oil and urea.

Que 15. Name two alternative arrangements for sewage disposal where there is no sewerage system.

Ans. The two alternative arrangements for sewage disposal, where there is no sewerage system are as below:

(i) Septic tanks

(ii) Composting pits

Que 16. A man travelling in a train threw an empty packet of food on the platform. Do you think this is a proper waste disposal method? Elaborate.

Ans. No, one must always put the waste in a nearby dustbin or carry it to the litter home and dispose it in dustbins there. Waste, not properly disposed may enter into the drains and choke them. It also makes public places dirty and unhygienic.

Que 17. Why should we not throw
  (a) used tea leaves into sink?
  (b) cooking oil and fats down the drain?

Ans. (a) We should not throw used tea leaves into sink because it may choke the drain-pipe of the sink.
  (b) We should not throw cooking oil and fats down the drain as it can harden and block the drain-pipes.

Que 18. Match the items of Column I with the items of Column II with reference to sewage.

Column I	Column II
(a) Inorganic impurities	(i) Phosphorus and nitrogen
(b) Organic impurities	(ii) Nitrates and phosphates
(c) Nutrients	(iii) Cholera and typhoid
(d) Bacteria	(iv) Pesticides and herbicides

Ans. The correct matching of Column I with Column II with reference to sewage is given as below:

Column I	Column II
(a) Inorganic impurities	(ii) Nitrates and phosphates
(b) Organic impurities	(iv) Pesticides and herbicides
(c) Nutrients	(i) Phosphorus and nitrogen
(d) Bacteria	(iii) Cholera and typhoid

Que 19. Given below is a jumbled sequence of the processes involved in a wastewater treatment plant. Arrange them in their correct sequence.
  (a) Sludge is scraped out and skimmer removes and floating grease.
  (b) Water is made to settle in a large tank with a slope in the middle.
  (c) Large objects like plastic bags are removed by passing wastewater through bar screens.
  (d) Sand, grit and pebbles are made to settle by decreasing the speed of incoming wastewater.
  (e) Wastewater enters a grit and sand removal tank.

Ans. The correct sequence of wastewater treatment in treatment plant is as below:

Step I. Large objects like plastic bags are removed by passing wastewater through bar screens.

Step II. Wastewater enters a grit and sand removal tank.

Step III. Sand, grit and pebbles are made to settle by decreasing the speed of incoming wastewater.

Step IV. Water is made to settle in a large tank with a slope in the middle.

Step V. Sludge is scrapped out and skimmer removes the floating grease.

Que 20. Three statements are provided here which define the terms:

(a) sludge (b) sewage and (c) wastewater

Pick out the correct definition for each of these terms.

(a) The settled solids that are removed in wastewater treatment with a scraper.

(b) Water from kitchen used for washing dishes.

(c) Wastewater released from homes, industries, hospitals and other public buildings.

Ans. (a) The settled solids that are removed in wastewater treatment with a scraper is sludge.

(b) Water from kitchen used for washing dishes is wastewater.

(c) Wastewater released from homes, industries, hospitals and other public buildings is sewage.

Que 21. A mixture (*x*) in water contains suspended solids, organic impurities, inorganic impurities (*a*), nutrients (*b*), disease causing bacteria and other microbes. Give names for (*x*), (*a*) and (*b*).

Ans. A mixture of <u>sewage</u> (*x*) in water contains suspended solids, organic impurities, inorganic impurities like <u>nitrates, phosphates and metals</u> (*a*), nutrients like <u>phosphorus and nitrogen</u> (*b*), disease causing bacteria and other microbes.

❯ Long Answer Type Questions

Que 22. What are the different types of inorganic and organic impurities generally present in sewage?

Ans. The different types of inorganic and organic impurities present in sewage are as below:
(i) Inorganic impurities – nitrates, phosphates and metals.
(ii) Organic impurities – fruit and vegetable wastes, oil, urea, human faeces, animal waste, pesticides and herbicides.

Que 23. The terms sewage, sewers and sewerage are interlinked with each other. Can you explain, how?

Ans. The terms like sewage, sewers and sewerage are interlinked with each other because sewage is a mixture of wastewater coming out of homes and other places. Sewers are pipes which carry sewage and sewerage is a network of sewage carrying pipes.

Que 24. Fill in the blanks in the following statements using words given in the box.

air, handpumps, cholera, water, large, ground

A very .... number of our people defecate in the open. It may cause .... pollution and soil pollution. Both the surface water and .... water get polluted. .... water is the source for wells, tubewells and .... Thus, it becomes the most common route for .... borne diseases like ...., dysentery, etc.

Ans. A very **large** number of our people defecate in the open. It may cause **water** pollution and soil pollution. Both the surface water and **ground** water get polluted. **Ground** water is the source for wells, tubewells and **handpumps**. Thus, it becomes the most common route for **water**-borne diseases like **cholera**, dysentery, etc.

Que 25. Think and suggest some ways to minimise waste and pollutants at their source, taking your home as an example.

Ans. We can minimise waste and pollutants entering the water and create less wastewater by taking following few steps at home:
(i) By not throwing used tea leaves, solid food remains, etc in the drain. We should throw it in the dustbin.
(ii) By not throwing chemicals like medicines, paints, insecticides, etc in the drain as they increase the pollution load of the sewage.

Ingram Content Group UK Ltd.
Milton Keynes UK
UKHW020909090423
419869UK00013B/246